—

*Ursula's gift has truly helped people to come to peace with their lives after being haunted by the mystical world of the unknown. I have witnessed with my own eyes the emergence of an evil spirit from one her clients when we went to the sweat lodge and the impact it has had on the patient and Ursula. Through her gift and sacred ceremonies and prayers, lives have been transformed.*

*Having read the book, witnessing dis-possessions, and being a client myself, has helped me to live a fulfilling life. One must always keep tapped into being well through light and love and know there is prevention and intervention measures to keeping well. This is a must read to helping you educate yourself about the mystical world.*

*Thank you dearest Ula for writing such a significant book that has touched my spirit, my heart and my entire well being... The education is critical to people's lives and pathways to quality health and happiness.*

*The world is blessed with your gift...*

*Hai, hai, in spirit and wellness.*
*Your friend,*

**Lise Robinson**
Mountain Woman

—

*I have known Ursula for over 20 years. She has made such a positive impact in my life without me realizing it at times. I have had readings from her the last 20 years and what she has told me has happened.*

*Even when she urged me not to do things because she said it won't turn out in your favo*r, I did *it anyway since it was a sure thing. It did not in the end turn out for me and became a very costly mistake.*

*Her energy and the energy she gives back is truly amazing. When my world has felt upside down and where nothing is making sense her energy and connection with me brings my energy and inspiration back higher than I imagine. She has had such a positive and moving impact on my life and I can feel a powerful shift when I talk to her.*

*When I have doubted her with her readings and even chuckled at what she tells me, they actually happened.*

*Ursula, you have a very powerful special gift and I am thankful you share it with me. I couldn't imagine you not in my life and you are here for a reason. Over the years you have become a precious and dear friend. You are an inspiration and Savior.*

**Susan Nowakowsky**

—

*We often know that something is not right, we feel things we do not understand, and are tormented by fears and have flashes of information we don't know the source of. All that and more affects our daily life, the choices we make, how we deal with people and life in general and how close we are to our true self. One thing I always understood, that there has to be a balance between the soul, body and mind in order to be content and not afraid of living .*

*I also knew I needed Ursula to help free myself from the traumas, pain and attachments of the past no matter the source. Her understanding of human complexity and life beyond our comprehension gives us an opportunity to choose healing and free ourselves from all that holds us back from being who we truly are and learn to trust our instincts. For we all have it. Ula, with her absolute devotion to the betterment of the human condition and tireless promotion of the truth guides us through this process of self-discovery and healing.*

*Ula,* I *thank you and commend you for sharing…you are the star that helps others shine and I love you for being you.*

**Lidia Anderson**
Abbotsford, BC, Canada

ursula111958@gmail.com
ursula111958@protonmail.com

Urszula
TERESA KUR

# Spirituality
## NOT FOR SALE

A Psychics Insight on
Past Life Regression and Healing

To Gabby with love
May healing bring
new best things
into your life

@B 23/04/2022

—



**Spirituality Not For Sale:**
*A Psychics Insight on Past Life Regression and Healing*

by Urszula Teresa Kur

Cover Design and page layout by
Ryan Goelzenleuchter, RG Design, LLC

Library and Archives Canada Cataloguing in Publication

Kur, Ursula Teresa, 1956-, author
Spirituality not for sale : a psychic's insight on past life regression and healing / Ursula Teresa Kur.

Includes bibliographical references and index.
ISBN 978-0-9958301-0-3 (softcover)

1. Reincarnation therapy. I. Title.

RC489.R43K87 2016 615.8'528 C2016-908226-1



First Printing, 2016

## CONTENTS:

# PREFACE:

The idea to write this book began over ten years ago and it has been in the 'gestation' period for all this time. None of the stories and experiences are fictional, they are very real and lived through, and as such have value. Since my husband and I moved to Vancouver Island in 2003, I have lost touch with many of the people in the book, but their sessions, outcomes of these sessions and lives are as vivid to my mind as they were when they were taking place. There are many, many more clients and experiences with the paranormal than are illustrated here, and the drama and importance of each one is not diminished if they aren't a part of this book. I have protected their privacy by changing their names (fictitious first names-no last names), places and circumstances. I loved and love working with, the people, and feel alive and energized when I do. It's like an adrenaline rush, even though I often find myself caught on the same emotional roller coaster ride as my clients when they course through their many lifetimes.

With the world today in such turmoil and being irrationally guided, there is a definite need for like minded people to work together to reverse the evil that is spreading like a cancer.

I think mankind is on the cusp of a new acceptance and enlightenment of the mysteries of the soul and the *true nature* of our existence, and am hoping and confident that this book will in some part help illuminate the way.

Ursula Teresa Kur

Qualicum Beach, BC, Canada

August 2016.

# ACKNOWLEDGMENTS:

I would like to thank the many people who have been a part of my life and contributed in no small way to the panoply of ideas and thoughts that are the genesis of this work. They have placed their trust in me, and helped give valuable lessons that made me a better, wiser and kinder person. For this I am very grateful. I want to express my undying gratitude to all my friends and family members who have supported me and inspired me.

In particular, and this list is by no means complete, Ewa Hartman, Dianne Konrad, Lise Robinson, my Sister Lidia Anderson, Gwen and Ken Short, Susan and Frank Kaspar, Elzbieta Zaborowska, Darcy and Misty Myers, my cousin Renata Kaczmarek, my parents Marian and Teresa Kur, Theresa Pound, and my three children Kelly, Sylvia, and Kimberly. And most of all I would like to thank my husband Michael, without whom completing and bringing this book into the shape and format that it is, and his editing input and belief in me and my psychic work, would not have made this publication possible. And also a special thanks to the Medicine Man Adrian Redcrow of the Saddle Lake Reserve who took part in my spiritual growth and helped protect me from the Evil referred to in some of the chapters in this book.

*Life contains but two tragedies.*
*One is not to get your heart's desire;*
*the other is to get it.*

— Socrates —

# CHAPTER ONE: SOPHIE

"Do you know why I feel this way? It's frightening to feel this way."

"I understand," I responded, trying to encourage my client to open up more.

"They all gave up on me," she said bitterly. Sophie, a petite size woman was sitting on the other side of my desk in an extra office chair.

"Who are they?" I asked although I knew that she was referring to medical personnel.

I asked her to bring her chair over to me and make herself comfortable.

"I would like to take a look at both your palms," I began, taking her two cold hands in mine. "Are you right or left handed?" I asked. This was a question that I always asked because that is an indicator of how to interpret the readings. For right-handed people the left hand is the hand where life potential is engraved, while the right shows how this potential is used. Logically, it would be reversed for 'South Paws.'

"Right." Came her answer, her voice sounding nervous. I peered closely at her hands.

The messages started to flow through me the way electricity flows through a wire. At least that's my interpretation of this phenomenon.

"Now listen, Sophie. Your hand of realization, which is your right hand, since you are right handed, presents the sadness you told me about at the beginning of the session. Your mind refuses to remember nine years of your early life, from the day you were born to almost your tenth birthday. This part of your life is wrought by sickness…"

"I think I was relatively healthy," the woman interrupted.

"I'm not speaking of your body, but of your emotions and your mind, in which repressed memories of uncomfortable events which until today, you could not and would not face."

"I knew that there was something very wrong, but I don't know what," she lamented, reaching for a tissue from the Kleenex box, which I always have handy. While she was busy wiping away her tears, I was plunging into her past. I immediately could see why the woman was not able to handle a job for longer than a month or two, or went through four unhappy, devastating marriages, and was now fighting off the cervical cancer she had been diagnosed with shortly before setting up her first appointment with me.

On one hand was this undeniable need in her to be with a man, and as soon as she was involved she had a strong urge to push him away and to free herself from the relationship. That compulsion included acts of infidelity on her part, to achieve a psychotic goal of punishing him and to make him leave. She could never explain her irrational behavior, which brought her tremendous guilt and shame.

As I spoke, Sophie's eyes filled with huge, shiny tears, which rolled down her face and dripped softly onto her elegant, knitted, gray dress. Since I was still holding her hands, she wasn't able to wipe off the tears, and wouldn't dare pull her hands away from me as that would break the steady flow of paranormal information I was receiving from her.

"How often have you had difficulty in recognizing or justifying your behavior?" I asked, arching my brows.

"A lot of the time I do things that I hate doing, but it seems, especially lately, that I have less and less control over that."

"Yes?" I urged her on. A long pause.

"Do you think that I am a bad person?" she asked.

"No, I don't feel you are. I believe that we can probably find a good explanation and root cause for all of this."

"What explanation?" She wanted to know.

"I can't tell you at this moment, we need to go back together in time and see for yourself. This is the only way you can free yourself from the burden of the past."

Throughout the reading, she received warnings about her health that needed to be looked after. A relationship with the man whom she was presently dating was another potential disaster. This man carried a seed of violence, planted from his early childhood, which began to sprout and grow, manifesting itself in frequent outbursts of rage, which were clearly directed against women.

"Sophie, this man can be very aggressive, so be aware of the possibility of violence against you." I felt it was my obligation to warn the woman.

"I know that he can be very violent, that is why I decided to end this relationship. I already told him to look for a place to stay," the woman explained. I was quite relieved to hear this news, since the visions I was seeing revealed a past life connection between Sophie and that man, and that past was not a happy or safe one for her. It carried forward a load of hatred and resentment, and demanded to be resolved.

Sophie took my words seriously, perhaps because I had been able to describe this man physically all too well and too precisely to be wrong about the rest of it.

At the end of our appointment, the woman asked me a few questions about hypnosis, past life regression and other things. She wanted to know if this form of therapy could benefit her. I told her that in many cases where defenses were created unconsciously, as was in her case, the best way to go about it is to communicate directly with the subconscious source which defined this defensive mechanism in the first place. Sophie decided to book an appointment for hypnosis. By the time she walked out of my office, I somehow felt she would cancel her appointments and she did, twice. And indeed, two months passed before I saw her again.

—

I will continue Sophie's story, but before I do, I would like to tell my own. The story is about my own struggle in life, the story about things, people and events that shaped me, the way I am now. The story has a happy ending, and this has nothing to do with things that happen in a physical manner but rather things that happen *within* myself, the great change and transformation of myself, that still continues, and it will go on until the day of my departure from the physical world. Why I used the word "departure" and not "death" will be explained in a later part of this book.

I was born in the year of the "Dog" (1958) in the month of Scorpio, constellation of the Small Dipper (a cluster of seven stars in Ursa Minor) which in Latin translates as 'Small Female Bear'. Incidentally, my name 'Ursula' translates in a similar way. Is this a coincidence? I don't think so. In the course of my life I have had a hard time believing in coincidences.

After my birth, it was noticed that my fine, bushy baby hair had a warm copper hue. My father's Polish family had difficulty accepting that and my mother was advised by those family members to keep my hair covered with a hat at all times. Seems strangely peculiar I admit.

Ever since the Middle Ages in Medieval Europe, red hair was thought shameful. People with red hair were considered dangerous and evil, automatically were said to be witches, and as such were (to be) avoided and feared. This aberrant behavior sounds outrageous and even racist in today's 'modern' world… Oddly enough, I was looked upon as someone who was a little different and no doubt unworthy. This, by itself was a hard enough burden to be carried by a young child. It was a tough thing for me to cope with. To make things worse, my psychic ability, which started to strongly manifest itself by the age of six, gave people even more reasons to fear me. Since I possessed psychic abilities, which by themselves were considered "the devil's attributes" in those mid -twentieth century years and, to boot, my hair was the color of copper, it was enough for some to think of me as a friend of the dark force.

Still, in spite of all this, there was another side to the way people would receive me. There was an ever growing group that would be drawn to me and would find my abilities and other attributes fascinating, even attractive. Needless to say this was a very potent factor that led me down my road to self-discovery and self-acceptance, often painful and confusing yet so exciting and intriguing. So, flying in the face of so-called public opinion derision leading to demands for my copper colored bushy hair be hidden by a hat or kerchief of some sort, my life started to show traits that were considered special, unique and desirable. Soon other gifts and skills started to render themselves and situate me even further away from what is thought of as 'normal' or average. This would include my obsession with North American Indians of which interest began around the age of six, and still continues today. With the only difference being now I know what to do with it, and also understand where it came from. I *am* glad and thankful that it came about.

Since preschool, I was told that I possessed leadership abilities, and had an uncanny knack to pull people in my direction. Whether driven by fear or admiration, or what I still can't put my arms around, people would flock towards me, and I would entrance them with my orations. I really had no idea where these words were coming from, and often it was obvious that due to my young age and inexperience, my own mind had no real means to generate them. I had remedies for kids with stomach problems, colds, their fears and insecurities. No matter what kind of problems were brought to me, I always seemed to have a way or an idea of how to fix them. As I grew older, my character took shape and out of "being different" I began to draw a great deal of strength and self-confidence from seemingly bad or unfavorable events. As I say jokingly today: 'From the strongest kicks in my rear end I derived the most confident and uplifting achievements.'

For examples of this 'Pied Piper' syndrome described here I bring you two instances I can recall: the first is at a friends house party in Calgary, Alberta we were invited to about 10 years ago.

It was a birthday or something like that, with lots of people milling about. My husband and I walked into the large kitchen, were served a couple of drinks and he drifted off to mingle with the crowd. A guest approached me and we started talking about past lives for some reason, as she had a few questions. Within 20 minutes, there was a crowd of around 15 women and men surrounding me as I went on about the psychic world and other esoteric topics. I spoke for over an hour. My husband wandered back to the kitchen and was astonished at this sight, like Jesus pontificating over the masses, he thought.

Another time, we were in Ismir, Turkey, and visited one of the fabulous archaeological museums they have there. Once more, the two of us got separated and I found myself wandering alone through the displays of Ancient Roman and Grecian Artifacts.

I heard a commotion coming from the other end of one of the large halls, looked up and saw a group of Turkish Junior High School age kids running towards me. They were gesticulating, yelling and pointing at me. I thought what the heck is going on?

The next thing I knew they surrounded me, still yelling wildly, and started to touch my clothes, hair and skin. Some of them knew a few words of English and I heard them say things like: 'Lady, we love you!" Over and over, still pointing, some jumping up and down. There were about 30 of them. I had never seen any of them before, and was mystified to be sure. This went on for about 5 minutes when their teachers turned up and dragged them away. When I met my husband a half hour later I mentioned this to him, and he had a time believing me. We went upstairs together and when we got to the top floor, the group spied me again, and the same exact thing happened again! This time my husband was witness, and said later he had never seen anything like this in his life. The teachers once again had to lead these children away, and many of them didn't want to leave me.

I have no clue what had occurred, or why, and am mystified to this day!

My "psychic gift" was something which I consciously hid from others. I never liked the way some people would change their attitude towards me after becoming aware of this strange ability. They would, irrationally, in my view, feel insecure and violated, speculating that all I wanted to do was to sneak inside their heads and drag out their deepest, most private secrets. I believe it is very hard to imagine how unsettling it is to find yourself wandering amongst other people's thoughts and feelings. So much of my life I kept running and denying my abilities, because I didn't want to go to those lonely, cloaked places hidden in other persons' minds or hearts.

I can't say how many times I thought I was going crazy, when the crystal clear images of my own and other people's pasts and futures would flash in my mind's eye, and I had no means or experience to really understand what they were, and even less what they meant. To make a long story short, I loathed and abhorred this so-called gift of clairvoyance, and for about twenty-six years I only gave readings to those who found a way of talking me into it, or tricked me into it. In my younger years I was convinced that I was an oddity and different, and the events I could foresee coming, were caused by me. Now I no longer flatter myself with this foolish idea, since I realize that I am too insignificant and powerless to cause anything at all. I can only detect it with my special "antennas". What took me longer to figure out was the reason for me possessing this gift, and the way in which this gift could and should be used in a beneficial and efficacious manner.

One unsettling element that accompanied my early readings was that I would often absorb the negativities that people would bring to me, and long after they were gone I still had to struggle with what they left behind (which could be anything: physical pain, fear, sadness, anger etc.) This was probably the most determinate factor that constrained me for years from practicing so called "psychic readings".

Among many things that fascinated me was an obsession with art and writing. The art interest began to manifest around the age of six and writing between the tenth and eleventh years of my life. From that time I also began to have powerful and so realistic dreams in full color! Many of these kaleidoscopic dreams were about the people of the Great Plains of North

America. Filled with astonishing details about their appearance, costumes, weapons, tools and traditions, my dreams could not possibly be explained from knowledge that came from the books or movies I had been exposed to, since such, even today, are very hard to obtain in my old country. This puzzled me for years, and until I came to Canada in 1986, I could find no rational explanation for what they were, or what was their ultimate source.

### Sophie continued

When she finally arrived at my office, I knew right away that she had reached the end of her rope. Her face seemed swollen and puffy, her eyes carried signs of restlessness and crying.

"Please help me," she despaired, wiping tears from her face.

"I will try. I will do all I can," I tried to comfort her and gave her a warm hug. Her shoulders trembled as she wept, her face pressed against my arm. "Let's go, let's do this," I encouraged her.

"I can't live like this anymore," she said, sitting down on the lazy-boy chair. "This whatever it is made me cancel our appointments twice, but this time I fought harder. I am here now, though and please make it go away. Otherwise, I'm sure it will destroy me."

Sophie was an easy subject, so it took me hardly ten or so minutes to bring her into a deep hypnotic trance.

In my work I try, in almost every case, using visualization, since it is a very helpful way to assist a person detach from reality and become more comfortable in turning inwards. There is also an image of a brilliant, warm, beautiful golden light I produce to create and consequently strengthen an enveloping feeling of safety and well being. It works as a shield that protects the person from negativity from the outside world, and from the unseen (which is more plentiful than the 'seen', in my view.).

I asked her to lay flat on the chair, and cover herself with the wool blanket we brought to the session. The hypnosis process began.

By the time Sophie was in a very deep state, her face became pale, serene and peaceful, her breathing slow and rhythmic. She was ready to begin her journey into the unknown.

"Sophie, I will now start counting backwards from twenty down to the number one, and on the count of one you will find yourself on your tenth birthday... Twenty, nineteen, eighteen...," The numbers were getting smaller and smaller.

"As soon as the first pictures start to emerge I want you to tell me everything that you will see, feel or experience." When I voiced the number "one", from the changes evident on the woman's face I concluded that she was regressing. Her head started to move from one side to the other and then the tears started. Her eyes were still closed.

"What is it Sophie? What is happening?" During readings and hypnotic sessions my voice always has a low, soft, soothing tone, which my clients find very comforting and calming.

"Where are you now? Are you at your tenth birthday party?" I asked.

"No," she sobbed, "my father was killed in an accident. Police were just in my home and brought the news."

"What kind of accident was it?"

"A car accident. My dad was drunk, and ran through a red light. He died on the spot." Sophie's speech was hard to follow as her head was whipping from side to side.

"How do you feel?"

"I'm really crying. Now there is nobody to love me."

"What do you mean? There is still your mother."

"So what!" the woman snapped angrily. "She only cares about my brother Tom. She doesn't like me."

"Are there any other siblings besides your brother Tom?'

"No." She shook her head.

"Sophie, I want you to go back to the time your dad is alive." She slowly nodded her head to let me know that she reached the time.

"Tell me about your father. How does he express his love for you? How is he showing his love?"

"My daddy hugs me a lot, and he says I am the most beautiful girl in the world!" There was a note of childish pride in Sophie's voice, but quickly her voice changed and the expression on her face became one of shock and disgust.

"I don't like this dad." The woman made a jerky motion as if she was trying to pull away from somebody.

"How old are you now Sophie?" Curious.

"I am five."

"Don't touch me there, daddy it hurts." The woman jerked her body and a grimace of pain appeared on her face.

"Where is your dad touching you?" There was a long period of silence. I waited patiently, since I knew the discovery would be gruesome and debilitating. But minutes passed and I still hadn't received a response to my question.

"Sophie… why you are not talking to me?"

"I forbid her to talk to you!" Came a strong, harsh voice, distinctly different from Sophie's.

"And who are you?" I had to make my voice sound more stern and serious.

"That's not your business. My daughter talks only to people I let her talk to!"

"What's your name?" I waited again for a long time for an answer to my question. I almost lost hope for getting any response.

"What's it to you?" The voice put on a nonchalant and cocky attitude.

"I want to talk to you, whoever you are. It would be easier to know whom I am addressing, unless you want me to treat you only as an imaginary voice."

"I am a man, not just a damn voice!" The voice barked, visibly disconcerted.

"So, if you are a man, you must have a name." I pressed on.

"Vince." Came the curt answer. "My name is Vince."

"Vince… when was the last time that you spoke with anyone?"

"It's been a long time since I could speak with anyone who could hear me."

"How long have you been you with your daughter Sophie?"

"She has always been my daughter."

"No, I don't mean that. How long have you been residing inside her?"

"What do you mean?" The voice betrayed some degree of unease. Uncertain.

"Well, I assume that you are aware, Vince, that your physical body doesn't exist any more… you must know that. You died in a car accident when Sophie was ten years old."

"What car accident, what the hell you are talking about! !?"

"You are dead Vince. Have been… for many years." Pause.

"Oh, my God. I remember it now." The entity was in shock.

"Vince. What was the reason that you failed to move toward the light?" There was another long pause before the voice responded.

"They don't want me there."

"What makes you think that way?"

"I wasn't all that good of a man, you know," the entity confessed. "I did things to Sophie, things that were bad, very bad…" the words trailed off.

"What things Vince?" I was pressing, watching the woman's face very intently for a reaction, which I was expecting to find. And indeed, in the blink of an eye, a grin appeared on Sophie's face, betraying the entity's embarrassment and guilt.

"Those things that fathers are not supposed to do with their daughters…"

"Did you abuse her sexually?" I put this to the entity.

"Yeah…" The voice answered nonchalantly. I felt a twinge of anger hearing this.

"I will tell you what I think, Vince," I began to speak. "I think you are not as bad as you think about yourself. And I think that I know why you did those things to your daughter."

"What do you know? These were bad things, terrible things."

"Yes, they were bad, but not evil."

"What do you mean?" I recognized that it was not the entity talking this time but Sophie. "He abused me and you are saying, that it was all right!?" The woman's voice was high pitched now and screaming.

"Sophie, what I am trying to say, is that your father didn't know any better, he was abused as a little boy, weren't you Vince?" I talked straight to the entity.

"How do you know that?" the incredulity evident.

"I know. I just know." I answered, then continued to speak to Sophie. "Your father was an angry man all his life, but he was never aware what caused that. Now he knows, and he can move on."

"And what about me, and what he did to me?!" Disappointment. "When will *I* be able to move on?" How can you side with *him*?" She was seething.

"As soon as you will be able to forgive your father for all he has done to you, this will end. Forgiveness is a must for you to heal."

"I don't know if I can do that." The woman sobbed. Her face in agony, it was hard to watch. "Daddy why did you hurt me, why?'

"I am sorry baby, I am so sorry…" This was the time for a conversation between Sophie and her father. All I could do was to sit back and listen.

"Daddy, I thought you loved me?"

"I did. I do, but there was no one else for me. Your mother chose to take pills to be away from me and from you. I didn't know who to turn to for love and I turned to you. It was so wrong. I didn't want to believe it was wrong. My father and his brother did this to me. Nobody ever told me I was wronged. I accepted it as part of life, the one that I didn't like."

"Dad… was it you who destroyed my relationships? How could you do that?"

"These men wanted to take you away from me. I felt lonely. I have only you."

"Vince!" I decided to interrupt. "Vince you cannot stay in Sophie."

"Where I am supposed to go? What I am supposed to do?"

"You have to go there where you belong. To the light."

"I don't see any light."

"Think about your love for Sophie," I led the way. "As soon as you do, you will see it. It is this light that brightens your heart. It is this love that is pure light. It is filling you inside and shines outside and around you. Can you see and feel it yet, Vince?"

Long pause, Sophie's head is moving from side to side, "Oh, yes" it whispered. "I can see it. It is so beautiful."

As Vince was beginning to feel the power of the light, I called my spirit guides and helpers from beyond to come and assist me to remove this lost soul to the place of peace. This is what I always do when working with forces from the other side. I don't think I could do it myself, without their special guidance and help. In fact it is really these otherworldly beings who work with people and not me especially. I am merely an instrument in their hands and the hands of the Divine Power that steers my life as well as others. This happens even if we are not ready or willing to recognize it as such.

"Vince. I have called some very special beings to come and help you to move into the light. Are you ready and willing to go with them?" A slight nod from Sophie gave me the answer, as the entity's mind was wandering somewhere in the light.

"Vince, can you see the beings of light that are right around you?"

"Yes, I see them."

"They are there to help you to go there with them where they came from. The place of peace and love. Do you want to go with them?"

"Yes I do, but I don't know if they want me." There was a frown now on Sophie's face.

"They do want you, that's why they are there with you now. Where they came from forgiveness is easy. But Vince before you go, I want you to do two things."

"Tell me…" the entity said nervously.

"They will not leave without you, don't worry. I want you to forgive your father and his brother for all the abuse that they put you through. And I also want you to ask Sophie to forgive you for all that you did to her."

"I forgave my father and my uncle while you were talking to me. You made it easy to see how it all works. Now, all I have to do is to ask my daughter to forgive me." Sophie was crying again.

"Sophie… please forgive me for all the pain and shame that I inflicted upon you."

"How could you do that to me dad, I trusted you?" Now she was really sobbing.

I decided to step in before the woman could bring the heavy weight of guilt back and drop it on the entity. This could unavoidably change his earlier decision to move on to the light.

"Sophie do you want to get better?" I asked her directly.

"More than anything."

"Then you have to forgive. It is the only action that can secure your healing. Without forgiveness you will make your father hang around in you, and your torment will never end."

Forgiveness is essential whether in the individual or to entire Nations for peace in man's soul and for the World.

"Then I have to forgive him." Sophie heaved a heavy sigh. "Dad, I will forgive you. I want you to go, I want you to be happy. And I want my life back." Her voice sounded now very determined. "When I get better, then maybe John will come back to me." She was referring to one of her past relationships. The one that she never managed to get over.

"Vince you can leave now, with Sophie's- and my- blessing. Go to the light and allow these beautiful beings who are surrounding you to guide you there. Go now!" The last instruction is always made in the form of an order rather than a simple request.

The moment of release of an Astral Being is the one that always amazes me. It felt the same way this time. In the moment that Sophie's chest rose as if something within her lungs was pushing too hard on her rib cage, I could see a mist made of a very faint cloud of fog forming above and then soundlessly melting into thin air. Then the woman's body became limp and still.

(This is interesting. When a soul leaves the body, I have noticed that it comes from 3 areas. One is the chest, or our Chakra 4. The second is the top of the head, and the third is out of the mouth. It appears as a very fine mist which rises a foot or so and then disappears. Only once have I seen a soul leave from the whole length of the body. Scientists have actually weighed a persons body before death and at the exact moment of death, and conclude that the spirit has the weight of 21 grams, or about 5 nickels.[1])

"Sophie how do you feel?" I asked after a sufficient amount of time had elapsed.

The woman lay completely still and quiet, there was no response. And then she began mewling[2], her arms wrapped around her stomach.

"Hmm…oh it hurts," she moaned. "My stomach hurts so badly."

"Sophie I want you to become aware of the source of the pain that you are feeling right now," I instructed her.

"She did it to me…," came a low, child-like voice. "She hates me, that's why she hurt me."

"Are you a boy or a girl?"

"I am a boy."

"Can you tell me who it was that hurt you?" The voice started to whimper.

"They cut me in pieces to get me out of her stomach. I hurt very bad now. She let them do it. She didn't want me inside her. She didn't want me," the voice cried.

"No, no that is not true." It was Sophie now who spoke.

---

1 *Snopes, Dr. Duncan MacDougall on Wikipedia, A Soul's Weight, New York Times archived article, March 11, 1907*

2 'Mewling', in case you're wondering, is a real *word* in the English language. When my husband was editing this book, he thought I had miss-spelled some other word or made it up. He looked it up in dictionaries and found to our shock that it is an actual word! According to sources, the word dates back to 1590-1600. I suspect that I somehow know the word from a past life, because *I* couldn't figure out what I'd written!

"You didn't want me. I heard you saying that you couldn't handle it," The tiny voice hurled accusations.

"Yes, I did, but it was an accident." Sophie started to cry. "They pushed me on an escalator, that's how I got injured in my stomach. You were inside me and they had to operate on me to save my life. I didn't mean to hurt you."

"It did hurt me, mom. I was in agony." A child's voice responded, but there was a less accusatory bent to it.

"I know baby, because I was hurting too. I wanted to have a baby, even though at the beginning I was afraid that I wouldn't be a good mother. I miss you my baby."

"Little boy," I involved myself into the conversation.

"Brad." Sophie interrupted. "His name was to be Brad."

"Now you see Brad that it was an accident that damaged your little body. It was not your mom's fault. This accident hurt her as much as it hurt you. You see she suffered a lot, she suffers now too, because you are inside her mind and you make her feel guilty about what happened."

"Brad did you see this man, who was your grandfather leaving with those beautiful angels?" I told the entity.

"Yes, I saw him. I didn't know he was my grandfather."

"Would you like to go to the beautiful place where those angels live?"

"Uhm…, but I am afraid to go by myself."

"I will call these beautiful angels back, so that they can take you there, all right?"

"Yes." A quiet, insecure response.

"Can you see these angels now?"

"Yes, oh yes!" There was noticeable rapture in the entity's voice. "They are smiling at me. They wave at me…"

"Brad, before you go with these angels, I want you to tell your mom that you will be fine, that you understand now what had happened, that you forgive her and that you love her. Can you do that?"

"Mom, I love you and I 'm not angry anymore. Don't be sad because I have to go. I will be ok. These angels tell me that they will take care of me."

"I love you Brad and I am glad that you are going. I know you are going to be all right. If I would decide to have another baby I want you to come back and be born again." After the boy's entity moved out, Sophie's body slackened and became visibly relaxed.

"Are you alone again Sophie?" I gave her enough time to accept the departure of the soul of her baby-boy, before I ventured further with her.

"Yes, I feel somewhat sad and lonely, but I like this feeling." the woman whispered.

"Sophie, would you like to continue or should we end this session?"

"I am tired, I want to finish."

The ending part of my sessions always consist of positive programming and confirmations which ensure the client to wake up with the best possible feelings, and the words that I use most commonly are as follows: Well being, peacefulness, harmony, safety, restfulness and relax. To reassure them and for the person's optimal benefit much of the time I program him/her to remember everything that their subconscious considers safe and valuable and to block anything that might cause discomfort or unease. At least until the next session, when I can work further on the underlying problems and issues. Then I count from 20 to 1 (backwards) and bring my client slowly back to the present time.

"Oh, my God what was that?" These were Sophie's first words, when she opened her eyes. She then wiped away tears that had fallen like rain during the session. "Who were those people? Where did those voices come from? Could I possibly have made them up?" The woman gave me a long bewildered stare.

"I suppose you could have…" I responded, "but if you had, there must have been a good reason for it. But I'm very doubtful, at least from where I'm sitting."

"I feel light," she commented. "The pressure in my chest, that I had for so long is gone. It seems that I can breathe much easier."

"I'm happy to hear that, but I have to give you a few tips of how you can protect this feeling of lightness."

"Uhm?" Sophie arched her brows, intrigued.

"You know what an Aura is don't you?" I asked.

The woman nodded.

"Now, since your aura is weakened, you are again very vulnerable to repossession."

"Are you saying that they can come back?" Sophie said apprehensively.

"No, those that we released shall be in a good place, but there are plenty of others lurking about. They are everywhere."

An aura is the vibration of the white light which I see surrounding people. Its vitality and strength depends on its intensity, brightness, and extension around the body. The health and well being of a person is reflected in the state and nature of the aura. The wider, whiter and clearer the aura around the individual, the healthier they are. If their auras are greyer in color, and diminished in span, generally there is a problem. Another amazing aspect of auras is the presence of so-called 'funnels' (my term - places where the aura vibrates with lower frequencies, closer to those of Astral Beings). It is my belief that these funnels are the entry gates of dis-incarnate beings.

Back to Sophie…

"You need to visualize at least twice a day, it would be a good thing if you would do it more frequently during the day, a bright golden light surrounding you, creating an impenetrable shield."

"How long do I have to visualize this light?"

"Your aura will eventually heal, yet one can always use some extra protection. I do it very often, especially when I work with people."

"What or rather who are those entities?" Sophie seemed fascinated with the subject.

"These are lost souls who due to their negative, heavy feelings at the moment of the death of their physical bodies, failed to move towards the light. They are earth-bound spirits caught between life and death, and belonging nowhere."

"What keeps them here?"

"Hatred, fear, anger, revenge, greed, attachments to worldly things such as places, people, food, sex, substances etc. A million things."

"This is all so new to me, but this is the biggest awakening for me." Sophie seemed quite moved. "I don't know how to thank you."

"Just get better and move on with your life."

"Thank you!" she repeated.

"You are very welcome." I smiled at her. "Go home now and try to take it easy for the rest of the day. What I removed out of your psyche has to still be flushed out of your body. It is important that you follow my advice, Sophie. You also have to practice proper, deep breathing. So remember, light and breathing are two things that I am prescribing for you."

"I will follow whatever you told me to do, I have to get better. I can't continue like this, I just can't."

"A positive attitude and motivation are the most important things essential to healing. I see you have both of them. I have full trust that you will be fine Sophie. Stay in touch and let me know how you are doing, all right?"

"Now I feel I can beat my cancer."

"Of course you can. I believe that you've already done that. In the course of my own life I learned that we have the power to create both, our illness as well as our health. Be your own friend and not your enemy, and you are on the right path."

Over a period of thirty years, and hundreds of people I have worked with, I estimate that in 95% of sexual abuse cases I find a clear karmic connection to past wrong doings. Other than that it was not easy to find karma as a common explanation for our bad luck or failures. In most cases it is simply a learning process that has to include learning through pain and suffering.

In many or rather, most of the cases where there was an extensive and often drastic abuse of some kind inflicted upon a person, a broad and panoramic view of past connections is often the tool that can bring about an act of forgiveness. Such is a necessary thing for true healing to take place.

Frequently I hear from people statements such as: "I forgave my parents for what they did to me," or "It doesn't matter, I don't care about it anymore." As I hear these words I still often detect a tone of pain, anger or sadness. I know that on a deep, emotional level the person saying it had never really let go of the past. It is only our mind, which subconsciously understands the need for forgiveness, which is trying to convince us that this is the only way we can move on and get better.

Part of us, though is not yet ready to let go, and that part will struggle to make us feel like victims, and will do anything to bring back the "rightful" anger and feed it to us so that we will insist that "justice" be meted out. Often we cry so long for it that we are no longer able to see what that justice was all about. We no longer see by having this justice served, we will benefit. Often we discover that there is no relief or improvement in how we feel, after said so-called justice, is exacted. Accordingly we should be free, fulfilled and satisfied, and yet we feel none of that. Even worse, we sense more frustration and disappointment, than we could have imagined. Time is wasted and the struggle we exert to achieve said "justice", completely fruitless. We have failed to understand the purpose of our experience. The reason that this happens to us frequently is that we understand our life experiences only as undeserved and unfair punishment, not as necessary and valuable lessons which are in place to facilitate our spiritual and emotional growth.

Still, the hardest concept for many is to accept responsibility for our own lives. How often have you heard: "If I hadn't married and had children I would be somebody now, my career would be flourishing." Isn't this a convenient way to excuse ourselves from our failing in life? We accept in our lives groups of people that we can blame, so that our ego can be excused from not putting any, or very little, effort into getting us to the promised land of success. Much of the time this success was not designed for us anyway.

Thinking objectively, no one forced us to make the decisions we've made. And beyond doubt, I know, that there were signs and symptoms which provided enough evidence that we were making a mistake. We failed to read those signs, therefore we have no reason to blame others for what we failed to accomplish.

There never is a wrong place to be. There can only be wrong ways of understanding why we are there, in the end.

If we would only look more expansively at the good side of life, we would more easily notice there is so much for us to be happy about. There is an old Polish expression that says: "If you don't have what you like you have to like what you have." This does not mean that we have to settle for less than we deserve. Much of the time we don't have any idea of what we deserve, or what is good for us. It would be more prudent and easier to allow the Divine Presence help us understand and accept what is there for us to accomplish. This simple act of surrender can turn our lives around and at least send us in the right direction.

It's instructive to understand that we are never in the wrong place, with wrong people, doing wrong things, because the Divine Power(God) wouldn't let that happen. God knows best where we are supposed to be. So all we need to do is to use God's greatest gift: choice. And could it be denied that this is something which we often throw back at Him? Especially in those times where life forces us to take responsibility for our own actions. We seem to have a genuine talent to twist things around making ourselves look like victims. Looking back at my own life I have to admit that I was sometimes *the* master of self-pity.

If a husband has been unfaithful is it not usual for society to see his wife as the 'victim' of his cheating rather than looking to see what that wife didn't do or could have done or failed to do to help keep her husband happy and satisfied? Or maybe it was God's plan to pull these people apart so that they both had the chance to experience life in a different way and learn the right things. We are always searching because a part of us knows what our chosen mission was in which we came into this life to fulfill. It appears that simply listening to that internal 'voice' would be best, and yet we often don't.

Over the years of working with regressions, I have learned that most people will search for the lifetimes in which they happened to be victims and martyrs rather than perpetrators and oppressors. Why is that, one would need to ask? I think because we want to look good, impressive, and righteous. Why do we want to look perfect to others? Simply to explain, we want to be accepted. We want to be accepted so badly, because acceptance equals love. And we all want to be loved. At times we want it so badly that we will resort to anything to achieve it.

It appears to me that the things we demand from others, we fail to give to ourselves. Therefore I often think that retrieving the lifetime of a perpetrator would serve us better than finding a lifetime where the image of us is easier to accept. If we could learn to accept the idea that we were not all that wonderful, and were capable of - and exacted-dark and cruel things, this would help to a great extent to see the progress that we have made. Realizing even that when we were tyrannical, God loved us just the same, this would set us free of nagging fears and doubts, and that could help us understand that the Divine Presence passes no judgment. Why shouldn't we do the same? We were, in fact, created in the likeness of God. I have no doubt that we all still carry His likeness. It is always easier to recognize it in others than for ourselves.

**Sophie concluded**

I saw Sophie one more time after our final session. When she came to my house, I hardly recognized her. There was an incredible glow I noticed on her pretty face. Her skin appeared clearer, healthier and her eyes were so much brighter. But what really changed was their expression, there was so much more life in her eyes, they were sparkling like stars.

"God, Sophie you look so beautiful. I can't believe my eyes."

"I feel even better, Ula!" she smiled at me. I realized that I had never had an opportunity to see her white and very even teeth, because I had never seen her smiling.

"So what brings you here today?"

"I just wanted to share how great I have been feeling and also wanted to thank you again for what you did for me." Sophie was deeply moved, and expressed that. "Before I came here I thought my life was almost over. I don't know where I would be now if I hadn't found you!"

"I'm happy that you feel this way, but it was not really me who did it," I responded.

"I am only a tool in the hands of someone much greater than any human being could ever be." I explained.

"I know, but isn't it possible that somebody else would not want to be that tool, or misuse your gift?" Sophie asked.

"That's possible, and does happen I'm sure. But if some are that way then they didn't grow to that gift. They simply don't understand that it will eventually catch up with them, because what goes around comes around. So if there is any wrong or evil done, there will be a time to pay the price for misusing God's gift."

"Will God punish them?" A simple but needed question.

"No Sophie, I don't think that God would bother to get involved in this," I laughed softly responding to the woman's words.

"Why not?"

"God doesn't have to do that, because in the beginning he created a natural law, that works independently of all human laws. And that is: if we perpetrate some wrong that wrong will inevitably come back and undoubtedly teach us a lesson of pain, suffering, fear, sadness or loneliness which we have inflicted upon others. At some point down the road. Or even in a future lifetime. In other words, nothing goes unpunished or unrewarded, we are held accountable for all we do, good or bad. If its wrongdoing that we did we bring punishment upon ourselves, if it was good we are rewarding ourselves with goodness that will be bestowed upon us."

"And God has nothing to with it?" Sophie didn't sound convinced.

"All he has to do with it, is the fact that believing in him and his teachings about love, compassion and forgiveness can be with great benefit and utilized in our lives to make things better, that's all."

"What religion do you practice?" the woman wanted to know.

"I am of all religions and of none." It was my usual answer, as evasive as it sounds.

"How is that possible?"

"I don't name the Divine Power I believe exists, like other people who call "him" God, Lord, Allah, Shiva, Manitou. To me it is a Creating, Loving Power, a Mystery which is all that there is beyond what we know, what we can see, touch and embrace with our minds. But it is only through our hearts that we can truly understand it's essence."

"I love listening to you. There is so much that I have learned from you since I came to see you the first time."

"Have you gotten that job I told you was waiting for you?"

"Oh, yes," Sophie nodded as she gave me her answer. "It is great, people like me there. I love being given more responsibilities. It is such a challenge for me."

"You know now that you can handle it, that you are good enough to do anything you put your mind to. It is so good to see such a transformation in someone's life and personality. This is my true reward to be able to be there to see that."

"Tell me something please." I could see hesitation in her glance, as if she was doubting I would answer her pending question.

"What would you like to know?"

"Are there many people who carry those dead souls around with them, the way it happened to me?"

"Unfortunately yes, in about 60% of people that I happen to work with, I found this external element that in great measure contributed to their problems and difficulties preventing their healing and improvement. For quite a few it was the only blockage they had that was separating them from achieving true healing and happiness. There were no other reasons that could explain the troubling conditions that were turning their lives into a chain of misery and suffering."

"Wow. It is that common?"

"Yes, it is almost like a flu, a common problem filled with symptoms which are unpleasant, often painful, but yet most people accept the struggle, and are convinced that it is a fact of life that cannot be changed for them."

"These lost souls would be then unavoidably identified and separated from oneself and furthermore given an opportunity to be extricated and moved into the 'spirit world.'"

"I'd better go. I could stay here forever and listen to you." Sophie raised herself up from the chair, "I will never forget what you did for me… I want to thank you, because it was you in the flesh who helped me. You taught me about God and so many different things and you showed me such a different perspective about God's existence that for the first time it makes sense to me. With this new understanding, I just might become a true believer." She gave me one of her warm and charming smiles.

"I think you've already become one, haven't you?"

"You will see how much clearer your life will be going when you allow yourself to accept things instead of struggling against them."

This was the last time I saw Sophie, but it wasn't the last time I heard from her. As far as I know she is doing great. Married now with her new baby-girl and an unfolding career, I hope she remembers the words we said that day before she left my office.

*The greatest discovery of my generation is that a human being can alter his life by altering his attitudes of mind.*

— William James (1842 - 1910) —

## CHAPTER TWO: KATHY

I met Kathy in my home where I was hosting an energy healing course. At that time she was at the end of her rope, on the verge of a nervous breakdown, unable to handle the strain of her life. She was over 40 pounds overweight, her hair looked dull and stressed and her skin was ridden with liver spots because she was drinking and taking too many antidepressants. She had to quit her job in a local bookstore due to her mental and emotional exhaustion.

I will never forget the comment made by one of the course participants, who said, "If I were you I would be careful with this woman, she is very weird." That callous comment struck me as insensitive coming from someone trying to embrace the art of healing, which in its essence is supposed to come from the heart born out of compassion.

When she approached me, I could sense that she'd been crying, her hands shook and she had a heavy, bronchial cough. I thought she may have overheard the nasty comment from the other course participant.

"I heard that you do regression work," she began earnestly. "Would you be able to help me?"

"I don't know, but I will certainly try," I answered honestly.

"I just lost my job…," she said.

"I know Kathy, I know. Don't worry about it," I said, cognizant of what she was hinting at. "You need help now, so we will see how can we make you feel better. How does that sound to you?"

People who come to see me are often tense and nervous, and many had never before gone to a psychic. A majority of them fear the worst, hearing and anticipating news about something terrible going to happen to them or their loved ones. They actually expect it so much that when they don't receive any of these kind of messages they become suspicious that I could be hiding something from them. It's unbelievable how negatively our minds work, how little faith we display in life, how much fear we learn to live with.

So, we began our sessions the very next day. When she arrived at my place unlike most of my clients, she appeared peaceful and determined and I knew she was ready for whatever the regression work was to reveal to be heard. Here I would like to mention that Kathy had had a few suicidal attempts during her struggle to overcome the effects of the sexual abuse she was subjected to. What we discovered during our regression sessions, proved that what she remembered was the mildest experience of what was done to her. Here again, we see proof that the suppression of morbid and distressful memories is our mind's defense mechanism for self-preservation and survival.

"Are you ready?" I asked Kathy when she was comfortably stretched out on the small sofa.

“I’m as ready as I can be,” she admitted, looking into my eyes intently.

Kathy was an easy subject so in ten minutes of relaxation she went very, very deep. The two full hours of our first regression were spent completely on reviewing Kathy’s childhood when the abuse took place. Something that Kathy learned during this session was the fact that her father was her first abuser and began to molest her when she was barely seven months old!

In every regression the most difficult part to handle, while working with victims of sexual abuse, is going back and moving through every detail and reliving the full horror and perversity of the abuse. This must be done in order for the victims to face their past and allow themselves to realize that it is only the memory which keep them prisoners. It is a time when the oppressed person realizes that at the moment they are completely safe. Regression into a past childhood is the time when I bring forward and work closely with the inner child.

It is very similar to learning math. One can’t comprehend and embrace higher math if you have missed important information that lays the foundation. One missing number can block you from ever learning math the right and easy way. When we do not understand we often dislike, and when we dislike we reject. This is what creates self-rejection and failure. It is often in cases like Kathy’s that I can’t help myself from shedding tears while leading the session through the abuse.

It took me awhile to realize that crying became my emotional savior, my own way of letting go and not hanging onto other people’s emotions, fears and pains. The sad and pervasive part of it which I realized at about the age of 37, was that due to my ESP abilities, I carried other people's feelings, physical and emotional pains long after they forgot about them. A lifetime of learning to protect myself and shelter my life and lives of my loved ones from what I was destined to do. Today, I still feel what people carry inside them, the difference is that I do not take it on myself, I dispose of it.

During the first session, there were two things that emerged very clearly; one that Kathy's father abused her sexually in an incredibly extensive manner, secondly that her mother let her down and chose not to do anything about it. There was no question that those two issues had to be worked on, but as time progressed I became convinced that it would be easier and faster to let go of the harm done to Kathy by her abusive father, than to let go of the feeling of betrayal that she suffered from her mother.

It is betrayal that cuts deeper into our psyche, our emotions and hearts than the actual wrong done to us, especially when we are children. Perhaps our vulnerability at that age, guarded by an ego responsible for our survival, is the key that can help us to answer why it is betrayal that is so hard to deal with and let go of, not the actual wrong-doing?

Betrayal is the reason for our subconscious mind to reverse our anger. That's where the confusion between our minds and our hearts sets into place. We contend that it is the abuser that we hate, but our emotions know and recognize that there was a way out. The subconscious part of us knows that there was someone who should have stopped these things from happening to us, yet they failed to do so. It is not relevant to the victim why that person or guardian failed, if it was a matter of his/her choice or something that couldn't be prevented (for example death or illness). The child still feels betrayed and abandoned. That betrayed and abandoned child sticks with us for life and cries within us, demanding "justice".

One would ask if there is justice? A justice that can make the hurt go away. I can answer this question right here, if it does exist it is only within us, not outside of us. We know the answers, our spirits know the answers, because they know that there is so much more to us than just the "here and now".

Our following four sessions which were set three to four days apart, brought an illuminating amount of revelation and discovery. Never before had I witnessed a more obvious and straightforward case of karma as it was in Kathy's case. She went on her internal journey and relived, as I remember correctly, 11 lifetimes. Only once did she perpetrate evil and hateful deeds for which she paid for in her other lives including in her present life as Kathy. It's essential to journey briefly through that lifetime in which Kathy managed to open a "Pandora's Box" filled with pain and suffering, in which my client was to pay for her wrong-doings.

She regressed to 17th century England where she had led a loose, immoral life as a woman by the name of Elisabeth. She was fortunate enough to have customers from the higher sphere of society, and this secured for her a relatively comfortable life (for the time period). While enjoying her profession, she came to know a noble man by the name of John. John fell in love with Elisabeth and wanted her for his wife. Strangely, the more John was in love with her the more Elisabeth hated him and was repulsed by him. On the day John came to Elisabeth's house to propose to her, she went mad and stabbed him several times. Immediately after that, she ran out of the house. While in her crazed state she bumped into a woman unknown to her. Without hesitation she grabbed a stone and begun to pound the woman's head, killing her on the spot. While in her killing frenzy she was apprehended, later on sentenced and hung. In her last moments these were Elisabeth's last thoughts: "I hate you. I hope you will all burn in hell!"

As I mentioned previously, for the next ten lifetimes including Kathy's present one, she paid a steep price for her hatred. As we were uncovering and peeling back the mysteries of her past Kathy began to feel better, more peaceful, happier and healthier. With my advice she started using herbal remedies to help her liver and kidneys cleansed from toxic substances that accumulated in her body because of the use of different pills and medications, which she took over the years she spent in depression and other mental and physical conditions. The conditions created by both her mental state and the side effects of the medications she was taking could be on the heads of her psychiatrists.

Kathy's progress was more than impressive. Her spirits were higher, anxiety no longer in place, her persistent cough almost completely gone. Even her skin started to clear and obtained a more glowing and healthy appearance. I was amazed and very pleased with her progress. It was all great until her fifth session. We had her next appointment set for the Wednesday as usual, but around 2 pm on the Monday of the same week, I received a phone call from Kathy. She was crying, and sounded in tremendous turmoil. I could detect fear even before she said anything.

"Kathy what's wrong?"

"Can you see me tonight?" she asked sobbing, "please I have to see you. I have to."

"But what's wrong?" I had other arrangements made for that day, and was trying to see if I could possibly help her over the phone, without having to change my whole day around.

"I think I am going to die. My life is in danger. I am paralyzed by fear, I can't even breathe. I can't make it without you. Please."

The first thing that came to my mind was that this had something to do with the trial that was happening while the sessions were in progress. Kathy was charging a Catholic priest with a rape that happened to her when she was thirteen years old. But I decided not to ask any questions until she got to my house.

"Ok, how quickly can you get here?" I asked.

"Right away."

"Can you drive by yourself?" I wanted to make sure she felt stable enough to get safely to my place.

"Yes." She hung up and fifteen minutes later she was knocking on my door.

"Please come in." I invited her inside and gave her a warm hug. "You are going to be all right," I tried to reassure her, as we walked towards my office.

Her fear was connected to the ongoing trial, but not the way I thought. I gave the Church more power than it had. I thought that maybe some church figure had tried to threaten Kathy and make her give up on pressing charges against the old priest. Eventually I learned all the facts from Kathy, and from that day on I gave up on trying to speculate about things and events.

"Tell me exactly what happened that made you feel your life is in danger?" I couldn't wait for her explanation. "Is this threat referring to your physical life or rather a lifestyle or relationship that you might lose? Did anybody threaten you in any way?"

"Physically…"she said slowly trying to calm herself enough to be comfortable to speak. "It happened this morning at 11 AM when I went to see this court psychiatrist," she carried on, "I have been waiting two months to get an appointment with this woman psychiatrist. Well, initially I was to wait five months, but it just so happened that someone canceled an appointment this morning, so right away she thought of me as the first who needs her help. I was very happy and excited when she phoned me. My court date is very close and I need all the instruction I can get. You know that they treat the victim like a criminal to discredit that person, so that the perpetrator goes free and unpunished. That's the reason I was to see that woman." She took a short break to summon her strength and courage to keep her emotions under control, so that she would be able to tell me the rest of the story.

"Take your time, we are here now, so we will try to fix whatever it is," I encouraged her gently.

"So, …"she sucked in a deep breath "so everything was ok until I went to her office where this woman psychiatrist was waiting for me. As soon as I saw her face I froze with the irrational and yet, as real as you're sitting there, fear that I am going to die. This dreadful feeling hasn't left me since this morning."

"How are you feeling now?"

"I feel a little safer now when I am with you, but it's still here." She pointed at her chest. "This strange tightness is still here."

I thought about this for a few minutes.

"Ok let's get started," I said, knowing that it was all we were able to find out at the moment.

As I mentioned before, Kathy was a wonderfully easy subject to work with. With every session after the first one all I had to do was to ask her to get in a comfortable position and then I counted slowly to ten. That was all that it took for Kathy to dive into a very deep hypnotic state. As soon as she was under I decided to go directly to the root cause of her malaise.

"Now, Kathy I want you to take me to the very beginning of the fear you were faced with this morning when you went to see the court psychiatrist."

"I see you...," she began, "I want to learn from you."

"Who am I?"

"You are an herbal healer."

"Am I a woman or a man?" I kept anchoring her gently to the moment she was reliving.

"You are an old man. Your name is Francis. You are poor, you live in the mountains, in a cave. I see lots of drying herbs hanging all over the place."

"How old are you?"

"I am twenty -one." Kathy had incredible ease in gathering information.

"Are you a woman or man?

"I am a woman. My name is Marie. I live in the village not too far from your abode. I asked you to teach me about herbs and healing. I want to do what you do. I want to help people to get better." Her voice was low and peaceful.

"Did I teach you about the herbal healing?"

"Oh, yes, you were very wise and patient, but I never got to know you better."

"Why was that?"

"You were just that kind of man I guess. No one ever knew you."

"And then what happened after you know the things that you wanted to know?"

"I went back to my village and began to help people. One day there was a woman who came to me to get something to increase her fertility. She couldn't get pregnant."

"So what did you do for her?"

"She was not a very strong woman, she was of a very ill health, so I advised her to strengthen her body first, so that she would be able to carry a baby." Increasing anxiety on Kathy's face and in her voice. "She got angry with me and said that it's not my business, and that she came to me with her fertility problem and that's what I am supposed to help her with."

"So what did you do?"

"I gave her a mixture of herbs to help her to conceive."

"What happened next?"

"She left, but I learned that she died a year later. You remember I told you she was not a very strong and healthy woman?"

Kathy's voice suddenly changed and sounded worried.

"Oh, God they are coming!" The woman was in deep distress, her face twisted in a grimace of fear and panic. "I didn't kill her, I did not kill her… nooo…!" She started to sob, folding her arms in front of her as if trying to protect herself from harm.

"Who is coming?"

"The people. People from the village, they want to punish me, because they think I killed her. I try to tell them what happened but they don't listen. They want to hurt me."

"How are they trying to hurt you?"

"They are throwing stones at me. Oh, God it hurts, I am bleeding from my head and face, and they will not stop. They are going to kill me. Somebody help me please!" Kathy is really sobbing now. I needed to come to her rescue.

"Kathy… you are dead now," I told her in a firm voice. "I want you to remove yourself from Marie's body. You don't feel any more pain or discomfort of any kind, you are now floating above the whole scene." I suggested. "What do you see?"

"They are still throwing rocks at me. They all went crazy. They hate me." She exclaimed in surprise, "Why do they hate me so much, I know I didn't kill that woman!"

"They act out of fear."

"What do they fear?"

"You."

"Why? I am not a dangerous person, I was always trying to help them."

"You possessed the knowledge they didn't understand, and that's why they feared you, they had to blame somebody for something they were not able to control."

"And what was that?"

"Death."

"Yes. I see it now, I understand it now."

"Kathy I need you to identify the woman you saw today at the psychiatrist's office. Can you do that for me?" Kathy was one of these people who had incredible ease in recognizing souls she knew in her past.

"Oh, yes I understand it now," she breathed out.

"What is that you can understand?"

"My fear. The woman that died and that I was killed for *is the psychiatrist*!" It was an incredible discovery. I was very impressed with the simplicity of the connection.

"She still looks fragile and not very strong, today." Kathy commented.

"How are you feeling now? Are you still afraid?"

"No, the fear is gone. I suddenly feel great."

"Ok. Kathy we have nothing else to do today, so I want you relax and listen to me for a moment, then I will bring you back to the present." I instructed her and for about ten minutes, programmed her to bring the most positive and uplifting feelings from the session.

When Kathy sat up and opened her eyes, her face still carried an expression of shock.

"That was incredible," she stated.

"I am surprised myself Kathy. Life arranges everything in the most unbelievable way. In your other life she indirectly caused your death, and in this one she came to support you in your struggle. She came to teach and instruct you on things which can help you to win your case in court. Wow! I will never forget this session."

I saw Kathy two more times in sessions. The last one, I felt had to help Kathy to deal with her guilt about an abortion that she was forced by the courts to go through when she was only 11 years old. The procedure took place in the fifth month of the pregnancy. I have to mention that the baby was that of Kathy's father. I am not aware if the justice system really attempted to find out who was the father of the child, and if they did, Kathy's father wasn't charged. As easy to imagine, it was a more than traumatic event, due to many factors, the pregnancy was high, the baby well formed, Kathy had no control or say in the matter, and no one ever attempted to bring to justice the man who was responsible for this. She didn't feel protected and safe even when there were other people around who were in the position to do something about it.

The baby was removed in pieces through a surgical procedure. What was left with Kathy over the next 33 years was a sense of guilt and loss, and the little baby clothing she was not able to part with until our last session.

While Kathy was under hypnosis I moved her through the abortion of the little baby-girl, and all the other accompanying events. We learned, that after the procedure, her father never touched her again. The little soul, by coming into Kathy's life, was able to stop the terrible abuse and humiliation Kathy suffered from her biological father. This realization was all that the woman needed to finally let go of her attachment to the lost baby and the guilt that came from the reality of its existence.

Additionally what we learned that day was that the spirit of the little baby-girl returned to her in the body of the younger of two sons, born about 15 years later.

I feel that it is important to mention that two days after our session Kathy made a trip to the mountains and there she buried the bundle of little clothes, with all the pain that was attached to it. She was at last able to grieve and set to final rest the memories of her lost baby.

I met Kathy later on and she offered to open her home to me whenever I needed to stay in the city. Her health improved, she became a Reiki master and was now in a position to continue the mission she began in Marie's life as a healer. She was able to forgive her father who came to claim a woman who rejected and killed him in another lifetime. It was an easy task for him since the one he was claiming was a 7 months old baby, his own daughter. The woman who was stoned on the street by Elisabeth, was Kathy's mother who came back to watch her daughter suffer for the death she caused many hundreds of years ago.

Kathy understood the law of karma, and accepted the payment she was to make in order to receive grace and be forgiven for all her wrong-doings. This was what helped her forgive her father and mother for what they had done to her. She gained the ultimate goal that enabled her to heal her life. She forgave and was forgiven.

Later on, talking to Kathy about my future plans at the time, the idea of writing "Spirituality Not for Sale," she asked me not to forget about her case. She believed that sharing her life story with other people who experienced abuse similar to hers, could help them learn from it and heal easier and faster by knowing how to deal with their pasts.

I will, definitely, never forget Kathy's case. She helped me to grow tremendously as a human being, while I assisted her on her path to wellness and recovery. There is always a place in my prayers for the woman by the name of Kathy. Even though her name for the protection of her privacy had been changed, she will know this is her story.

She said: "If only one person can be helped because of learning about my life story, it was all worth it." These were some of the greatest words which I was honored to hear in my life. I thank Kathy for that.

It's not easy to write this book since I am sharing much of my private life with all of those who will read this book, and many of them who also know me from personal encounters. I want to share parts of my life with my readers for one reason: if there is anything that I have learned in a hard or painful way I hope they can use that to spare themselves suffering. I do not, personally, believe that pain is an absolutely necessary element of learning. I am also convinced that nothing belongs to us, not even our own talents, gifts, skills and experiences, not even our lives. We were given them so that what we have learned can help others to live their lives better, healthier and be happy.

*Your primary goal should be to have a great life. You can still have a good day, enjoy your child, and ultimately find happiness, whether your ex is acting like a jerk or a responsible person. Your happiness is not dependent upon someone else.*

— Julie A., M.A. Ross and Judy Corcoran —
*Joint Custody with a Jerk: Raising a Child with an Uncooperative Ex*, 2011

## CHAPTER THREE: LUCIA

I came to know Lucia through a psychologist who for some time tried to assist her in her attempts to resolve her problems. He told me he had run out of ideas how to help his client.

Starting out, I would like to describe Lucia at the time I met her. She was of medium build, a dark haired woman who appeared to me around fifty -years -old, though I learned later that she was a few years younger than me at the time. She was only thirty-six, and through most of her life, struggled with loneliness, depression, and physical aches and pains that would affect her entire body, at times leaving her unable to function normally for days on end. I must add that medical tests done were unable to find anything wrong with the woman, so eventually after a series of those tests she was told that it was all in her mind, therefore they (medical personnel) sent her to see a psychiatrist. She went to see a psychologist instead. After long months of attending his office, she gave up.

Lucia immigrated into Canada from Italy at the age of twenty-two, where a few years later, she met her husband and had two children.

I learned that she was not happy in her marriage, though she had nothing against her husband, who appeared to be quite a decent and honest man. She was also not very close to her children, because she had a hard time bonding with other people. Her few friends described her as a nice, though difficult person to be around. Most of the time depressed, negative in her opinions and insecure. Lucia would tell me that frequently she also had to fight parasitic infections, not a pleasant prospect.

I always, or usually, have a reading or initial talk with the client before deciding if past life regression would be the right direction to take. While I was reading Lucia and obviously hitting many of the important issues of her past including an abortion, the woman stared at me with disbelief and then she exclaimed.

“I’ve waited for you for a long time. I just knew somebody like you must exist, so when Patrick, my psychologist, mentioned you, I knew I had to see you. Now I know I was right.”

“What do you mean?” I was not convinced I understood. “What is it about me that makes you feel I am the right person?” I wanted to know.

“You know there are things that cannot be seen, and you can see those things that no one knows about, like you could see my abortion and the sense the guilt that I still feel about it. I know you can find out what is destroying me from the inside.”

"I will most definitely try. When do you want to set the first session?" I asked, having in mind my next trip to the city, which would happen in the next two weeks.

"Today. Right now."

"Now?" I repeated, a little taken aback.

"I will not leave this room until we have our session!" I was truly surprised by Lucia's words.

"I don't want to live any more."

"Lucia how can you say that?"

"I tried it before, it is not so difficult to end a life you don't want to live." From the tone of her voice and determination on her face I knew she was deadly serious.

"Ok, I have some time, let's proceed." I surrendered. Eagerly, the woman laid down on the blanket spread on the floor and covered herself with another one to keep warm.

The session began and until today I can not stop reminiscing over the discoveries we made that day.

When she was regressed and her body visibly relaxed I began to notice a slight change on her face. A sort of twitching, making her face look even older and angrier.

"Where are you Lucia?"

"In this damn country!" the voice saying these words was definitely not my client's.

"Who are you, and what are you doing inside Lucia?" I made my voice sound hard and firm.

I am Antonio, Lucia's father." As I listened to the answer to my question, I remembered that Lucia's father was still living back in Southern Italy. It was my first spirit possession by a still living person (most commonly found in parent-child relationships).

"Antonio…why aren't you in your own body?"

"My body is doing fine. I don't need to be there. She is my concern. She should have listened to me. She should have stayed in Italy with me where is her rightful place. No, …she didn't listen, she had to come to this stupid country."

"On what basis can you say that?"

"I know. I came here and I couldn't stand it. The people are stupid here," the entity barked.

"Your daughter's husband is Canadian, your grandchildren are Canadians so what is wrong with them?"

"I hate that stupid man, and his kids won't be good because they grow up here."

"Antonio," I interrupted, "do you love your daughter?"

"What a stupid question that is," the spirit snapped at me. "She is my daughter, of course I love her."

"So if you love her, why then are you are destroying her?"

"What do you mean?" the entity's sounded incredulous.

"I know that Lucia likes this country and she loves her husband and children. Why can't you accept that?"

"A daughter's place is by her father," the voice regained its cockiness.

"No, your daughter's place is by her children and by the husband of her choice, that's where her place is. Your place was by the woman you chose to live with. You do not own your daughter and her life. Only a sick in his mind father would want to tie his daughter to him. You cannot serve her as a man, can you?"

"Of course not!" the entity howled, outraged.

"Antonio, I don't think you truly love your daughter. You are selfish and you display no concern for Lucia and her life."

"I love her," the entity became defensive.

"Why don't we then ask her about this?" I suggested.

"Ask."

"Lucia." I addressed my client's personally,"you heard your father talking, didn't you?"

"Yes," the woman voice uttered, she was undeniably upset and angry. "You never loved anyone, least of all me. I hate you for what you are doing to me, do you hear me?"

"Lucia you don't mean that," the father's voice responded.

"Yes I do. You make me feel sick, old and tired. I am thirty-six and I feel and look like I am sixty. I feel miserable… like you."

"No, this is not true I am healthy. I am in a good shape for my 86 years."

"And you know why, Antonio?" I interrupted this dialogue between father and daughter.

"No, why?"

"Because you derive and sap all of Lucia's strength, health and vitality."

"This is not possible, is it?" the entity's question displayed its increased doubt.

"Yes it is. You are draining your daughter's well of life."

"I want only good for her." It was the first sign of surrender, that sparked a little hope in my mind. From previous experiences with the cases like this, where the possessing spirit belongs to the living body (usually a parent), I learned that it is much harder to remove this kind of presence than the one that is a lost soul of the deceased person simply because it usually has much stronger reasons to be where it is. The motive is a need to control the child's life.

"You are talking strange. How this is possible?"

"Well, let me explain. Where do you live?"

"In Italy of course, you know that."

"Where does your daughter live?"

"In Canada."

"So how do you know what is happening with her. How can you hear me? I am also in Canada." I challenged the spirit.

"I don't know, I don't understand that," the voice admitted.

"I will help you to understand. Your spirit that belongs to your body lives in Italy, most of the time, but sometimes it moves into the body that belongs to your daughter. It is your daughter's strength that you are taking away when you go back to your own existence. That explains why your body is flourishing and your daughter's is withering. If you continue doing this, then Lucia will die. You also confuse her life, her feelings and her thoughts. She doesn't know who she is or what she wants. She has already attempted to take her own life, because she cannot live this way anymore."

"She is my daughter. I have the right to be with her." The entity's arguments were getting weaker.

"No, you don't." I said pointedly. "The only right you have is to love her. You don't have a right to destroy her life."

"I know my father. He would never let other people be. He had to order them the way he expected them to be, isn't that right dad?" Lucia interjected.

"Is this what you think about me?" the spirit said defensively.

"Yes."

"I just want to see you are happy."

"Is that what you tell all your friends?" Lucia was not trying to hide her sarcasm.

"They know me. They know that I want only your good."

"Then leave me alone," the woman pleaded.

"You," the entity directed this to me.

"I am listening." I said.

"You too think that I am destroying my daughter's life?"

"Yes." I gave him a straightforward answer.

"So how can I prove you both are wrong?" the spirit challenged me.

"By removing your presence from your daughter's body and mind, and going back to reside permanently in your own." I instructed.

"Are you sure that is the right thing to do?"

"Ask your daughter."

"Lucia, do you want me to go?"

"Yes, I want you to go and leave me alone." the woman almost shouted.

"Will you write to me? I have only you, your mother is gone."

"You have all your well-off friends." Lucia was angry and couldn't help herself not to display it.

"They don't mean much to me."

"It is your life father, you live it." there was nothing in Lucia's voice that would betray any positive emotions towards her father. "I just want you to go. Go." All of a sudden the woman started to sob. "You ruined my life."

“Ok. I am going back, you don’t want me to stay. I go,” the voice died down.

“Is he leaving?” I wanted to make sure it was not a trick.

“Yes, he is. Oh my God, his legs are shaking, he is an old man now.”

“And how do you feel now?”

“I feel lighter and somehow stronger. He was eating me up, wasn’t he?”

“Yes, he was.” I decided that there was much more work left to do, so I asked Lucia to lay down for a moment breathing deeply, then I asked her to walk inside herself searching for other reasons that were contributing to her problems. As I was directing her, I noticed that she clasped her palms over her ears and her face became distorted by pain.

“What is it? What is happening Lucia?”

“I should not have done it!” I heard all of a sudden. This was not Lucia speaking.

“What was it that you should not have done? Who are you?”

“I know who she is.” Lucia came to my rescue. “Her name is Katerina Catelioni, she made me very sick when I was six months old.”

“Yes, I should never have agreed to do it, even though it was her parents that requested it.” The entity opened up. “I pierced her ears when she was six months old, and she got a massive infection that made her very ill. I cannot forget her incessant crying. It haunts me even after all these years.”

“Where are you now?”

“I am attached to Lucia.”

“Are you inside her?”

"No, I am outside."

"Katerina, do you still have your own physical life?"

"No, I died of a heart attack twenty -seven -years ago."

"So, when did you find Lucia? Was it right after your death?"

"Yes, I couldn't rest in peace, I needed her to forgive me."

"Katerina it was not your fault. It was my parents who asked you to do it."

"Yes Lucia, but I still had a right to say no. I didn't because I wanted to get paid. I hid behind the fact that I was only doing my job. It was wrong. I caused you so much pain, and you were just a tiny, innocent child." I saw tears trickling from under Lucia's eyelids. The entity was truly in great distress.

"Katerina I am not angry at you, I forgive you." There was undeniable compassion that I heard in the woman's words. "Go to rest."

"Thank you." the entity said, deeply touched. "I told you she was too young to have it done, but not you. You had to follow your traditions, so that you could feel important." I was surprised at this, since what entity just voiced, was not directed at either me or Lucia."

"Katerina who are you talking to?" I asked.

"To Lucilla."

"That is my mother's name!" exclaimed my client in shock.

"Where is she?" I was excited. This session was taking a very unexpected turn. It almost seemed that the presences were taking charge in their own hands.

"She is right here, inside Lucia. I can see her." This happened to be a very helpful hint, that allowed me to move on and work with the next presence.

"Katerina, I want you to leave now and proceed to the light, it's time for you to depart to your resting place." I turned my attention to the attached spirit of the woman. "Are you ready to go?"

"Yes, I do feel at peace now." she said serenely. "I want to thank you for your help."

"It's ok, that's what I do. Go now Katerina!" Unlike in other experiences of the release of an astral being, I did not notice the client's chest rise while the entity departed. I realized that the spirit of the woman was not residing inside but was barely attached to Lucia's aura, therefore, as I concluded, the fourth chakra had not taken a part in the process.

Since we already knew about the third presence residing inside my client, right after Katerina's departure I began to address Lucia's own mother. I knew the woman had been dead for about fifteen years. And from the reading I knew that she had spent most of her life being or feeling sick, and continuously seeking medical attention.

She married Lucia's father at the age of 16, through a marriage arranged by her father. It was evident to see that after their only daughter was born, the woman learned to use her illness to keep her husband away. Further, she became detached from her daughter as well. I believe that she never allowed herself to bond with her child from the moment she arrived in the world.

Lucia became an object of blame that she received from both of her parents alike. Her mother saw her as an element that was tying her strongly to a man she did not love and who, in her mind, was causing her misery and unhappiness. Her father saw her as the reason that caused his wife's health problems, which led to his banishment from the bedroom. These were some of the main factors which contributed to Lucia's loneliness and inability to bond. Her subsequent detachment and loneliness was the main cause for her vulnerability to spirit possessions at any stage of her life. In spite of no physical or sexual abuse I could conclude that in this case neglect and emotional deprivation of the child could have caused even greater damage.

Here, I would like to add that with many people I work with, neglect, abandonment, emotional deprivation and mental cruelty can be deemed forms of abuse which are as damaging as sexual and physical abuse.

**Lucilla's case continues.**

"Lucilla can you talk to me?"

"I don't want to talk."

"I think talking about it will help you to feel better,"I suggested.

"What do you want from me?"

"I want to ask you about your daughter."

"I don't want to talk about her. I haven't seen her in a long time."

"So, Lucilla…," I took my time, "You are not aware that you have been occupying your daughter's body for many years?"

"What nonsense are you are talking," the voice snapped. "How could I occupy my daughter's body? I am dead."

"Well, yes I should put it differently. Your spirit occupies it. You didn't depart to the light as you should have done."

"That doesn't make sense." The woman was still resisting that she was indeed inside her own daughter's body.

"Lucia," I directed my words to my client. "Can you help me to explain to your mother that she indeed inhabits your body. That after her death she didn't depart to the light."

"I couldn't see any light." the entity complained. "Everything after I was free of my body, was as bad and sad as before. Nothing changed. I was hoping death could rescue me from my misery. It didn't."

"And would you like to know why?"

"Of course, didn't I suffer enough?"

"Lucilla, you suffered because you chose to, and…,"

"What do you mean?" the entity wouldn't allow me to continue.

"Are you telling me that my forced marriage was something that I wanted? You are out of your mind!"

"No, I am not saying that. What I am saying is that after awhile you could have done something to remove yourself from this unhappy situation. You didn't live in times of Spartacus, and Roman gladiators."

"And what is that supposed to mean?"

"It means you were not a slave or prisoner. It means you could have left your marriage."

"You know what people would say?"

"What are they saying now? Do they even care?"

"No, no they never did," she knew this was true, and didn't like it.

"You stayed with your husband because you needed someone you could blame for your unhappiness, and passiveness. If you had left him that would have forced you to take responsibility for your *own* life. And that would require some hard work on yourself and your life. It was much easier to put all the blame on your husband and your only daughter. That was your excuse to push your child away from you, too. Honestly, Lucilla, I don't think you ever tried to learn to love your daughter. She was such an easy object to blame for your own failures."

"You think I was cold and heartless, don't you?" the entity didn't like this line of reasoning.

"No, I don't think you were especially that way. All I think is that you have to stop feeling sorry for yourself and help your daughter to heal from the damage you contributed to. It is time to help yourself to see the failures of your life, so that you can make some needed corrections. That can help you to move on with your own spiritual growth, and perhaps get you a better start next time around."

"Can you help me get out of this mess?" she sounded remorseful.

"Yes, that is the reason why I am talking to you. I am not here to blame you or make you feel guilty, I am here to help you to become free of all that, so that you can finally move to the spirit world, and be able to rest in peace… Lucia, I want you to make peace with your mother." I was talking to her daughter now. "Can you do that?"

"I'm sure I can." Lucia said this in a peaceful and serene tone.

"Can you tell your mother what you want to say?"

"Mother, I was very lonely and you were so distant and absent, I wanted you to hug me and comfort me but all you were able to do was to cook food and wash my clothes. I learned to live pretending you didn't exist, and in a way you didn't. You gave me my physical life and maybe that was all I needed from you. I think I love you, but it is like loving a stranger. That's the best I can do. I don't carry any anger towards you. I feel a little sad, but it will eventually go away. I want you to go now and allow me to be alone, this is my life and my body and I want it back."

"I will go, but I need this woman," the entity referred to me "to help me to do that."

"OK," I agreed. "Lucilla I want you to relax now, think of nothing, just feel the peace that surrounds you."

"Yes, I can feel it."

"If you slowly turn around and look behind you, you will see the light I was talking about." I took a short break, got up and walked around the room to stretch my legs, and to allow the spirit to collect itself.

"Can you see it?"

"Oh, yes I can see it. It so beautiful and peaceful."

"Can you think of any deceased person who you know cared for you a lot?"

"My Grandmother Rosa." came her immediate answer.

"I want you to call for her, she is going to come and help you move to the light. Can you do that?"

"I don't have to, she is already here. She is smiling at me."

"Is she saying anything, listen to her carefully." I gave her another instruction.

"Yes, she says don't worry everything is going to be all right."

"I want you to take her hand and start walking towards the light, but before you go I want you to say some last words to your daughter. Can you do that?"

"Yes, Lucia I am so sorry that I failed you as a mother. I hope next time around I will do better. Can you forgive me this failure?"

"Yes, I already did. Now just go, and be happy."

The releasement happened the same way as in so many other cases, except that this time it was just Lucia's head slightly rising, and then resting back on the pillow. The woman's face remained expressionless, but this didn't last long. All of a sudden Lucia began to whimper as if being in a great deal of pain and distress.

"What is it Lucia?" I reacted immediately. "What is happening?"

"Oh, my stomach it hurts so much," she moaned, pressing her hands against her stomach.

"I address to whatever or whoever it is causing Lucia this pain."

"No, no don't do it, oh please! ." I realized immediately it was a child speaking.

"Who are you?"

"I am Antonio."

"Are you a child?"

"Yes, I am Lucia's son."

"What happened to you?"

"He killed me." The voice exclaimed. "This son-of-a bitch killed me."

"Who are you talking about, and how could he kill you?"

"I am talking about my father. He forced my mother to abort me. It hurt. It hurt so much. I will not rest until I kill him for what he has done to me." I was very shocked, since I didn't remember anything about Lucia's describing her husband as a man who would be capable of doing such a thing. However I knew she did lose a baby through an abortion. It was hard for me to respond and not to show my confusion. I did my best to hide it.

"Antonio… do you know where you are?"

"I am in my mother's belly. I am her baby."

"Do you feel anger at your mother too?"

"No, I love my mother, she did what she could to protect me."

"How do you know that?"

"I heard her fighting with him and crying and begging but he wouldn't listen, he said he could not let the bastard be born, because his father would kill him. And it hurt so bad, so bad…," the voice broke and began sobbing.

"I want him to know how much he hurt me."

"Antonio, I want you to listen to me, can you do that? You said that you know you are in your mother's womb?" I began. There was an answer that came with a slight nod of the woman's head. "Did you know that your mother is hurting very much because you are there?"

"No, why?"

"Because she feels your pain, she suffers a lot. She also blames herself for not being strong enough to prevent your death."

"I love my mom. I don't want her to feel pain."

"She can only stop feeling this pain if you leave her body, and go to join the angels in heaven."

"If I go my father will never pay the price, he will never know what he did to me."

"There is a way he can learn about it," I suggested carefully.

"How?"

"I can talk to him and tell him how much he hurt you. I can make him understand what he did to you." I figured that this was the best way to approach the situation. It could not be that difficult to set up appointment with Lucia's husband and bring him the news.

"Will you do that? the entity was encouraged.

"Yes, and I will do everything so that he will understand and regret this terrible thing he has done to you."

"You promise?"

"Yes, but you have to promise *me* that you will leave to the light where you will be with these beautiful angels."

"I am afraid to go there by myself."

"I will call them and then they come to take you there. You don't have to be afraid. They are very special and loving beings, they will teach you and protect you, you don't have to fear them."

"Call them, I want to go," the spirit, himself, declared his readiness to depart, and that was a very good sign.

"Antonio, do you want to say anything to your mom, before you go?"

"Mom, don't worry he is going to learn that what he has done to me. This woman promised me to talk with him. I love you mom but I think I want to go. I can't stay anymore. You are not angry?"

"No, Antonio I am not angry. I want you to go and be happy and safe there. I don't want to suffer this pain and guilt anymore. I am going to die if it doesn't go away."

"I am going, they are waiting for me. I will be waiting for you on the other side. Good bye Mom."

Here I could see that my client was tired, and emotionally exhausted. We had been in the session for two hours and fifteen minutes, and I felt very fatigued and drained.

Even though I felt there were even more presences left, they would have to wait until our next meeting. This woman was a bottomless well of issues stored in the heavy luggage she carried from her near and far pasts. They will all have to be addressed and worked on when the right time comes.

When Lucia came out of the hypnotic trance, her entire face appeared younger, I would say years younger.

"I feel so much lighter," she commented while returning to a sitting position, "I don't remember ever feeling so good and peaceful, Ursula."

After Lucia left I spent some time reviewing all that we learned during our first session. It was an overwhelming amount of information, which required time to process and understand. Aches and pains, uncontrolled and unfounded outbursts of anger and frustration, spells of depression, feeling old and tired, the inability to focus and many other problems were, incontestably, rooted in the number and character of the possessing spirits Lucia carried. Her father's presence could explain the woman's anger and outbursts of rage and her need to have the final word. Her mother's spirit was instrumental in her numerous but medically unfounded health complaints, an incessant feeling of gloom and unhappiness. The spirit of the aborted baby contributed to her anger and feelings of guilt and hopelessness. Perhaps, I thought, it was also a reason why Lucia had such a hard time bonding and getting closer to her husband. But this was what one would call a twist of fate, about which I was to find out in a weeks time, during our second session.

There was one more thing that caught me in a trap called a "promise". I learned from Lucia herself, after our session was finished that little Antonio's father was not her current husband, but her ex-boyfriend. It happened back in Italy, when she was seventeen years old. I felt very uneasy realizing that, at this point, I had no means to arrange the meeting I promised to the spirit of the little boy, therefore I was unable to keep my promise. Failing to keep a promise had rarely happened to me and I was upset about the whole thing.

**Lucia's second session.**

As usual, it's generally easier the second time to bring a client into a deep state of hypnosis, than initially. I had allocated another two hours to explore more mysteries in Lucia's life, more reasons that could explain her problems.

This is the place where I want to tell my readers about the twist of fate I mentioned earlier.

"Lucia, is there anything inside you that doesn't belong there?" I began our second session.

"I feel that there is."

"Any of those that we released last week?"

"I don't think so." She shook her head and pinched her eyebrows as if trying to get a closer look at something or somebody inside her mind. "What are you doing here?" Her brows arched in disbelief.

"Who are you talking to?"

"Andrea, my ex-boyfriend, you know, the father of the little boy."

"You never mentioned he was dead."

"I am not dead." This wasn't Lucia who said this.

"I'm sorry, "

"I heard you talking to Antonio. I feel very bad. I never realized that it hurt him so much."

"Andrea, where do you live now?" I changed the subject wanting to learn more about the man to whom this spirit belonged to.

"I live in Palermo. I have a wife and two children. I went through the University of Rome as my father ordered me,"

"Are you happy?" I asked.

"No, but I have to live with everything I've done."

"Do you love your wife?"

"No, I married her because my father decided she was right for me. The only woman I ever loved was Lucia." This voice sounded sad and resigned.

"If you loved her as you say you do, why did you force her to have an abortion, why didn't you marry her instead?"

"Because my father hated her, and he forbade me to have anything to do with her."

"Why did your father hate her so much?"

"I don't know, he just did."

"And there was no strength in you to oppose that decision?"

"I guess I am a coward."

"So what do you want from Lucia now. Why you are obsessing over her?"

"I want to be with her. I feel we belong together."

"No, Andrea you don't belong together, and it was you who made the decision about that a long time ago."

"Lucia," I addressed my client and asked her to take a stand.

"Can you forgive, Andrea?"

"I don't know, he hurt me so much. He betrayed me. He was the reason I had to leave Italy. And the worst is what he has done to Antonio." She was very hurt.

"Lucia," I reasoned with the woman, "if you will not let him go, you are going to continue to feel pain and anger, you will prevent your own healing. It will be *your* life that will suffer. Is that what you want?"

"No," the woman almost shouted, "of course not."

"Then you have to order Andrea to withdraw into his own body and set you free."

"I want him to go, it is over between us. It was over a long time ago."

"I want you to tell him that yourself."

"Andrea, go back to your life, leave me alone. You have your family and I have mine. I want my body back for myself."

"Then you have to leave my body too." the entity objected.

What the hell was this?

"Just a second," I interjected, "Lucia, were you aware that you were possessing Andrea's body?" I wanted to know.

"Yes, I missed him. I felt that I was supposed to take care of him. I don't know why I felt this way, but I did."

"Andrea, I want you to go back now to another lifetime and search for the life that connected your destinies, so that you may learn about your feelings and attachments to one another." I suggested.

The entity had no problem to move back further in time.

"Yes, I found the life you asked me to find!"

"Where are you?"

"I am in our house."

"Where is that house?"

"It is on one of the Greek islands. We live there."

"Who is we?"

"My mother, father, and me."

"How old are you, and are you a boy or a girl?"

"I am six years old, and I am a boy. My name is Spiros."

"If you look into your mother's eyes very carefully, can you tell me if you recognize her as anybody you know in your present life?"

"Yes, it is Lucia."

"Do you love your mother?"

"Yes, and she loves me too. Even though my father says that I should be a girl, because I act like one."

"What else does he say?""

"He says that this is my mom's fault, that she made me to be that way. I don't believe him, it is not her fault. It is the way I am."

"Now Andrea I want you to move a little bit ahead in time and find events that change your life for the better or worse." I gave the spirit the suggestion.

"Yes."

"How old are you now?"

"I am six."

"What is happening. Is it good or bad?"

"My mother is going to have another baby. It doesn't feel good."

"What is causing this feeling?"

"My father is hitting her and shouting that he is not going to raise somebody else's bastard. He thinks that she is fooling around with another man."

"OK. Spiros, move forward again, and tell me what is happening now?"

"My mother is having a baby, but there is a problem. I am scared, there is lots of blood." The voice was terrified.

"Is there anyone with your mother?"

"No, my father said to her that this is her time to pay the price for her sins. He doesn't want to call anyone who can help."

"What are you doing? Are you crying?"

"No, he doesn't allow me to cry. He says only girls can behave like that, and I am not a girl."

"What happens next?"

"It is only me and my mother, because my father left the house. There is lots of blood, my mother looks very bad. I don't think she can hear me.""

"What makes you say that she can't hear you?"

"She doesn't answer me. Mom please say something. Oh, no, no!" there was a cry of desperation and despair that tore from Lucia's throat. "Mom, mom don't go, don't leave me please!" Strong sobbing drowned out the words and left the entity in a state of shock. I pulled the entity out of there.

"OK, Andrea I want you to come back to the present moment." The crying ceased almost immediately after the entity was called back.

"Andrea I want you to tell me if you could recognize the soul of your father, who is he in your present life?"

"Yes, he is my father now." Understandable surprise in this sentence.

"Do you know the soul of the baby that your mother was to have?"

"Antonio." The answer came instantly. "God, it was Antonio. Now I can see the reason why I did not want Lucia to have the baby. I was afraid that she would die and I will lose her again. It all makes sense now. I hid behind my father so I could blame him for the abortion. You know what he called Lucia from the first time he saw her."

"What?"

"A damn whore."

After all these incredible findings I convinced Andrea to move back to his own body, which he agreed to do without resisting. I also had to make sure that Lucia would call back her spirit that was possessing or obsessing Andrea's body and mind. They finally released each other from the claws of mutual and destructive obsession, that was eating up and destroying their lives.

After I was done with Andrea I regressed Lucia to other past lives, at least those that would confirm Andrea's experiences. She managed to bring more detail to what we already knew. For one she said it was her husbands baby, she had never fooled around, the second important information shed light on the hatred that Andrea's father felt towards her.

Lucia came from a wealthy family when she married her husband, who had an unhealthy gambling habit. Lucia learned the extent of it when her son was about four years old. She threatened her husband that she was going to tell her father about it. In return her husband made up a few stories about Lucia being unfaithful. Knowing her father as she did, didn't leave Lucia any illusions that he would ever forgive her for that. She also knew that it would be her husband's words that would receive more credibility than her own. In a final vicious abomination, after Lucia's death, her husband slandered her name to her father. In addition to inheriting all her money, all he had to do was to promise never to say anything about her alleged crime of adultery.

Here, a sad conclusion emerges, about how poorly he had lived his present life, and how much deeper he plunged into an ocean of hatred and treachery.

Lucia's friends noticed that she looked better and some of her aches and pains diminished. The most common remark she could hear was that she looked so much younger. I knew that there was more work to do, and as often happens, many clients after seeing the first signs of improvement, stop attending the sessions. Some of them would come back later but only when their problems started to rear their ugly head once more.

Through the times I have worked with people I learned one of the most important things is to allow them to make their own decisions, and that makes my work with them possible and so much easier. And respecting those decisions no matter what they might be. Respecting them without judgment.

As I said it before, the healing power is within us, and I believe, it is passed on us from the Great Divine. I am only a tool, catalyst or facilitator of the whole process. What I tell people is that I can show them where to go to find what they seek, but I can't walk with them to get there. It's everyone's lonely walk through their own souls, minds, dreams. It is there on that lonely path where they learn to recognize their own spirits, their own destinies, their own truths.

My next case will prove to those still in doubt, those who insist that it is only a matter of belief that brought many of my clients to recovery and healing. I couldn't agree more, because I know that everything in life which we consider real, it is only real for those who believe in it.

However in what I do, I only need one kind of belief. I need to believe that my clients want to get better. This is all that is necessary to make our mutual efforts effective and successful.

Other than this they don't have to believe in reincarnation, spirit possessions, karma and other ethereal topics. They don't have to know anything about altered states, hypnosis, even relaxation. Those who don't know about those subjects and those who do can be equally helped through age and past life regression, as well as through the process of releasing into the light the astral presences.

Tracy's case will be one of those who didn't believe and did not know anything about regression, she didn't even know the meaning of the word "hypnosis" when I met her.

*Never discourage anyone…*
*who continually makes progress,*
*no matter how slow.*

— Plato —

## CHAPTER FOUR: TRACY

Tracy was a 21-year-old native girl. She looked to me to be quite skinny, somewhat rugged and pretty worn-out for her young age. Her motley appearance could be explained by relating the following story of her so -young life. Tracy grew up in a very abusive home. As I- and she- learned in a later hypnotic session, she was born as only one of two in a twin pregnancy to a mother heavily addicted to cocaine and other hard drugs, which she used even during that pregnancy. In her later years her mother would lapse into long spells of deep depression. She would be frequently hospitalized due to her mental and emotional condition, which was exacerbated by continuing heavy use of drugs and alcohol.

Tracy, in due course and following in her mother's footsteps started to use alcohol and many other dangerous drugs by around the age of nine. Over the next 10 years she was in and out of various drug and addiction treatment centers. Around the age of 13 she finally ended up on the streets working as a prostitute. She, unbelievably, carried 6 children to full term, five of which were given up for adoption. The oldest child was six years old, and the youngest eight months. This child was still in her care. The girl was experiencing frequent paralyzing dives into deep states of depression, enduring outbursts of rage, and daily bouts of fear and anxiety. I had a suspicion that she was still using drugs, though she had denied this when I asked her about it. She did not have a steady job and most of the time was on Social Assistance.

I met her at the private office of my friend, Lisa, a government social worker, who had asked me if I could do anything to help her client. She ran out of ideas herself of how to help this young girl, and to assure the safety of her young child.

"Hello Tracy, do you know who I am?" I began.

"Yes, Mrs. Martin told me about you."

"Do you know what we are going to do today?"

"No, not really." The girl resignedly shrugged her shoulders. "It doesn't matter, I want to try. Maybe this will work. Nothing else has." She sighed.

After I spent a few minutes explaining the process of hypnosis to her, we began the session to see where it would be taking us. She sat back in a comfortable la-z-boy and without much effort drifted fairly and easily into a deep hypnotic state. This was her first time, and I was pleased to see that she was so responsive.

"Now Tracy," I started in, "I will count slowly backwards from the numbers 20 to 1, and when we get to 1 you will move back in time to the day of your *fifth* birthday." Time slowly passed as we reached the last number. Then suddenly:

"I don't want you to do that to her!" came an unexpected, surprising utterance, which was definitely not coming from my client.

"Who are you?" I asked the voice.

"I am her friend."

"What is your name?" I queried.

"Melissa. Melissa Zeviak."

"How old are you Melissa?"

"I am six years old."

"How long have you been with Tracy?"

"Since 1913." I was expecting anything but this. For a brief time I was very confused. With help of simple math, I figured out quickly that Tracy's year of birth was 1977. How could they possibly have been together from 1913? I had no time to ruminate on this, and needed to move the session forward.

"Melissa, I want you to move back to the time that something made a big change in your life happen." I gave the entity a moment to regress, then I asked, "How old are you when it happens."

"I am six."

"What is the year when you are six?"

"I think it is 1919."

"Where are you?"

"I am in the basement of the house."

"Is it a farm house?"

"Yes it is, we live here."

"What are you doing in the basement?"

"My mother sent me there to bring her some jars. But I think that she really didn't want me hear them fighting."

"What do you see in the basement of your house?"

"Nothing much. We mainly store things in here."

"Can you tell me what do you see?"

"There is an old sofa, a table, some shelves with jars, boxes. My father keeps his guns here."

"Are they secured?"

"No, they just stand, leaning against the wall."

"You never touch them, do you?"

"No, I know better than that. My father would kill me if I touched them."

"Can you hear anything from upstairs?"

"Yes I can hear footsteps, and their shouting. They are still fighting. My dad is drunk as usual. I hear the door slamming."

"Who left the house?"

"I don't know. I think it was my mother who ran out of the house, but I am not sure."

"What were they fighting about?"

"I am not sure. I think it had something to do with me. My mother shouted that if he dares to do something she is going to go to the police. I don't know what she meant."

"Melissa. What is happening?" I noticed a visible change on my client's face. Her features tightened and her eyes widened as if afraid.

"He is coming down to the basement."

"Your father?" I wanted to make sure I was following and understanding the events the right way.

"Yes."

"What does he want from you?"

"He is pushing me onto that old sofa. He stinks of alcohol. He makes me sick." Tracy's face exhibited disgust.

"Keep telling me what is happening." I instructed the spirit.

"He wants to pull my panties down. I don't want him to do that. I am kicking him. I kicked him in the groin. He slapped me across my face. He says I am the same damn whore like my mamma."

"Where is your mamma?"

"I don't know, she must be upstairs…" the voice began to break.

"What is happening now?"

"He is dragging me by the hair towards the wall." The entity was now in great distress, therefore I had to make more frequent comments so that she would feel more comfortable.

"What for?"

"He is reaching for the gun. Oh, my God he wants to kill me! Mom, mom help me!"

"What happened?" I intervened.

"He put the rifle to my forehead and shot me. Oh, there is so much blood everywhere."

"Melissa. You are here, now. It is ok. calm down."

A long pause.

"Where am I?"

"You are in the body of Tracy, my client who is not doing well, because of you being there. Do you like Tracy?"

"Yes, she is ok."

"What attracted you to Tracy?"

"I don't know. It just felt right to come in." The entity was honest." I thought she needed me."

"Melissa, you are not supposed to be inside someone else's body. You are dead, and your spirit is to move to the light."

"Where is that?"

"Did you go to the church with your mom?"

"Yes, every Sunday."

"So, you for sure heard about angels and heaven?" Expression indicated the affirmative.

"That's where it is."

"You just called it light." responded the entity.

"I call it light, some people call it spirit land, some heaven. It is a very beautiful place. You are going to be safe there. You can grow and play and have many beings around you who will love and care for you."

"You wouldn't lie to me, would you?"

"No, I wouldn't. Melissa if you will not like it there, then you can always come back here. Though I know, you will like it there very much."

"I want to go, can I?"

"Yes, I asked the angels to come and take you to the other side. Are they there yet? Can you see them?"

"Oh, yes I see them. I never imagined they would be so beautiful." A broad smile appeared on Tracy's face.

"Melissa, I want you to go with these angels."

"I am going now." These were the last words I heard from the spirit of this six year old girl.

The session continued.

"Tracy did Melissa leave?"

"Uhm." The girl nodded her head. "I think I will miss her."

"It will be all right, don't hold her back." I advised, knowing what could happen if the possessed person would chose to hold back the soul ready to leave. This could end with the entity deciding to stay, even if it was against its own choice. This would completely negate my efforts of releasing the lost soul into the light.

"Melissa is going to be fine."

As the hypnosis progressed, I found three more presences inside Tracy which had to be released, before we were able to explore my client's own past, to try to resolve her numerous problems. The presences were not strong ones so I didn't have too much trouble convincing them to leave. Right after that I asked Tracy to take a few deep breaths, then I instructed her to start moving backward in time in her present life to a time as a fetus still in her mother's womb, just shortly before her birth. I again counted down from twenty to one. I couldn't hear myself sounding the word "one", because Tracy began screaming in terror, and trying to cover her ears with the palms of her hands.

"Oh! What is this sound, it hurts my ears? Oh, please make it go away…"

"Tracy I want you to focus on this sound and when I count backwards from five to one, you will become aware of the source of this terrible sound and every other sense that will help to explain what you feel right now. What is this sound?"

"It is a sound of a shotgun."

"Tracy, where are you?"

"You told me to go back to my mother's womb, shortly before my birth. I don't want to be here!" She exclaimed. "There is so much blood."

"Tracy what happened to cause so much blood. Is your mother in labor?" I asked.

"No, she shot herself through the stomach. She killed my brother, oh God I am so scared." My client's body keeps wiggling around as if she was trying to escape.

"You never told me that your twin brother was dead." This time I had a very tough time to understand the facts she was uncovering.

"There was another baby inside my mother's stomach. I was not a twin I was a triplet." It was an incredible shock and Tracy had difficulty overcoming it. "I had another brother and she killed him," she cried. "Why did she do that, did she hate him?"

"Are you and your other brother harmed physically?

"No, we seem OK. They are trying to save her and our brother."

"Did you mother survive the accident?"

"Yes, but she should have died. She is not a good mother."

"Tracy can you repeat your last sentence."

"She is not a good mother."

"Do you feel sometimes this way about yourself?"

"No." Came the first response, then immediately she changed her mind. "Yes, I think that way about myself. I am not a good mother. I gave three of my children away. One day I am going to get my kids back and be a good mother to them," she said in a low, determined voice.

"I think you may be able to do that one of these days Tracy, I really do. But now, let's not worry about it." I knew there was so much more to explore, so I didn't want to waste more time. Our most important discovery of Tracy's present life was made, so we needed to move on.

"Tracy, once again as I count backwards from twenty to one, I want you to go back to your most recent lifetime before this one." I gave her these instructions and then began to count down the numbers.

Again without any trouble the girl regressed even more deeply.

"Have you found it?"

"Yes," she answered curtly, "I am right here in my house."

"Who are you?"

"I am a woman."

"How old are you and where do you live?"

"I am 29 and we live on the farm."

"Can you locate this farm?"

"Yes, it is in Southern Alberta, not far from the border of the United States. There are maybe forty miles to the border." In spite of my expectations, she gave me some very precise and exact information on where her farm was located. Now I began to wonder if she would be as precise with describing the time when she lived there.

"Could you tell me the date of the day that you see yourself right at this moment?"

"Yes, it is July 17th 1919." Amazingly, this information unbelievably came quickly and without hesitation.

I have to mention here, that it's not often that clients can provide detailed information like this. Usually, the most I get are names, perhaps a partial date (usually a year), not much more.

As Tracy named the year 1919, a red light of recognition, flashed in my mind. It was definitely a familiar date.

"What is your name?"

"Trudy Mechelen." Again, I was just stoned by the provided information.

"How long have you been married?"

"Too long," she sounded frustrated.

"Do you have children?"

"Yes, I have a six year old daughter." Again, seemed familiar.

"What's her name?"

"Melissa." This just bowled me over. I, all of a sudden, understood the meaning of Melissa's words. When I asked her how long has she been with Tracy, she responded right away; "Since 1913". In 1919 Melissa was six years old so that would make 1913 the year of her birth. Since my client was her mother at that time, it made perfect sense why she said that they have been together since 1913. It was for me one of the few sessions that had more then one twist. One thing which in my experience doesn't occur too often, was that the entity was drawn to my client due to the connection from a past life.

"Tracy, what happens to your daughter?"

"I believe her father shot her."

"What do you mean, by 'I believe'?"

"On the 17th of July we had a big fight, he was drunk...," she began to explain. "He wanted to have sex and I refused him. He got mad and shouted that if I didn't want to do it, he was going to get it from Melissa. He said the women in his house were to serve him. I told him that if he dared to touch my daughter I would report him to the police. That's when he slapped me hard, and I ran out of the house."

"Where was Melissa?"

"In the basement. I sent her there to be out of her father's sight."

"Ok, continue. What happened next?"

"After I heard the shot, I ran into the house. He was standing in the kitchen. His face, clothes, hands and shotgun were covered with blood. I knew he killed Melissa."

"Then what happened next?"

"He shot me through the lungs. The last thing I remember is him bending over me and shouting: "You stupid bitch, you made me do it!" In spite of the gruesomeness of the described events, my client remained surprisingly calm.

"Do you think that you were responsible for his crime?"

"No," she shook her head. "I didn't do anything wrong, except marrying that sick man." This answer reassured me that there was nothing to undo, since Tracy managed to understand the events the right way.

"Tracy, if I ask you now to try to recognize the soul of your husband who killed you and your daughter, in someone you know in your present life, would you be able to do that?"

"Oh yes. It is my mother." The answer came so quickly, that I had no time to swallow it, without choking on it for a brief moment. I couldn't believe in this almost uncanny chain of connections that were displayed in this case.

"Oh, my God." There was incredible shock in Tracy's voice. "She didn't want to kill my little brother, she wanted to kill me, so that I wouldn't go to the police. I can't believe it."

In her altered state Tracy was exhibiting high and unquestionable sharpness of her mind and she could really verbalize in a very proper and logical manner, something that I didn't notice in her conscious state. She would display a lack of education, as well as a rather poor and limited way of expressing herself.

"You know...," Tracy face brightened with a smile, while her eyes fluttered under her closed eyelids.

"Yes."

"I think I knew about that, that's why I decided to come in a crowd." The girl almost giggled. "Three is a crowd isn't it?"

"Yes, you could say that." I saw her point.

"Ok Tracy, now I want you to go and find a lifetime in which you have done bad things that later on you had to pay for, perhaps including your present life."

It was amazing how quickly and easily the girl would dive into the deepest ocean of memories and fish these that carried answers to all the questions she came here to find.

"Yes I found it," she reported.

"Who are you in this life?"

"A man. I live in England. It is 1723. I am 34 years old." It was unbelievable how quickly Tracy was able to provide information.

"What is your social status?"

"If you ask me if I am wealthy, yes I am very wealthy. My social status is not so good."

"What are you doing at the moment?"

"I am chasing an animal. I am in the bush."

"What animal? Can you describe it to me?"

"It is all black, but no hair on its body. It somewhat reminds me of a human. It uses only hind legs to run, very strange I never saw anything like this before."

"Maybe it is a human?"

"Are you joking? It is black like coal. People don't come in such a color."

"Maybe they do, you just didn't see them yet."

"Oh yes, like you did." There was undeniable sarcasm in girl's voice.

"Are you able to catch this animal?" I returned to the questioning.

"Of course, we have to catch lots of them. It is good money." I was now completely sure that my client was reliving a lifetime of a slave-hunter.

"What is your name?"

"John."

"How old are you at this moment when you are chasing this black animal? How long have you been doing this?"

"Well I am 26 now and it is my first hunt. I like it."

"John, I want you to face this as you call it, animal. Look into its eyes."

"Yes, you know if I didn't know better, I would say they are almost human. Wow, it is a female, I see her breasts. I will get good money for this one. They need females to reproduce."

"What are these animals used for? What do you do with them after they are captured?"

"They are put on ships and send to the New Country."

"You mean to America?"

"I have heard this name."

"You know now John, that these are human beings that you hunt. They are people like you, the only difference is that they have black skin and they live differently than you."

"They are savages, primitive savages."

"Nonetheless, they are people. Do you think it is right to enslave them? Do you think it is right to treat them this way?"

"Since it provides for my wife and two children, it must be good."

"Does your wife knows where the money comes from?" I attacked his point of view, again.

"Why should she know, women don't need to know about these things."

"I want you to move forward to the years when you are no longer a slave-hunter."

"How old are you?"

"I am 48."

"Why did you stop?"

"I got some physical ailment, from this damn country, and my wife said that she would leave me if I didn't stop. So I stopped. I am not that young, you know."

"Now, I want you to move towards the time of your death, right before you take your last breath." I instructed. "How old are you now?"

"I am 48."

"Where are you?"

"In my bed, sleeping."

"Where is your wife?"

"She is sleeping in another room."

"You don't sleep together?"

"Not for the last five years, since I got that ailment, she refused to sleep with me. She didn't want to get the disease from me."

"Could she get it from you?"

"I suppose so. But it doesn't matter I cannot get it up anyway."

"So what happens that night? Are you sick?"

"No. This male servant that I brought from Africa, came at night to my room."

"And then what happened?"

"He put a pillow on my face and suffocated me. He was a strong bugger. I've got no chance."

"So what do you feel about what he did to you?"

"I deserved it, he got me to pay my debts. I guess it is fair."

I was very impressed with Tracy's understanding of the law of karma and repayment. "I guess the payment was not big enough, to pay for all the wrongs. I needed a few more lives to pay it all up. Do you think it is over?"

"That only depends on you," I responded. "It depends on you."

"So if I let this life to be screwed up to the end, then I'll be even?"

"No it doesn't work this way." I was trying to explain one of those questions that most of my clients ask me. "Undoing the wrongs is not equal to senseless suffering and pain."

"What do you mean?"

"What I mean is that at any time we can change our punishment into grace, if we choose to live with compassion and love. If we choose to actively do something for others, for only one reason, because we care. This could be the fastest way to pay our karmic debt, rather than allowing our lives go to waste." I explained. "Senseless suffering leaves us in a limbo called self-pity, instead of helping us to get motivated to bring about some self-changes or self-improvement. The only things that could help us to move from the stagnant places in our spiritual growth."

"That makes sense." The girl heaved a sigh, and her lips twitched in a pale smile of understanding while listening to my speech.

"We often might have to accept our pain as a part of our pay back, but it is not good enough. Why, because it often doesn't come with recognition of our guilt, and instead we learn to feel sorry for ourselves. Even worse, we learn to manipulate it, so that we might get attention, pity or even control over those who were not careful and gave into our lies."

"Well it does make perfect sense," the girl whispered.

It was the time to end our session. So as usual before bringing my client back, I did my part of positive programming, and confirmations then counted back from ten to one and asked Tracy to open her eyes. When she declined her chair back to its upright position all I could see on her face was astonishment.

"It was all so strange," she commented, shaking her head.

"How do you feel?"

"Pretty good! Better than in any other time in my life." She answered.

"Now take some time, then if you decide to see me again you know where to find me."

"Ok, I will do that."

I didn't seen Tracy again. Years have passed since our session, and from what I heard, she moved to the city and went back to school. At the moment she is trying to get two of her children back. How things will go for her is very hard to predict, but it seems like this one session enabled some big changes in her life.

I guess this is the way life is supposed to unfold. Each of us has a mission in someone else's life to fulfill. We come into someone's life for a brief moment with a package that contains a lesson that we needed to deliver, and then we leave. I believe that the lesson stays, even if sometimes it takes a very, very long time for a person to pick up the delivered package and see what is inside.

One word, one sentence, sometimes one glance is all it takes to change someone else's life forever. Therefore it is so important that we weigh our every word before it leaves our lips, that we weigh every thought before we think it, every act before we act it, because if we fail to do that, we are catapulting into the Universe a huge bundle of negative energy, that has uncanny and frightening ability to spread disaster everywhere it will reach.

But it is important to know that in the final analysis what we send out will come back to haunt us. Even if the sound of the voiced words have long since died out their energy never ceases to exist.

I would like you, all my readers, to think for a moment and perhaps count in your mind, the many thoughts, words and actions that we all direct against others with cold premeditation and without a shade of consideration or understanding, send away in one day. If you can do that then you will be able to see the gruesome picture of cruelty, selfishness and greed, that we all possess.

Think about the bad wishes against others that we foster in our hearts even for a split second, that come through. How did they make you feel? These dishonest words of blame or accusations which we cast into other people's faces, that disgraced them and broke their lives.

Did we have a right to do those things? Many of you would probably shout with anger: "They did those things to us. They deserved their punishment!" Yes, they probably did some of those terrible things to us, but as you can see through the cases I presented, no one really knows who started it all, who threw the first stone. Maybe it was not them, but us? And even if we have a justified reason to blame, what is the difference between us and them, if we decide to avenge what was done to us? We ourselves are equally evil and cruel. How can one killer accuse another killer? Is there a difference in the value of a life that was senselessly lost? Where and when does the wrong start? And who is to be the judge of that?"

If we choose to look only at one lifetime, then it is easy to make these judgments, but if we look deeper, we no longer feel we can pass judgment. It takes a great effort to look further and beyond, that's why most of us will only look at the surface and judge it for it's face value. It is easier this way, it doesn't require anything, moreover, it gives us a position of power and control, which most of us, one way or another, want in our lives.

What I hear frequently, is: "I want to be in control of my life and myself." The question that comes to me when I hear this statement is: "Why do we have such an incredible drive and need to be in control, and what makes us feel that we can control anything or anyone?"

Throughout the course of my life this is the most significant lesson I have learned. The first is that we are never truly in control of anything. All there is to it is the illusion that we are in control. An example comes to mind. Let's say we are steering our career in the direction of our choosing. We were lucky enough to have the necessary education or training, without interruption. We are very proud and happy to begin to work for a successful company. We start to make lots of money and gain deserved recognition. As soon as we gain this illusive impression that we are in control of our career, the company that we work for goes under and is forced to lay everybody off including us. There was nothing that we could control about the external events, which leads to us this feeling of vulnerability. We feel like fallen leaves pushed in every direction by the wind. The only difference between us and those leaves is that they don't struggle against the wind, they allow the wind to take them where it might. And what we do is exactly the opposite. We want to wrench ourselves away from the wind, hoping we can fly against its current. There are two lessons that we could learn, if we chose not to struggle. The first that we could get a free ride, and the second that we could be able to see the places where the wind would take us, which we would never visit otherwise. Other possibilities and alternatives can enter our lives.

How can I translate this metaphor so, that what I am trying to say, might become clearer.

We could look at this layoff as the vacation that helps us to recuperate our strength. We threw ourselves into our job and poured all our energies into it. During this vacation we could meet someone who might offer us a better opportunity, or perhaps we could learn about another activity or function that we would love to do. We could even decide the change our career.

All it would take from us would be faith and humbleness to accept the fact that a higher force had different and better plans for us than we did.

Why is it that in these low moments we blame God, whose existence we suddenly remember? And why is it when things are going well we choose to behave as if He doesn't exist?

It is this place where we can clearly see an undeniable difference between our ego and our spirit. The ego feels that we deserve it all, tells us what is best for us, and demands it with cold detachment, while our spirit knows what truly is the best for us(even if our own ideas are different) and asks for only one thing: the strength to accept.

It doesn't push us, it doesn't pressure us, it gently leads us there, where we have to be, to learn our lessons, which we have (perhaps conveniently) forgotten about. The spirit never competes, it only assists. And this happens only if we decided to follow its guidance. The Spirit always respects our power of making decisions, it doesn't force us to do things we don't want to do. It also doesn't do something else. It doesn't judge.

This judgmental part of us is the most unfair and also the one that makes the good things hard to see, even less, appreciate. It is this part of us that makes it very hard at times and even impossible to forgive and through this heal ourselves. The healing that I am talking about may be physical or emotional in form, yet very spiritual at it's core.

I believe beyond a doubt, that it is only through our spirit that we can achieve the improvement that we seek, and not before we accept all that came with the teachings, which we would often call failures, suffering, defeat, downfall or loss. Yes, that is because we prefer to treat life as punishment and not as learning. As long as we are fixated in this way of feeling, we can never take one step forward.

There are many questions that I am frequently asked. One of them is: "Can you heal me?" This one is often the most interesting since it is hard to even imagine how anyone could possibly not know the very simple and obvious answer to this question. By searching for another doctor, another pill, another medicine man, or another psychic, people are predisposed to searching for a quick fix. The answer to this question is: "No, I can't heal you, and there is much more to it, nobody can." The power and ability to heal sits deeply within each of us, thus it is only our own selves which can unleash it and put it to work. This power is not ours, it belongs to the source that issued it. Call it as you will. I call it Creator. God. Divine Presence. Translating it into simpler language for those who choose to call themselves atheists or agnostics, it is the presence of Love that heals us, and the absence of it can destroy us.

Through the many hundreds of people I have regressed in my life I found that the biggest devastation in their lives was done in the absence of this mighty and most powerful feeling of all. Love. Its starts with learning to love ourselves first. For that we need good teachers. The first teachers are always our parents, those who raised us or those who abandoned us, in either way we learned our first and most important lessons. If we are supported and accepted it tells us that we are special and good, because these nurturing people love us. We identify completely with those around us.

If we see our parents putting themselves down, struggling with their self-worthiness, self-confidence and self-respect we are more likely going to have serious problems with the same things. They are our role models so, naturally, we imitate them in every possible way. In plain words it can be said that we have become copies of our parents. Settling only for that (meaning being only what our families were) will not give us a chance to grow. Like every copy, even those coming from the best copiers, we will be worse quality and clarity. Quality means making the same mistakes and feeling that because they, seemingly, work for our parents, they must inevitably work for us as well. I use the word "seemingly" on purpose, to pull your attention to an important fact that our parents are not the only ones standing in line. There are many others who came before them, whose mistakes *they* are recycling. What I just proffered is a picture of a vicious circle. So if we copy and not make any effort to improve, we are poorer copies of the very old "original". The clarity can be explained by the fact that the "original" had at least different external conditions and reasons behind which it could hide, therefore had some excuse from not doing the right things. We don't have these excuses, so we have nothing to hide behind.

The world doesn't stay the same, in stasis. It advances, it creates better conditions which makes it easier to express ourselves. Consideringly, if our fathers were taught that men don't cry, it cannot apply to us, because we live in times when men do cry, and even more, are respected for it. We have the power to break away from old beliefs, laws, rules and ideas. All we need is courage.

Leaders are those who have the courage to break away from the old, and we should be grateful for that trait that can allow the change to take place. Every one of us can be a leader, there are few limitations to that. However, not too many of us have the temerity to lead. But, yet, we don't have to be leading crowds, it is plenty good if we can be our own leader, subsequently directing ourselves in the right direction and allowing the changes to take our lives where we want them to be. In this sense, we become believers in what we are incapable of doing

Sometimes thinking small is better. I say if each of us could change the way we are, we can become a living proof to others that change is possible, and not especially difficult to achieve. Small change is a warrantor for bigger change

This is all possible yet often so unreachable for most of us, not because it is impossible but merely because we are too passive to try, too stiffened by the old ways to attempt to break free.

Hiding behind these false walls we often call security, we continue to live lives that we learn- and accept- to hate, and as a result we often come to believe that we are truly unable to do anything right. This conviction has nothing to do with our abilities or capabilities, but rather is rooted in our fears, which we have allowed to overpower us.

It is important to understand one more thing, that not only achieving our goals but also *not achieving* them can be our victory. This, I realize, may sound to the reader like a conundrum. The real strength shows in our ability to retreat with dignity and deeply believing that one lost battle doesn't mean we have to lose the whole war.

There is also another way to deal with that what we truly cannot achieve. This would allow us to accept without struggling, and move on accordingly.

There is no need to treat the unreachable as failure but merely consider it as guidance provided for us, so that it can help us to find the right way to go. Unfortunately, more often than not, we choose to feel badly about what went a different way from our expectations.

In many situations, we gravitate more towards anger and resentment than toward objectivity and healthy self-criticism. If we would choose to look at the big picture, we can see the reasons for which events occurred in the first place. Which makes it easier to accept and adjust. All that struggle would be spared us and with it a great deal of suffering and pain.

Here I would like to present an example to illustrate this philosophy, and pursue a more expansive view, and magnify the detail at the same time.

*The glory of friendship is not in the outstretched hand, nor the kindly smile, nor the joy of companionship; it is in the spiritual inspiration that comes to one when he discovers that someone else believes in him and is willing to trust him.*

— Emerson —

## CHAPTER FIVE: NORMAN

At some point, several years ago, I had the pleasure of working with a well known public figure in a couple of sessions. Our first encounter- a reading- had an important highlight. I could see that this man had a future as a writer, yet he himself was stubbornly insisting that he wanted to be an actor. Ironically, though he had unquestionable acting talent, bigger and more important roles were dearth in coming about. This was a continuous source of frustration and disappointment for this lovely, deep and gentle man. At the time of our first reading, he was just about to give up on his dream of "Hollywood". I had no doubt that his calling was locked in writing. As soon as the reading began I received a strong and very clear vision of a beautifully bound grey jacketed book and the face of this man was on the rear cover of the jacket. The difference was that he had a bushy yet well groomed beard in that picture. Shortly into the reading when I revealed the vision to this man, he looked at me quite astounded and said that he had a beard like this barely three months ago. For some reason he shaved it off, though he somehow felt it was not the right thing to do. I had no difficulty in giving him more information about what kind of book it was to be. He listened and then left my place still not convinced, and not delighted with the premise that mine and his visions of his prospective artistic future were not well matched. Regardless of the dissonance, he was intrigued enough to further pursue this subject, and we set an appointment for past life regression work.

A week later we got together and we were both blown away by the findings of this single 2 hour session.

Among the many things that we discovered, including the fascination for my client with native spirituality, most became easily explainable. As it turned out, he had had two lifetimes where he had lived as a native man. These were profoundly deep lives, filled with wisdom that seemed to have a weighty influence and impact on the kind of person my client came to be in his present life. He was born in the United States and traced his blood links to the Indian people of the eastern regions of that country. I believe them to be the Shoshone and Mohawk. He was actively involved in native ceremonies and practices. But this wasn't surprising to me, since it is not unusual to find connections of this type. What is intriguing was the discovery of the most recent life he had in France at around the turn of the 20th. Century.

Born to a very poor peasant family, as a young child he was sent to live and work in one of the many Catholic Churches in Paris. The Church gave him a formal education and used him as a writer. Education that otherwise would be considered a blessing became his tormentor and enslaved him to the people who gave him his dream, yet took his life away. He didn't live long enough to become an old man. In his mid-forties, disconsolate and disappointed he became ill, and withdrew from life. Tuberculosis didn't take its time moving him to the other side.

His last thoughts and wishes on his deathbed were those of having a chance to live again and write from the depths of his heart and not take orders and instructions from others. After this discovery, it was apparent to see that he got the chance for life he wished to have. Upon coming out from under hypnosis, the man was startled and puzzled by all that he retrieved through the course of the session. He could remember everything in this session. I knew it would take him awhile to overcome the surprising revelations of his deeply buried past, place them in his present life and come to terms with them.

A couple of months after our session, the man phoned me up and said that he was excited and happy to announce that he had decided to take a screenplay writing course in Los Angeles, and he was hooked on the subject. After returning from the States, he had no doubt that writing screenplays was what he wanted to do for living.

One would have to ask, why then do we struggle to push life in the direction we want it to go, if instead we would let destiny take its course and lead us on the waves of life, for a free ride to the destinations we didn't realize were meant for us to pursue? If we would allow that, yes, that could save us much pain, suffering and disappointment.

Is it in our human nature to challenge life? What part of us demands those challenges? Does the spirit need to challenge? I think we can sense the answer to this question.

The Spiritual Dimension is searching all the ways which we have arranged for ourselves, before returning again to this Earth, so that we can determine the absolute truth of our human existence and move us to higher realms of our spiritual destiny. The Ego, alternatively, searches for the ways in which it can challenge the very reasons for which we exist.

Thinking back of my own life, it makes me want to laugh at the times when I was swimming against the current, ending up exhausted and lost on the shores of this river called "life". It took me years to understand the simplest human law, that acceptance and humility protects us from struggle and pain. Many years after that realization became clear to me, I learned to utilize my knowledge and wisdom that, I realized, was always there and at hand. Have you ever wondered how silly it would be to live in a dark house, in spite of knowing that there were light switches in every room? And it was only our fear that wouldn't allow us to try to find them. This is exactly what happens to so many of us, who are searching for the wrong things in the wrong places.

So much had changed since the day I left the country of my birth, Poland, thirty years ago. All the years that have passed since 1985, when I emigrated to Canada, have had the most profound influence on my character, philosophy, humanity and my spiritual growth. Each event could by itself be a road sign for so many people who are lost in the vastness of the ocean of life and its tidal waves of change and never ceasing motion.

What is true today for so many people will not be so tomorrow when changes of life will wash away all the illusions of today and bring new hopes and dreams of tomorrow.

The idea of change is one most feared by so many people, yet is one that secures for us the possibility to grow and advance.

A long time ago, I was one of many bleeding hearts who would throw in God's face these questions: "Why do you allow this to happen to me? What have I done to anybody to deserve all this?" No matter how anxiously I would await for an answer, there was only static silence, emptiness in my mind and dejected disappointment in my heart.

Then, I would feel even more anger and disgust at God's apparent attitude of doing nothing about what was happening to me. I felt that He had decided to dump me and focus on others. I was sure those others, of course, didn't deserve his attention the way *I* did. I also speculated, frequently, that their problems were not half as bad as mine. Then as a result of all this self-deprecating thinking, I would become depressed and hard on myself, since somewhere along the way I came to the simplistic conclusion that I was unworthy and that is why God had let me down. Countless times I doubted in the existence of the Divine Presence altogether, other times wondering why God would decide for such a worthless person to be born. (Pathetic thinking, I admit).

Well, at some point about the age of 25, I became pretty much an expert in this game of self-pity. Today, I am very thankful that God has given me more credit than I have earned.

Thus, I can now express my deepest thanks for all that He has sent my way. He knew better that these were important lessons which I needed to learn to get where I am today.

What I am trying to illustrate here is "surrender", something that I have finally learned to some extent, and became very grateful to God for being so patient with me. Surrender is what protects me from feeling helpless, angry, frustrated and feeling that the whole world had turned on me. Many of you have felt this way at one point in your lives, at least.

I know that many of you, my readers, would argue here with me, but please allow me to explain how it works. Let me bring you an example that would illustrate what is the direct correlation between expectation and disappointment.

How many of you after meeting somebody new and hoping for something extraordinary and different from anything that we have ever experienced, thought naively that we could change these people? In the face of common sense, we begin thinking that we can change these people to match our perfect image of them, assuming when this is perfected we can live happily after.

You know how this story ends? I know. I made a couple of these foolish attempts just to learn that I couldn't change anybody. So instead, I ended up blaming these people for making me unhappy, because they refused to match my fantasy about them. In the final count it was me ending up with two and not just one disappointment. Firstly, the people I wanted to change were who they were and not what I wanted them to be. Secondly, I was disappointed in myself since I thought I could do better.

If you think you can stop an alcoholic from drinking, or a drug user from using drugs? Think again, and accept that you can't. But there *is* something you can do... That is, to deliver the lessons that you were meant to deliver. The lessons would stay in person's mind and heart, long after you are gone and forgotten. It is these lessons passed in the form of a gentle smile, one word, one sentence, in a fleeting moment or in years of being together, that can do what you couldn't. The lesson may help the person to decide that they want to change, and they and only themselves have the power to change.

The best we can do is just let them be and accept them for what they are, knowing that the way they are, and us being with them is all we need to learn our own lessons. When we are done, and still can't accept the people we are with, there is only one way for us, to have enough courage to leave them behind or pray and ask that they will walk away from us and set us free.

Nothing in life happens without a reason, I have no doubt about that. Perhaps sometimes it is difficult to see the reasons why things happen, but if you are armed with two things, faith and patience the reason will soon be unveiled

What is faith? Can we define it? What happens if we do?

*Faith* is tight adherence to sets of beliefs and personal convictions. Faith is the trust, confidence, and complete acceptance of truth which cannot be demonstrated or proved by the process of logical thought.

What is *destiny*? Can it be changed? Is it written for us in the stars?

*Fate* is a power that supposedly predetermines events. Fate can refer to an individual as well as to the whole social group, nation, race, country, universe etc.

*Destiny* is the power of fate (one's predetermined lot).

Now, let's take a look at these three concepts:

*Fate, Destiny and Faith.*

Do they relate to one another and if so, how are they connected? Should they be blindly accepted or can they be defined and changed? How do my readings relate to fate, destiny and faith?

The simplest way to look at this is: Yes, there is such thing as Fate, but how completely it applies to us is based, in many cases, on our Faith and what we chose to accept as our Destiny. We have incredible power to change things and destinies, and all we need is faith, and to believe that we can do whatever we set our minds to.

After all, the expression "You are what you believe you are" has to have some relevance and truth, for being as popular as it is.

Unfortunately, in my practice I have seen too many good people visit other psychic readers before they came to see me. Regretfully, I have found some of these clients damaged by those readings. They were given such nonsensical information as, 'that they are going to die in the near future', also told they had deadly, terminal illnesses, or some terrible accident was waiting to happen to them. Others were told that their spouses were unfaithful and planning to divorce them. Yet others were told that their children had cancer or other dreadful diseases, and that they were not to survive their 10th birthday.

In many years of my work with people I have yet to meet anyone who was in a position to handle this kind of information.

I say to clients when asked about any purported or potential bad news, that they should expect that if God meant for them to know such things. He would find the right way to deliver to them the information they are supposed to know. At any given time I would rather be an Angel of Mercy than a Messenger of Death.

I am convinced that God has chosen to use me as a tool for healing and not distraction. I believe I am to point out to people who are seeking help how they can heal, find their happiness, and find ways to prosper and live their lives in the most purposeful, successful and prosperous way.

I don't feel I am put in their way to judge them, or to remind them how insignificant, lost and useless they are, but rather to help them to use their resources to be the best that they can be.

So many times I was asked by my clients how to distinguish this guidance from other ideas which might not be coming from the best sources. The voices of temptation and ego often pose for the voice that guides us. How to discern the difference? It's not that difficult. At once, the guiding voice will never be the one that pities you and reinforces your own feelings of being a victim. It will not be that which will try to turn your attention to the negative side of our actions and which could have contributed to the outcome of events which make us unhappy and sad.

Ego, in contrast, rejects objectivity, and causes us to feel much self-pity, so we come to one conclusion, that the world is against us and everyone around us is trying to pull us down. In such an arrangement there is never a place for a fast recovery or healing. In a perverse way our ego imprisons us and takes control of our destiny.

Ego: Definition: a person's sense of self-esteem or self-importance:

Let's accept this as an immediate danger. It is the Ego part of us which causes us to fight or flight, so in this sense, it is essential in securing our survival, but that is where Ego stops being our friend. Further continuation of the use of Ego as a guide will allow us to be totally controlled by it and become completely unresistant to the destructive effects of hate, resentment and jealousy, thus compromising and disabling our chances to heal. I would say here that this phenomenon can even be extended to entire nations like Nazi Germany in the 1930s and even to the Neoconservative Movement in the United States today.

I would like to bring forth yet another danger that Ego can pose on us. While the core of our personality is overtaken by our Ego we have no defenses against the unknown to gain access to our "inside" psyche.

The easiest way to illustrate what I am trying to say is the following:

There is a knock on our door one day and when we open it we are standing face to face with a stranger who seems oddly familiar. He introduces himself as a distant relative who is trying to get back in touch with us. We trust him and allow him into our home. We then permit him to stay after hearing his story that he has been facing some life difficulties. One day becomes two, then three and the next thing we know is we have a permanent fixture in our precious household. This is also a time where we have to go about our own lives, we have to go to work and do the other things we normally do. After we leave the house, our new guest begins to make some mysterious phone calls, which we eventually find out about through our telephone bill. When asked about this, he answers that he is looking for a place to live. We accept this as a good thing, and really are relieved, since we do want the guest to finally abandon our good home. Instead of him leaving, though, there are yet more phone calls, followed by secret meetings taking place. Darker and darker looking individuals, unbeknownst, visit the home while we are not there. And then one day we come home, and discover that there is crowd of ominous looking, strange people inside and they are telling us that we no longer live in our house…

What I am describing is *Spirit Possession.*

The phenomenon has three stages:

**Stage One**: *Shadowing.* That would be the first telephone call made from our house while we were absent. The Discarnate Spirit does not yet have a key to our house but just having him close to our door sends chills down our spines and keeps a dark cloud on our doorstep.

**Stage Two**: *Obsession.* Would be correlating to the first dark visitors into our house, who visit but do not stay. In this stage the discarnate spirit enters our mind and is quite capable of influencing many of our thoughts and also can have an impact on our decisions and actions.

This stage seems to have a more permanent character. We begin to feel more confused, lost and displeased with ourselves and many of our reactions are very bizarre and irrational. We have difficulty with self-identification. Often described by clients as not being oneself, a feeling of mental fogginess and fatigue, and there is also noticeable forgetfulness, and a hard to control irritability, frequent changes of mind and swift mood swings.

**Stage Three**: *Possession.* In this stage the discarnate spirit actually inhabits the body, as if it was its own. Has no problem to influence the body, mind and emotions with great intensity. Often described by clients as: not really 'being there', feeling dead, indifferent, feeling split within and having no energy and will-power left. In this stage rarely before experienced aches, pains, difficulties or health conditions occur, often detectable through medical tests, yet having no previous medical background or symptoms can appear. Some of these spirits come and go, some stay permanently. Feelings of total helplessness, a lack of interest in the meaning of life, clinical depression, suicidal thoughts or even attempts at murder can be evident. It is a very dangerous stage, because the client feels totally out of control over his/her own life and destiny.

I will attempt to illustrate the destructiveness and dangers, in cases of my clients with whom I had the honor to work with over the past thirty one years. I will present different ways in which discarnate spirits can be detected and removed, so that anyone who is affected can again begin his/her journey to wellness and health.

Often I have been asked how common is spirit possession? I have to posit that I feel that it is as common as the flu. I believe that most of us, at some point of our lives, have experienced spirit possession at some stage and degree.

*We can easily forgive a child who is afraid of the dark; the real tragedy of life is when men are afraid of the light*

— Plato —

## CHAPTER SIX: MOST TERRIFYING AND INTERESTING EXPERIENCES OF MY OWN

What follows is my own account with possession in Stage One, however what shadowed me was not a regular human discarnate being but an "It"... an Elemental Evil. I am referring here to a veritable demon. As I mentioned though it was only Stage One possession: Shadowing, what was causing it was more dangerous than the stage three possession of any other entity.

Let's begin this interesting story, which will reveal the true horror of what I went through and how it affected me and others around me.

Darlene, a 38 year-old young lady with a Sociology degree, was referred to me by my good friend, a Doctor of Psychology and a Chartered Psychologist with a well established practice. On many occasions before that, Jonathan referred clients to me with whom, as he would say, he got 'stuck'. Darlene had had several suicidal attempts, and was severely depressed and negative. My Doctor friend had exhausted his other resources for healing this girl, and I became her last possibility to get help. I had an initial reading with her over the telephone (as I usually do, before deciding if hypnosis would be an appropriate direction to take in order to find what is the underlying problem). I learned about the physical and sexual abuse that she had suffered from men she was related to in some way from her early childhood and teenage years. After leaving home and starting University, her self-esteem improved slightly and she became quite a "popular kid on the block". This was also when she started dating and soon learned that sex could be used as tool for punishment and control. She began indulging in numerous affairs. Her sexual rampage finally came to an end with her obtaining her degree and settling into a more established adult life. In her work environment, she couldn't find as many willing, naive young men to be used and abused through sex. It was then that her depression manifested, and she lost her "spark", as she would say.

Things worsened after she befriended another woman who got her involved with heavy drinking, and the bar scene was on her daily agenda. One day her friend complained about her own state of depression and Darlene offered to help her with a session of Reiki, a technique she had recently learned in a night class. Through this, she contracted from her new friend this demon which attached to her and became a part of her everyday life. It was also when her first serious suicidal thoughts began. On at least two occasions Darlene was taken to an emergency room, after attempting to poison herself, or to cut her wrists. She stopped sleeping, and over-exhaustion deepened her depression and withdrawal.

"This disgusting, ugly thing!" as she would describe it "sits on my bed every night, giggles endlessly and tells me to do all these terrible things to other people, especially men. It tells me that I should tie them to the bed, rape them and make them suffer as my mother made me suffer. If I refuse to listen, it threatens to hurt me and even kill me. I can't live like this anymore. I think it is better to be dead than live and be forced to be afraid of this thing. It is going to kill me, I just know it." I could hear the conviction in her voice and knew she wasn't kidding.

I agreed to take on the case and traveled by myself to Northern Alberta where she lived. We settled down in a room next to the doctors office and began the session.

"Well," I said, "let's see if we can do something about your problem." I wanted to give her some hope, but she didn't seem to be listening.

When she was comfortably reclined, I adjusted the lighting and pulled up a straight back chair close to her. As I took her through the relaxation process, I couldn't help but think about her self destructive tendencies as well as her penchant for hurting others, which particularly was worrying.

I was instructed by Walking Bear, my main Spirit Guide and teacher, who always appears to me as a noble, sweet and wise native man, with beautiful flowing white hair, one of twelve Spirit Guides that are constantly around me, to light sweet grass braid. I usually never use sweet grass during my sessions. I do burn it before and after, but this time I did what I was instructed to do. It was the smoke of that sweet grass braid that protected me during this session. I laid it on the floor between us.

As soon as the woman was relaxed and in trance, I noticed a strange vellication - a sudden muscle spasm on her face, almost as if there was an invisible hand distorting her features. As she went under more deeply, Darlene said:

"I am scared. It's here. It forbids me from talking to you."

"Well, we are going to see, aren't we?"

As I said that, I suddenly felt a very strange and unpleasant chill run down my spine and at the same time began to notice the foul odor of rotting meat. The first thought that came to me was that she hadn't washed her feet. Then the temperature in the room dropped at least a couple of degrees (this would not be too strange, except that it was such a hot summer day, and I had the window wide open to keep the room well ventilated.) I had experienced this terrible smell only once before and it was connected to a place where, in a previous case, I was to help dispossess an entity in a client. I didn't hang around for that at that time. But this was my first real case of demonic possession, as will be described below.

"Try!" the screechy, unearthly voice coming from Darlene's mouth had a very raspy and threatening sound to it. "I am the one this fool has to listen to, unless she wants to be punished."

My confidence was shrinking at an alarming rate. I also knew I could not show the fear I felt to whatever it was that was residing inside my client.

"Well," I stated firmly, trying very hard to hide my emotions. "I don't need your permission, whatever you are, to talk to Darlene."

"We will see about that!" I forced a laugh.

"Darlene." I directed my words to her, trying hard to ignore the presence. "I want you to talk to me."

"It won't let me." There was definite note of horror in her voice.

"You don't have to listen to it. What can it do to you?"

"It says it is going to kill me."

"Can you let me talk to this thing?" I suggested.

And then suddenly: "What do you want, you bitch?" These words blasted me away.

"I want to tell you to get out of her and leave Darlene alone."

"Not a chance!" The thing hissed through my client's lips.

"I am the strong one. I am going nowhere. I am going to punish this damn bitch and you better stay the hell away!" it warned.

"What are you going to do?" I challenged the demon.

"I am going to kill you too…" At this point I had a, pardon the expression, 'devil' of a time trying to suppress my fear, but decided that for the sake of my client (and me) I couldn't afford showing that I was in any way affected by this threat.

"Really, you think you can do that? What the heck is your name; I might as well know what or who I am addressing"

"Aphresor"[1] The demon barked out this ancient Biblical name.

"Darlene, can you describe this thing to me?" I wanted to "compare notes", meaning I wanted to compare Darlene's' description with what I was now seeing as it sat cockily on her chest. I wanted to confirm what we both were seeing: A gory, horrific looking 1-meter-tall creature with the face of a goat, huge curved horns, serrated sharp teeth, red flashy beast-like,

1 The isn't the actual name of this demon, but it's dangerous to call or name the demon by its name, as one could be calling it from the nether region.

slitted eyes. It's body was covered with something between skin and scales. I was forced to examine my own perceptions and even my own sanity. But I could clearly see what was sitting on its haunches on her chest as she lay deeply hypnotized on the bed. I saw its dark bat-like wings draping down behind it. It also had short, stubby arms with sharp looking talons and a tail as well as cloven hooves. Then, it swiveled its head toward me and I gazed for a moment into its terrifying, and inexplicably hypnotic red eyes, a sight which I will never forget as long as I live.

As much as I tried to rationalize the situation, I couldn't think of anything that could convince me that this was a dream, that what I was facing couldn't possibly be real, yet I knew I had to handle it somehow. What then saved the day was an instruction from Walking Bear. I was told to put the demon in a steel cage with square bars 10 inches thick and spaced only an inch apart.

"Darlene I will need your help!" I spoke to my client.

"What do you want me to do?" she asked fearfully.

"I want you to look at that cage that I just placed behind you. Can you see it?"

"Yes, I can see it… What is it for?"

"For our unwanted guest."

"It says you can't do that."

"Aphresor," I directed my words to the demon. "We can do whatever we want, just watch us. In a moment you will be locked up in this heavy cage and you will not be able to bother Darlene. And the next time I see her we will remove you from her and throw you and your cage into the abyss where creatures like you belong,"

"She is not going to help you to do that!" the demon argued.

"Just watch me. Darlene, you can do this. You have to do it. Lets put it in the cage. We can wait until my next visit, and then we will get rid of it for good." I encouraged her.

"I can't, it will not let me, and its too strong," she cried.

"Darlene," I made sure I raised my voice, "It is only as strong as you allow it to be. You can do it, I know you can. Grab that pole that is leaning against the cage."

"Yes I am holding it now." She seemed more confident now.

"Hook him by his ugly wings, and push it inside the gate..."

"Yes, yes it's inside. I pushed it inside." There was noticeable excitement in her voice now.

"Now shut the gate quickly and lock it!"

"Oh, my God it's squealing like a squished worm. It can't get out! I locked it in the cage."

"It will make lots of noise, but just tell it to shut up and not to bother you."

The session and its findings was not the worse of the events that unfortunately followed. What happened in the days after the session was and still is one of the most frightening occurrences that I have ever experienced. Even behind the shield of time that has passed, I still dread thinking or writing about it. Is there a safe zone when it comes to things of this character? Honestly, I do not have an answer to this question, but I definitely wish there is a safe place for our sake.

### Darlene Session number 2

Because of other pressing appointments in Calgary I had to go back home for awhile and during this time had a chance to collect myself, and reexamine and evaluate Darlene's situation and try to determine what course of action should be taken to try to help this woman finally free herself of this demon and again go forward with her life.

I embarrassingly admit now that practically every day I was praying that she and Jonathan would find that somehow they did not need my help anymore and the case would just disappear and go away. No chance of this for Darlene would call me almost every day asking when I was going to return and perform another session that could finally cast this demon away for good. It was squealing like a pig almost constantly and uttering non-stop threats against both of us!

At the time I had had no real experience in the field of demonic possession and had never before performed an exorcism. Although I had witnessed a depossession executed by Medicine Men during native ceremonies in a healing sweat lodge. Through these fascinating rituals and rites I was exposed to these Medicine Men who would relapse into sudden and violent thrashing about after having cast out the possessing demon. The Shaman then had to perform a ritualistic self-purging ceremony before it was finally all over.

During this same event I witnessed the miraculous and rapid return of the depossessed person to good health.

I knew I would have to sooner or later decide what to do with Darlene's pleas for help.

Early on, during these two weeks after that first session I had several conversations with my talented psychologist friend. He, as I, knew an experienced Shaman and the two of us, along with my sister who was by my side through this came to the conclusion that what was needed was to perform an exorcism with Darlene pretty bloody soon before the demon could find its way out of the cage. I contacted this medicine man whom over the years had looked after me during my annual fasting and had been assisting in my spiritual growth. I felt much better and more confident about the upcoming exorcism once he agreed to participate in this process. We also had a few short days respite which gave the poor man a little time to prepare for this and help develop some protection from the inevitable wrath and harmful intentions of the demon.

One last frantic call from Darlene told us that the demon seemed to be gaining more and more power and soon might be strong enough to extricate itself from the cage. It's squealing had turned to roaring. It was enraged. Darlene told me she couldn't sleep. I was very concerned for her life if this should happen.

I found out the next day that our plan was going off track as our Medicine Man couldn't in fact assist me in performing the exorcism as his wife had developed a strange and unexpected illness, which I realize now was initiated by this demon.

So I was again on my own.

When I told my fiancée what was going to happen, he offered to go with me. But then he found out he had conflicting business and couldn't come with me after all. He tried to talk me out of it.

My sister and I arrived late in the afternoon the day before the scheduled appointment that was set for 10 the next morning. My psychologist friend Jonathan offered us his apartment to hold the session as well as gave up his place for my sister and I to stay the night.

As the three of us sat in his living room chatting about the outcome of the previous session with our client, the attack came without warning. I felt a sudden inability to move or even utter a single word. It felt like somebody was holding me under water trying to drown me. I couldn't keep my eyes open, my face went totally numb and to pronounce even the simplest sentence proved a challenge. It felt that I was surrounded by a thick glass wall, shutting me off from the outside world and at the same time rendering me completely inarticulate. I watched my sister and Jonathan talking to me, could see their lips moving but there was no sound. It was one of the scariest times of my life. I had never before felt such isolation and vulnerability.

It was my sister's frantic shaking of my shoulders that helped extricate me out of this catatonic dead zone. I was completely lost.

That same evening the demon (it had to be) did the same thing (put them in a zombie-like state) to my sister and to Jonathan, in turn, without success. This lasted at least 45 minutes! It attempted to threaten all of us in this same way to force me to change my mind about carrying out the session with Darlene the following morning. I said a prayer out loud and asked for guidance and protection, which seemed to work. More than ever I was determined to cast out the demon and free my client from this evil and destructive presence that took over her life.

Never in my darkest thoughts have I ever contemplated such a presence straight from the depths of hell and encountered its insane power.

I was anxious all night and didn't get the good nights sleep I was hoping for. My anxiety level increased even more when my sister and Jonathan left for a few hours, leaving my client and I alone for our morning session.

As I waited for Darlene to arrive, hoping lamely that maybe she might lose her way, my Spirit Guides instructed that I needed to prepare my smudge[1] for purification and protection from the incumbent threat at hand.

So I did this and waited nervously, my heart pounding, for the session. I was still debating canceling this exorcism and wait for the Medicine Man to be available another day.

As expected, Darlene showed up a few minutes earlier than agreed, eager to get this over with and back to her old life.

"Hello Darlene, and how are you feeling today?"

I met her at the door and tried to put a big smile on my face. I put as much confidence in my voice as I could muster under the circumstances.

"I am very nervous. I am so anxious to get this over with and be free of this unending nightmare." As she said this she lowered her voice slightly, remembering that the demon could hear her and that could bring a renewed attack from the demon, "It can hear me can't it?" she whispered.

---

1 Smudging: A mixture of sacred herbs such as sage, sweet grass, cedar, and sacred protective fungus, ground up or shredded, to be burned before performing Sacred Ceremonies such as Sacred Circle and Sweat Lodges.

"Yes it can, but it feeds off your fear so don't show it how it effects you. We are going to cast it back to the hell where it belongs!"

"Thank you so much for doing this for me. "

"It is going to be OK. I know we will free you from this but you have to try to stay strong and help me do it. "

"Just tell me what I need to do."

After this I asked Darlene to join me in smudging and cleansing herself, the first time in a long while where the client had joined me in this ritual.

I prepared another dish full of a mixture of sweetgrass, sage, and cedar to burn right through the session. I placed the petri dish on the floor between the bed and the chair I was sitting on. To my great surprise the herbs burnt strongly, producing a thick veil of smoke that became a shield. I felt that this was going to be a very tough session to get through. I never truly realized how dangerous and unpredictable in the end it would turn to be.

The session began the same way as happened during the first one. A most foul odour filled the room, assaulting my senses. I was grateful that the smudge was really burning and to some extent managed to screen the full discomfiture of the stench that reminded me of a decaying human corpse. I call this the smell of death. One can never forget this smell once exposed to it.

Over the years this odoriferous scent would be the very first indication and alert of someone I know departing from this world. And even a distance as far as the space between continents cannot diminish its strength and potency.

It took me a few years to stop dreading this dynamic. I simply have to accept that the famous concept of the Circle of Life that doesn't end and should not be tampered with. Since then it has become easier for me to just acknowledge the reality of this malodour and simply let things unfold as they would in the end, at any rate. Oddly enough, I think of it as an uncanny ability to tap into death in advance of others, as dreaded as that is.

To my relief the session went better and easier than I thought it would. Darlene appeared to have gained more strength and confidence over the previous weeks.

It took about an hour. The holographic steel cage hovered over and through my client, the trapped demon screaming awful insults and foul mouthed recriminations my way. We never wavered. I told Darlene to gather her strength and mentally push the cage over the edge of a smoldering volcano and into the boiling magma in the chamber, which is what she did. The demon went crazy.

After the session ended I felt completely drained and sleepy.

When Jonathan and my sister returned later, Darlene had already gone home. As I was saying goodbye to her I took notice that she looked so much better than at the beginning of the session. Her eyes were clear and focused, her face and demeanor appearing younger and for the very first time I noticed that she really was quite pretty. She had light in her blue eyes which was not there before. She gave me a big hug and expressed how grateful she was for what I had done for her.

I was sitting on the sofa in the living room when they returned to the apartment.

"Are you OK?" my sister asked me.

"I think so," I answered "Why?"

"You look very tired and pale..."

"It was a very tough session, the worst I have ever encountered,"

"Are you OK to drive?" she asked me. "If not I can drive at least part of the way back..."

"No, I think I can drive." I said in response. I also felt that the 5 hour long drive to Calgary would seem longer that ever.

We left about 1:30 PM and for the first 100 Km we chatted, talking about the session and its fantastic and successful outcome. We were happy for this woman, knowing that she could now heal her wounds, get past the abuse and other issues that had plagued her life. As always this awareness is the most satisfying part of my psychic work. Beating the odds and helping someone turn their lives around.

As I drove on, though, I started to feel detached from our lively conversation and a heavy atmosphere seemed to envelope the car. As our journey continued I began to somehow feel more and more isolated and a dark and grey cloud was affecting my mood. The closer we got to the City the darker and more ominous this cloud became. To the point that my dear sister and I didn't exchange a single word between us for over 4 hours. She was afraid, she told me later, to say anything to me, and thought I was angry with her. I told her later what had happened, that I couldn't even speak.

As I pulled into the garage I asked my sister to take our things inside the house and told her that I would be there in a few minutes, that I needed to be alone for awhile.

She did what I asked and as soon as the garage light went off I sat there in the darkness.

Now this: "You stupid bitch did you think that you could get rid of me that easily?" The disembodied screech of the Demon. Sitting in the back of our van!

Without looking back into the dark recess of the van I grabbed my sacred pipe carrying bag, and opened and slammed the door shut as fast as I could.

Instead of going to the kitchen where I could hear my sister unpacking our bags I quietly slipped down the staircase leading to our half finished basement where we had a threadbare spare bedroom set up with a single mattress on the floor.

I felt chilled, a totally isolated feeling with that dark cloud closing tighter and tighter around me. I knew that this same demon had somehow come back in the van with us. It was shadowing me and was attempting to get even closer to take complete possession. At first it had disarmed my will to fight. Instead of resisting I gave in and quietly laid down on the bed, my face turned towards the daylight of the only window down there, . I felt as if I was under water and the sounds from upstairs were muffled and undecipherable. I wasn't aware of time and hadn't realized that 5 hours had passed. Nor did realize that I had been crying most of that time.

I heard my fiancée coming home and caught part of his conversation with my sister. I knew she told him that she had gone downstairs to check on me few hours earlier, which I was not even aware of. When he came downstairs and sat on the edge of the mattress I felt like my world was just about to collapse.

"What is happening to you? "He asked, gently taking my hand in his. It took me a while to respond.

"I think I'm in trouble, Michael."

"I was worried that something terrible might happen to you on that trip up there. I should have been with you…"

"There was nothing you could have done."

"Was Adrian the Medicine Man working with you on Darlene?"

"No, his wife fell unexpectedly ill and he could not make it…" My voice trailed off…

"I thought I could handle it myself."

"I told you I thought it could be dangerous, did I not?…" his voice rising.

"Please stop… it's too late now."

"What are you going to do?" he was quite worried now. I didn't tell him anything about the demon. By now I realized that this thing must have attached itself to my aura. I had no idea how it could have escaped the hell I thought we had cast him back into.

"Please ask Lidia to call Adrian and tell him that I will need his help! Ask her to tell him that I am in big trouble".

My sister did just that and a 4 PM time the next afternoon was set. The Shaman Adrian would attend the ceremony by telephone from Northern Alberta. A consult for freeing my aura from the demon. With Adrian's assistance on the phone we should be able to beat the demon and send it back to the recesses of hell where it came from.

I slept very poorly that night, even after performing a prayer ceremony, doing some smudging, and smoking my Sacred

Pipe. I also asked the Creator for help and protection. During sleep one's defenses are weakened. I did a prayer ceremony and smudged myself once more before going to bed. I also asked the Creator to surround me with a huge ball of golden light so that nothing from the demonic world could get to me. In spite of all this I still felt vulnerable and would not allow myself to slip into a deep sleep.

I got up somewhat rested the next morning but my mood was heavy and oppressive. I had trouble smiling. All I could think of was the ceremony that day. I had no appetite and had barely touched food. Even coffee tasted bitter and weird. My fiancée had to return several movie rentals that day and he asked me if I wanted to go with him. I agreed and went upstairs to have a shower and dress.

Our Master bedroom had a bathroom with a large double shower stall.

As I stood alone under the welcoming stream of hot water, soaping the grime of the last day off my body. I suddenly heard a guttural, growling sound coming from behind me.

"You fucking, stupid bitch, you think you can ever get rid of me, ...*ha ha ha!*".

It was an animal-like howl that was not human, yet I understood these words all too clearly. I looked over my shoulder and saw this meter tall thing sitting on its haunches in the stall!

Without thinking I pushed the glass door open and jumped out of the shower, slipping and falling hard on the cold tile. As I sat there the demon stared back at eye level at me with those devil-like red eyes! The same thing I released from Darlene. I was paying particular attention to the goat-like split hooves on its hind legs and the short sinewy arms, each with their 5 long black claws.

I burst out of the bathroom ignoring the throbbing pain in my knees from the fall, grabbed my clothing laying on the bed and took the stairs three at a time, .

My fiancée looked at me surprised, not expecting me to be ready in such a short time.

"You're ready? You did not put on any makeup." he noticed.

I don't know how he hadn't heard the commotion. He was probably in the garage.

"Well, we're not going anywhere special," deciding not to tell him about my experience in the shower. I knew that he would question me in depth. He couldn't know that merely talking about the demon would give it more power, maybe even compromise the loved ones around me, and this I would not do.

The demon slowly materialized and sat in the rear seat of the van, boring its red devil eyes into the back of my head as I took the front passenger seat on that sweltering Saturday afternoon. My husband couldn't - nor could anyone else - see it. The only indication for him was the foul smell he noticed.

"What is that awful smell?" my fiancée asked, "It stinks like a rat or mouse got in here and died..." he commented.

"Probably that's what is causing this stench," I lied, concealing my little secret.

Later, waiting for the 4 PM meeting I prepared everything we needed, got my smudges and peace pipe together for performing the demon casting out ceremony. At the same time, 500 km further North, Adrian would be performing a similar ceremony to add more power and to protect me during the process. My sister called him and made sure our 2 ceremonies were accurately synchronized.

I lit the smudges 5 minutes before 4 PM. Smudged and purified myself, asking the Creator to give me strength and protection through the entire ceremony and afterward.

I suddenly felt a surge of strength as I prayed to the Creator for protection.

The entire ceremony took about 35 minutes during which I had put myself in a deep trance, connecting my mental and spiritual strength with Adrian's as we proceeded.

I could hear the demon growling and throwing out threats of destroying me and everybody who was attached to me. It continued delivering threats of killing me and forcing my life to go straight to the nether region and other similar insults, but when it realized with every ensuing threat its power over me was diminishing and my strength and confidence increasing it began squealing again as it did when Darlene had managed to lock it in the steel cage. I knew then that I was going to be all right. My very last prayer was:

"Please Creator banish this creature back to the hell it came from so that it will not harm anyone else. Ever." After that and a last puff of my sacred pipe I felt the dark energy beginning to grow weaker until the gray cloud around me shrank and vanished all together. It was as if the sun just showed up in the sky and our entire house became bright and peaceful. I could now breath freely and knew my ordeal was over.

I spent another 15 minutes expressing thanks to the Creator and Adrian for their assistance and help. And with that I also promised myself never again to attempt another exorcism alone. I would cancel any appointment if the circumstances would align the same way as they did in Darlene's' s case.

I want to express a dire warning to every healer who deals with demonic possession and let them know that no one is safe from this, no matter how strong, spiritual or separated from the situation they feel they might be. It is always better to ask another healer for assistance and make good preparations before tackling such cases. After this particular experience I can really understand and empathize with anybody who is possessed by disembodied souls that have failed to find their peace after death and instead roam the darkness that exists between life and the spirit world and which I would call their own earthly hell. In religion, one could use the famous term Purgatory to describe same. I have personally encountered and dealt with hundreds of these cases, the oldest disembodied beings having had been in this state for as much as 700 years. I was only shadowed not totally possessed by the demon yet the darkness that it plunged me into was the most frightening I have ever experienced. I pray this never happens again to myself or anybody close to me.

Later on my fiancé, having finally been apprised of what had occurred, was completely taken aback and fascinated. He thought it might be expedient to have me draw as best as I could recall this Demon in all its horrifying ugliness, if only to add another layer of truth to this book and insisted that I make a sketch. I have had a reasonably good career as an artist in my past, and many of my works are in private collections, so drawing this thing was not an issue. I sat down one day and started to draw. The memory was as vivid as if this creature was still right in front of me. Somehow it felt that an invisible hand was leading my pencil on the paper to bring forth as many details as possible. I will never know. The plan was to put the sketch in my book. It would probably have happened the way we wanted if the sketch had not mysteriously disappeared. There was no one in the house except myself and my fiancée and he swore he did not touch the drawing after seeing it for the first time. It really was a terrifying visage. The drawing was never found and in a way I was very relieved that it has vanished for good. I was asked many times after that to redraw it, but I just refuse to.

The devil is a most skillful shape shifter and without effort I believe it is able to get closer to oneself by taking on a familiar face, one whom you already know. Then it can take advantage of your trust and ignorance to get what he wants. What does he want? This question each one of us would like to know the answer to… And in so many ways we do know what the devil is after.

This Devil is the lawyer suggesting that we sue our business partners or take our ex-spouses to the cleaners, or it pushes us to take a bribe to increase our bank account or even worse to try to conceal a crime we have committed whether premeditated or by accident.

It is sometimes easier to go for the glitter rather than the mundane and pedantic, for instant 'pudding' as my late father-in-law used to say rather than hard and honest work, or to take the easy way out rather than take responsibility for our actions. Is the Devil behind human evil? I believe it is, but I do not blame the Devil entirely for our nefarious actions. I would put the blame on ourselves, since at the end of the road these are our decisions which determine the direction we go. Free will. These are our own choices that matter.

Thus, this book will be published without my sketch of the Demon but I hope the description of this thing works well enough for you. Which suits me fine.

What is in us that makes us more or less accessible to such forces?

As mentioned earlier a weakening of our aura is often a reason in which we attract unwanted disembodied astral beings that use us as their host. The first and probably least noticeable signs and symptoms of spirit possession are a lack of energy, heightened irritability, depression, and frequent and dramatic mood swings. This then can devolve into the appearance of illnesses, aches and pains, headaches, nausea, a lack of appetite or the opposite, uncontrollable eating binges, to mention only a few. Later, radical and inexplicable behavior can began to wreak havoc on the person's personal and professional life. Extra marital affairs, and one night stands began putting a strain on marriages, often leading to separations and divorces. In cases of people who never drink or used substances, heightened usage can lead to tragic overdoses. Car accidents and violent behavior can lead to self destructive actions, posing danger to those around us.

*Slow down and enjoy life. It's not only the scenery you miss by going too fast - you also miss the sense of where you are going and why.*

— Eddie Cantor (1892 - 1964) —

## CHAPTER SEVEN: PSYCHIC ATTACKS. GINA.

This is a subject that I deal with more frequently than any other. An interesting part of this phenomenon is that we might very well be under attack and yet we are completely unaware about what is happening to us. What is "psychic attack"? I would define it as an invasion into our own spiritual psyche by living or dead spirits. It could happen through an actual physical presence that is attached to the outside of our aura[1] or one that may have gained deeper access through a weakened aura. Or thought energy that is angry, hateful, ill-wishing, resentful or jealous. Everything is energy. Our thoughts are powerful energies that if positive can enhance and enrich our lives, or destructive and hateful which can take life force from us. They can drain our physical health, make us ill and depressed, influence our thoughts and actions, and frequently are directed against ourselves in negative and dangerous ways. Hexes and curses have a similar effect, but can also have a darker side to them. Curses have opened the gates to hell and summoned demons to infest and plague our lives. I have dealt in my

1 Aura: an energy field that is held to emanate from a living being

practice with such cases, and have also experienced the effects of this phenomenon in my own life. These memories remain very fresh. They remind me to remember that I need to always place protective shields of light around myself, my home, my loved ones and friends. I not only put those shields around me but I make sure that I strengthen them everyday. I always try to remember to reinforce them the first thing before I get up from bed and the last thing I do before retiring for the evening. One has to be aware that when we are asleep, we are more vulnerable and exposed. We need to have the protective shields especially when we are sick, sad, unconscious or intoxicated. The aura should be re-energized every day to function properly.

One of my clients I will call *Gina*, a Native woman living on one of the Reserves north of Red Deer came to see me in 1996 because her life had begun spinning out of control and she was becoming more depressed after she left her violent and alcoholic husband. When they married, he left his Northern Saskatchewan Reserve lodging and moved into my clients Alberta home. Soon after they married, he became quite violent, his drinking got much worse and she was truly afraid for the safety of their two small children. After four attempts she managed to escape her abusive husband and moved by herself with the kids to St. Paul where she somehow learned about my work with Native People and came to see me. When I saw her the first time, she had hardly slept, and her face was covered by a red rash that would come and go. She would have days where she would pull out handfuls of her long hair. She had persistent flu-like symptoms that lasted for three months. She was depressed and some days couldn't get out from bed to look after her children. Luckily, she had family close by who helped her out. I spoke with her briefly on the telephone and we set up an appointment. All this started shortly after she had left her abusive husband. When we hung up I began seeing flashes of three people: a young man who I believed was her ex-husband, an old man who appeared to be performing some kind of Shamanic ceremony and an old gray haired woman who had an angry and hateful face. The images kept coming until Gina walked into my house for her appointment, a half an hour later.

She was a nice woman, I thought, in her late thirties, but really looked 10 years older. Dark circles under her eyes told me she suffered from chronic insomnia. The dull and blotchy skin and dry unmanageable hair testified to her illness. Her sunken brown eyes really had no expression, and were subdued and expressionless like the glass eyes of a plastic doll.

"Hi Gina, please come in." I welcomed her and tried to make her feel comfortable and at ease.

"Hi Ula… I have heard about you so much from many of my friends. They recommended to see you."

. "Let's sit down. "I led her to my office where our reading was to take a place."

"Well, Gina…" I started." Right after we talked on the phone I started to see images of three people, and they are still here, so I want to ask you about them."

"Ok." She nodded. I didn't catch any surprise in her voice.

"I see a Native man in his early forties, with long hair, and who a wears baseball hat backwards. Quite dark skin…"

"That's Alfred…" she pointed out. "My ex."

“All right, we have one… There is another older man who I believe is a medicine man or shaman. Do you know anything about him? She shook her head letting me know that she could not identify who I was talking about, so I continued. “And I see an old native woman with gray long hair and very cold and hateful eyes, do you…?”

“Yes, I know who she is. She is my ex mother-in-law. She lives on the reserve in Saskatchewan, where my husband was born. He is her only child and she is very controlling and abrasive”

“Do you have a relationship or contact with her?”

“No…I am really afraid of her, always have been afraid. She actually has told me she wishes me to be dead”.

“Tell me now about your insomnia. Have you always suffered from it?”

“No, it started shortly after I left Alfred. I began having this recurring nightmare. I would be sleeping for a short time and suddenly something wakes me up and I feel there is someone standing in the room. I sit up on my bed and try to peer at it through the darkness. As soon as my eyes adjust I see a dark form standing at the foot of my bed. Then the feature starts to solidify and I see my mother-in -law pointing her finger at me. She has these hateful eyes and stares at me without moving. Then I hear her high pitched voice call out:

“You are not going to escape, I will kill you!” As she says this she slowly starts floating toward me. I am so frightened I start screaming, reaching to turn my night lamp on. When I do, she is gone, but I can hear her chuckling followed by this evil laughter like an old hag.”

"And three weeks ago I noticed a very strange thing." She pulled her hand out, turned palm side up and pointed at her fingertips. I bent closer to see what she was trying to show me and noticed a number of black lines in the fleshy part of her fingers. They looked like dark slivers"

'What are those?" I asked.

"These started to appear everywhere! ... On my fingertips around my mouth, and around my nipples."

"Are these some kind of sliver?"

"Yes and no." She confused me with her answer, but gave me an explanation.

"When I squeeze them out they slide like you would expect slivers would, but as soon as they are removed, they disappear!" I was shocked, yet incredulous. She offered to show me. She asked me to start squeezing one of the dark marks on her index finger.

"It doesn't hurt, please don't be afraid. I want you to see. I know you don't believe me, nobody does but when they do this, they easily see that I am telling the truth." I took her finger in my hand and started to squeeze. A dark tiny spot appeared on the surface of her skin and as I continued applying pressure, I could see the body of this dark sliver slowly emerge from the tip of her finger. It was a shiny black sliver. I could not believe what I was seeing. I managed to push it to the surface of the skin when all of a sudden it just disappeared!

"Oh My God, is that ever weird." That was all I could say.

"You see now what I mean?"

"I see." I was still trying to overcome my shock, but as I held her hand the dynamic visions slowly began again each trying to get my attention. I saw the old woman with the old man talking and exchanging something. I believe she was giving him alcohol and some money. He was nodding and smiling and there was a sinister expression on both of their faces. Then I saw the man walking around gathering bushes of thistle and digging from the ground some small fragmented bones. I was aware that these were chicken bones, that were in use for whatever dark purposes the shaman needed them for.

"I know what is happening to you." I said, trying to control these chaotic thoughts

"Your mother in law paid this old medicine man to put a Hex on you. He used thistle for the ceremony he performed to make you suffer. You are right, this woman is full of hate and she especially means to try to kill you through these ceremonies."

"How can I stop this?" She started to cry. "Why is she doing this to me. I *had* to leave her son because he would have killed me in one of his drunken stupors and would have hurt my children. I got a restraining order to protect me. Right after, everything got worse. I was so sick that my sister had to drive me to Edmonton to a specialist to take tests to find out what was wrong with me. I have always been a healthy person. I hardly ever got the flu or a cold. Now I am sick all the time. My entire body aches. I feel like a 70-year-old woman. I don't know how long I can take it. And I was diagnosed with Systemic Lupus Erythematosus (Lupus). The doctor said that all the symptoms are related to Lupus."

"Gina, they found the symptoms that manifest the same way as Lupus, but it is not Lupus. I know it."

"We will remove the hex and put protection around you and your children. I believe that even if you do have Lupus, your symptoms will soon vanish after we reverse the hex. Take my word for it."

"I think I am ready, when can we start?"

"We'll start right away…" I got up to fetch my sacred pipe bag and everything else I needed to perform my ceremony to send the evil attacks back to those who unleashed them on my client. I always use my sacred pipe and native herbs such as sage, sweet grass, cedar, sacred fungus (I always use for extra protection) and of course, Kanic-anik tobacco for my pipe. The ceremony took about 2 hours, and was a success. I had another short session with Gina to program her to be positive, and teach her how to use protective shields and the small bundle of sacred herbs that I prepared for everyday smudging and clearing.

When we were done I was exhausted. But I knew that we had sent back to the senders their dark energy. Gina's face was bright and her eyes alive. Her skin had lost its blotchiness and we looked at her fingertips. There was not a single sliver anywhere to be seen.

"Oh my God…!" She gave me broad smile. "Thank you, thank you. I feel so light and my cough and cold symptoms are so much better. The pain in my body is going too…I don't know how to thank you, Ula!"

"But it's not over yet."I cautioned her. "You will still have to protect yourself. You have to smudge every morning and night before going to bed. Keep this little bundle of clothed herbs I prepared for you always on your person, or on the night stand when you sleep. Have your children smudge with you and prepare for them little bundles like yours and have them carry them during the day and put them on their night stands when they go to bed. You are their mother, that is why you have to prepare these bundles by yourself. I am sending you extra sage and one braid of sweet grass. I will pray for you and if you need to talk or see me again, please call me anytime." I gave Gina these instructions, she took some notes and put them in her purse.

"Thank you again. People were right, you are a real medicine woman. You have such a good energy around you."

"I hope so." I smiled at her. "If I didn't, I wouldn't be doing what I am doing. Please take care of yourself and let me know how you are doing."

I never saw Gina again. I heard from her a few times over the next few years. She confirmed that her Lupus symptoms did actually vanish and her health recovered and she felt better than ever. She moved to Edmonton and enrolled in University for full time study. She said she would never forget what I have done for her and will always keep me in her prayers. She did find out from a third party that her mother-in-law had taken ill and passed away three months after we reversed the hex she had put on her ex-daughter in law. Gina never did find out what became of the medicine man who had facilitated the process.

*Many persons have a wrong idea of what constitutes true happiness. It is not attained through self-gratification but through fidelity to a worthy purpose.*

*— Helen Keller (1880 - 1968) —*

# CHAPTER EIGHT: MORE OF MY MOST TERRIFYING AND INTERESTING EXPERIENCES

The next time I had an encounter with the dark side was in April 2003. As my husband has an interest in history one of the things he is fond of doing is to visit museums and cemeteries. I must say that due to my heightened psychic sensitivity these places would not be on my list of priorities, but nevertheless I agreed to go with him. We visited Calgary's Glenbow Museum at a time when a very large exhibition of Chinese artifacts was on display. At first we decided to see the art exhibition which was the only one I would have preferred to see that day, but as we walked through the large rooms of the Museum, without noticing we entered a huge display of ancient Chinese Culture. At some point we became separated as my husband had to read every little information plaque or explanation posted by the artifacts. I'm the opposite and like to breeze through. I was passing a glass case behind which a large Chinese soldier in uniform, headdress, and mask was on display. For some reason the mask seemed a bit strange to me. I drew closer to see if the sign on the wall had a description about the mask. As I started to move away from the case I froze in place and looked back at the display. In the blink of an eye I thought I saw red eyes looking out at me from the black mask. Goosebumps covered my arms and my scalp tingled, forcing me to suck in my breath and shut my eyes. When I looked back again there was nothing. I looked around to see if someone else was in the room with me but it turned out I was alone.

I didn't spend any more time, and decided to sit down on a bench in one of the corridors to wait for my husband to finish his visit. Of course it was another two and a half hours before he was done with his tour.

On the way home we talked a bit about the Chinese exhibition, but I never mentioned what I had seen.

That night I felt more worn out and tired than usual which often happens when I visit hospitals, cemeteries, funerals or historic places. I decided to go upstairs to bed around 11 PM, leaving my husband watching TV downstairs in the family room. I fell asleep quickly when all of a sudden I was jolted from my slumber by an eerie feeling. I opened my eyes and tried to adjust to the dim light coming from the open door of the bedroom. What I saw next made the blood drain from my head. Right above me by the ceiling was a dark mask with the frighteningly red eyes hovering ominously. I reached to my left to find my husband but realized he wasn't in the bed. Then the mask dropped down and I felt two strong hands push me violently down on the bed. The strength of these invisible hands was so powerful that I had the feeling they would crush my shoulders. I was pinned down, unable to make a sound or fight back. I remembered trying to scream but couldn't. Funny, irrationally, I realized I was furious at my husband for not being there to protect me from this evil force. Then as quickly as it began it ended and I could breath again. I called out to my husband and he answered from the stairs as he walked up to the bedroom. I could still feel the coldness on my shoulders where these invisible fingers had dug in.

I described the attack to my husband and he said he was sorry for not being there for me in the bedroom when it had happened. I knew that something- or someone- must have followed me home from the Glenbow Museum and I realized that could have been the case because, carelessly, I had failed to perform my usual basic level of protection before we went there. I am well aware of the dangers of the unseen world, yet sometimes I drop my shields and leave myself vulnerable and open to unwelcome forces. From that moment I became more rigorous about making sure a protective bright light is always around me.

The third time I could not explain as easily the source of a psychic attack that took place just about 2 years ago in our home on Vancouver Island. My husband as usual was sitting long into the night on his computer, and I decided after my meditation to lay down in bed and maybe watch some TV. After an hour or so of watching some programs I turned off the TV and nestled under the covers. Though I normally sleep on my back, this particular night I laid on my left side and began to doze off when I heard a sudden loud screech like a slaughtered pig and something suddenly latched onto the side of my neck. I could feel sharp teeth sinking into my skin and muscles. I jolted out of the bed with both my hands trying to pull it away from me, something that looked like a pear shaped raw red muscle-and-skin skull with an elongated jaw protrusion and sharp front teeth that were sinking into my neck. My eyes bugged out as I clearly watched this horror. Struggling, I ran out to the living room still frantically attempting to stop whatever this thing was from hurting me. During that whole time, my brain was desperately trying to figure out if I was still asleep or awake. Even after finding myself standing in the middle of my softly lit living room I was still not sure what was happening to me. As an almost automatic response I began breathing deeply hoping it would calm me down and prove I was only imagining all this. My mind was telling me to use all my knowledge and purge this entity out of my consciousness. Strangely this was not working, the whole damn thing was still there, and with the corner of my left eye, I continued staring at this bloody, dark veined skull, it's angled dark eye sockets seeming to be as two black tunnels leading to hell. It had elongated exposed nasal cavities as an animal skull could. In the frenzy of this titanic struggle I became aware of a voice ordering me what I needed to do to stop this vicious attack. I followed the instructions and mentally placed a collar made of bulletproof thick glass, looking like a funnel sitting on my shoulders, the widest part reaching the top of my head. I could see through it but my neck became protected from the attack that continued for another 15-20 minutes! I was so distraught that I didn't even look for, or call, my husband! He asked me to explain this in this book, as he doesn't want people to think that he had done nothing to help! During this time, which seemed to last an eternity,

I could hear the clicking sounds of the serrated teeth hitting the glass. Quieter and quieter screeching was still assaulting my senses but slowly died away as the head started to dry, shrivel and shrink to the size of a tiny raisin. It stopped moving and the attack would finally stop. It must sound crazy, but I decided to keep my glass collar on just in case. What I need to add as very important information is that three or more weeks before this debacle I contracted a sinus cold from my brother in law. The worse of it lasted three days, and with my natural remedies I thought I had beaten it. But I was wrong. My cold or whatever it might have been was lingering and I had difficulty with breathing, the cough without substance would plague me for three more weeks, and so would shivers and pains in my entire body. It felt as if something was draining my energy and preventing my body from getting better. I must say I am hardly ever sick and had not had any colds or flus for almost ten years. It appears more than obvious to say that after this unexpected psychic attack ended, my symptoms disappeared within a day and I finally started to feel better.

As mentioned before this sounds even to me as a far fetched fabrication but it did happen and is still very vivid and real in my mind. I am still trying to figure out how to classify what had attacked me, this was a first such experience. I have dealt with more than a few weird and strange situations and entities which have molested my clients, but never once have I come across such a creature such as this one that was trying to drink my blood! For now I have decided to call it a Psychic Parasite, a presence that to my mind was neither human nor demonic. It was something between the two but without a doubt I would place it closer to the demons than just lost souls that are trapped between the plains of existence and unwilling to move on.

I pay very keen and particular attention on placing important protection on myself when I go to bed and before I start my day.

I really do not think that I will be ever be free of the abject horror of this attack or the image of what attacked me.

To close this subject I must say that I have helped many clients clear their auras and their bodies from the effects of psychic attacks. I should add the fact that we can also be psychically attacked by the negative energies of living people who harbor angry, hateful, resentful feelings toward us. These thoughts are very potent and to an unsuspecting victim can wreak havoc to their health, love life, careers, relationships, prosperity and more. My advice to everyone who reads this book is: make sure that the protective veil of light is always around us, when we are asleep and when we are fully awake. Evil does not sleep and is always trying to find a new victim and devour him or her to feed its own malicious existence.

Here, as the subject introduced is extensive I will continue with more personal and other eerie and mystical experiences with the unseen.

The first I can remember were appearances of dark shadows during my early adolescent years, in a bedroom that my brother and I shared for several years. The shadows would hang over me in mid-air and would pull me out of the deepest sleep and were terrifying by just being there. I was neither able to move nor make the slightest sound. My entire consciousness was locked inside my immobilized body and I was forced to face and go through the entire experience with a feeling of total vulnerability and isolation. These terrified events plagued me for three years of my life from 12-15 years of age. I was unable to understand, deal or stop this until many years later when I began to learn about what I am describing in this segment of this book. These were night terrors that were replete with total sleep paralysis which was a key ingredient which made them so much more frightening. I can see now that the deterioration of my physical health at the time was quite understandable. Whatever was attacking me meant me serious harm and I was lucky that the damage done to me, even though extensive was not irreversible. The worse of all this was that I felt so alone and isolated. I have never mentioned these events to anyone, not to my 2 years older brother who I believed would have teased me mercilessly or to my parents who I assumed would not sympathize with me on a subject that was purely forbidden by their religious beliefs. I am not sure what arrested these night terrors, but I know beyond doubt that my experiences were the direct reasons behind my decisions to write my first book at the age of 12 on the subject of ghost hauntings. Regretfully that 375 page hand written manuscript, written in Polish, vanished without the trace and I was never been able to locate it.

**Ursula: Another Example.**

Another, perhaps deemed less terrifying and certainly a more 'entertaining' ghostly encounter took place the first year my husband Michael and I began dating. On one occasion I was asked to stay for the night in Michael's beautiful home. One night we were in his bed having some tea and just talking into the early wee hours. Somehow that night I felt as if we were being watched by someone. I propped myself on the bed and saw the figure of a man standing by the right side of the large dresser and in the opening leading to the master bathroom. He was not tall, rather a slimly built man dressed in a worn out tweed jacket with baggy pants and large boots. He had a Lenin-type hat on his head. Before actually seeing the apparition my nose noticed the piquant smell of manure mixed with dry straw, a smell I was quite familiar with from my frequent childhood visits to my maternal grandparents farm, where I spent many summers.

"What is it?" my husband asked, looking into the direction where I was staring, trying to understand what I was looking at. "What are you looking at?" He asked me, a bit spooked by my behavior.

"There is a man standing next to the dresser," I stated simply.

"I don't see anyone there! What does he look like?" I sensed that my husband's skeptical nature came forward and he was going to probe and see if I was mistaken, that I could not possibly see something *he* wasn't seeing.

I described the man to him and by that time I became aware of the man's name. He told me his name was Frank.

"Can you ask him some questions?" I nodded in response. "Can you ask him what he is doing here?"

I directed my thoughts to the apparition.

"He tells me his farmhouse stood here before."

"Can you ask him what year his house was here?"

"He says it was 1919." I could see that though my husband was getting more and more excited about the communication, there was a somewhat undercurrent of disbelief and doubt in his tone.

"He says he is very mad at you..." I began conveying what the spirit was communicating to me.

"Why is he mad at me?" Michael was really intrigued now.

"Because, he says you cut all the trees down." After this sentence my husband became silent. I felt he was for whatever reason quite shaken by what I just said.

"Oh my God, you are seeing him aren't you?! What else is he saying?"

"He says he did not like your ex. He says if *his* wife did what *she* did he would have kicked her out of his home and town..."

"Wow!" It was all Michael managed to whisper. By then the apparition had melted into the soft shadows of the room.

"He is gone." I announced laying back on the pillow.

"I believe that you saw whatever it was..."

"Why is that?" A pregnant pause at this question.

"Well, when he told you about the trees."

"What about them?" I interrupted. "What about the trees?"

"You would not know, nobody knew that except for me... When I bought the lot to build the house it was all covered with trees, hundreds of them, and indeed I had them all cut down, except for 5 or 6 of the bigger ones."

What I learned in time about Frank was that he was a hard working farmer whose farmhouse stood a bit to the right where my husband's present house, at the time, was built. All the land around belonged to Frank as well. He was married but no children were born into the marriage. May I point out here at the possible parallels to my husband's previous marriage, which was also childless. They later adopted a lovely girl, my step daughter. His wife died before him at 59 years old. Frank himself passed away in 1929. Michael and I checked later in the archives of the Glenbow Museum that would verify that there were several farms around that area but we could not find any solid facts or written history connected to Frank and his life.

I should include here a rather humorous incident that happened with the spirit of Frank, perhaps a week before I became aware of his presence. We both were in the bathroom one morning getting ready for work. I was standing close to the open entrance to the bathroom very close to the wall where the large dresser stood. My husband was further inside the bathroom at the far end where there was a medium size walk in closet. He was getting dressed after finishing his shower and shaving. I was already dressed and was bending down and putting on my tights as the last piece of my wardrobe that morning. I was blocking part of the opening from the master bedroom to the master bath. At some point I felt two hands land on my backside and lifted my skirt. I jumped, startled, thinking that my husband was again in one of his amorous moods.

"Michael, we don't have time for this now!" With these words I jumped out of the way, looking over my shoulder. To my great surprise Michael was not behind me instead, hearing what I said he popped his head out of the closet door, quite genuinely puzzled by this.

"I'm right here." he announced.

"Weren't you trying to pass by me into the bedroom just now?" my brows lifted in disbelief.

"No, I am here getting dressed, why?"

"Somebody just touched my butt and lifted my skirt. I was sure it had to be you!"

"No! That wasn't me I swear. I actually caught a glimpse of you leaning over and then almost bolting upright, while looking at me and I had no idea why."

From his expression I gathered without doubt that he was telling the truth.

**And this one…**

Another rather humorous incident took place the same year during a trip to Edmonton, where we decided to stay for two nights in the old prestigious Macdonald Hotel, built in 1915. The first night we stayed there we went to bed around 12 AM. With the bathroom door opened and a little nightlight on, the room was not pitch dark even though the blackout lining of the drapes were pretty much blocking out the street lights. We had barely laid down and I was starting to doze off. Something made me look to the foot bed on the side where Michael was sleeping or so I thought, until I saw a tall figure standing right on that side of the bed.

"Michael, what are you doing standing there by the bed?" I asked.

"Dear, I am right here next to you." my husband's voice sounded a little muffled by the fold of the comforter underneath which he was hiding. I took note of this.

"I raised my head further off the pillow and could see the figure much clearer than a moment ago when I thought it was Michael standing there for some unknown reason. This large framed man had a round cherubic face, a balding head and was dressed in a double breasted formal long coat. The next morning during our breakfast we discussed what had happened the previous night. Michael of course being so inquisitive and curious to learn about the paranormal asked me for a detailed description of the man I saw. Breakfast was served so that there was no further discussion on the subject. As we were walking out of the restaurant, the hallway leading to the lobby from there had many old historic photographs of the early days of the hotel hanging on both sides. I stopped all of a sudden in front of one of them and immediately recognized the man I saw in our room the night before.

"Here he is." I pointed at one of the five men in a group photo I was standing in front of. "This is the man I saw in our room last night."

"Macdonald." There was a small plaque under each photograph explaining the details that were accompanying each picture. Michael read the name that pointed at the man in the middle of the group of five on the old yellowed photograph.

"Who is Macdonald?" I asked, unaware of any of the historical facts pertaining to the hotel we were staying.

"He is the guy(architect) who built this hotel", eyes brightening with approval as he said that. "Wow, you saw him in our hotel room last night, how fantastic!" In many respects Michael was like a little boy in a huge candy store where he could not stop marveling over all the candies that he could have if he was able to eat them all. It is one of the qualities of him that would always warm my heart as much as it could annoy me, when he would bombard me incessantly with endless questions he wanted the answers to. He sometimes would not accept the idea that there could have been facts I did not have explanations or answers to. He remains the same to this day and continues his quest for learning as much as possible on the subject of the paranormal and supernatural. He once told me that the famous American Philosopher William James once stated that, if had his life to live over again, he would lead it studying the paranormal.

**And this one…**

Over the years we have experienced many of paranormal events that I am often reminded should be described in this book.

One of the most interesting occurrences took place in an old part of Winston-Salem, North Carolina where a well preserved historical Moravian village is kept open for the public to experience and learn about the past of this interesting group of people who once inhabited the area. The monument has been dubbed 'Old Salem.' and dates from the 18th and 19th Centuries.

The tour is kept as authentic as possible by many volunteers in period costumes who serve as interpreters or enact in role playing that perform day-to day lifestyle chores, the same way they were done centuries ago. One of the houses we decided to visit, was the Old Inn or Salem Tavern, a brick building first built in 1784. The main room of this house was the kitchen with an old style fireplace and furnishings that were either part of the original house or were brought in from other places that would match the era and that remain consistent to the historical period of the Moravian Village. A volunteer woman dressed in simple colonial era clothing was peeling potatoes and demonstrating the methods of cooking of the historic period. As Michael began conversing with her and asking his many questions. I wandered around the room, then noticed that there was a natural slope of the dirt floor leading to a lower, cellar level. It was dark down there, so until I reached a smaller room where historically the colonists would store their food supplies, vegetables, grains, meats and such, I couldn't see much detail. As my eyes adjusted to the gloom, it was a few moments before I realized that what I was seeing was not real. My first thought was that this re-enactment was a bit excessive. I saw a stocky man in old, quite worn out simple clothing kneeling at the far end of the cellar He was vomiting violently on the dirt floor. I stopped and stared for a moment before I realized that it was not a re-enactment but an apparition I was witnessing. I knew that the man was poisoned with arsenic and this was his fate because he had done some terrible deeds in the past which brought this punishment upon his head.

The sound of the man's retching as he continued throwing up was pitiful and hard to ignore. At one point he stopped, lifted his head and looked *straight* at me. There was tremendous pain and despair showing on his face. It sent shivers racing up and down my spine. The room got all of a sudden very chilly, and I turned around and ran back up to the main room as fast as my legs would carry me. The experience must have still been showing on my face, because both Michael and the volunteer woman looked at me, very concerned.

"What has happened? You looked scared."

"Nothing, I just went to where I was not supposed to."

"Tell me."

"There was no Volunteer down there was there?" I asked the woman.

"No, it is only me in this building." The woman stopped peeling the potatoes and wiped her hands on her long skirt. "I can check it for you, maybe I am wrong, maybe some other volunteer came in and I did not notice, being too busy talking with your husband." She seemed apologetic.

"No, that's not necessary." In spite of my protests both the woman and Michael went down to the cellar to check it out. I did not follow them, choosing to wait until they came back.

"There is no one there." Michael said. I knew that they could not possibly see the earthbound suffering stuck in a time long past, a soul that was paying some kind of Karmic debt.

"Who did you see?"

I described what or rather who I saw and that stopped the questions until later on that day when a second incident happened as we were leaving the Moravian Village.

As we left the main entry and were walking towards the parking lot where our rental car was parked it began to rain. As we walked side by side I stepped on a metal plate covering a sewer drain. I felt two hands on my back with great force pushing me to the ground. Unable to regain my balance, I went down on my knees and knuckles. It all happened so quickly that my husband did not have enough time to grab me to break or prevent my fall.

I was too shaken up to gather myself and stand up.

"What happened?" Michael hauled me to my feet, and looked at my bleeding and badly shaking hands.

"Something pushed me down and made me fall on this rusty plate," my voice quivered partially from pain and partially from fear.

"Let's get out of here."

"We had better stop at a drugstore and get some first aid to disinfect your wounds. I don't want you to get a Tetanus infection." We got to the car and drove to the nearest Pharmacy to get the necessary medications to look after my messed up fingers and knees.

In spite of using a peroxide antibiotic covered bandage and cleaning my knuckles I managed to get quite a nasty infection on my fingers that left visible scars that are still here.

*He who is of calm and happy nature will hardly feel the pressure of age, but to him who is of an opposite disposition youth and age are equally a burden.*

— Plato, The *Republic* —

## CHAPTER NINE: MARTY'S CASE

Marty was my long term friend's 25-year old son. He was well built, handsome and well mannered and made the strong impression of being well grounded, confident and successful. And all this would have been very close to the truth except for the migraine headaches he had suffered from about the age of four. They would show up unexpectedly and incapacitate him to the extent that made him unable to get up from bed, go to work or even socialize. What was very interesting was the fact that during the parties he attended, after a few drinks his personality would change to such an extent that from this soft spoken young man would emanate the most horrible, vulgar things and would go even to the extreme of using obscene language and had no problem insulting people at will. For which he would apologize later. This radical behavior ensured that he stopped being invited to parties and other social and family gatherings.

Marty became withdrawn and depressed. He would push away anyone who became involved with him. And this was the way he managed to destroy two of his recent relationships. It appeared that there were mostly women who could trigger the outbursts, but what tipped the scales was an incident that happened when he was driving towards Banff on the old highway. At one point he noticed a semi-trailer coming from the opposite direction. Suddenly he heard an angry voice in his head saying, "Why don't you just pull the steering wheel to the left and hit this truck head on?". "End this senseless stupid life. Get it over with." It took great restraint from Marty to resist this thought and pass the semi safely. He pulled over onto the shoulder and sat there shaking for a while. He was so scared and shocked at the power this voice had over him. Once he got home he told this to his mother, who flipped out and immediately contacted me and asked how quickly I could have a session with Marty. She was seriously afraid for her son's safety and wellness especially since in recent months his migraines had grown more severe and frequent.

We set up the session for the upcoming Saturday since I had my monthly trip planned and I was to stay with Geraldine anyway. To make sure that Marty was first in line for the session, I rescheduled a few less urgent cases and set his session for 6 PM that Saturday.

I arrived at Geraldine's place shortly after three. My other girlfriends were already there and we had a nice dinner at Geraldine's home, after which we sat drinking coffee and talking about Marty.

She was seriously worrying about what was happening in his life. It seemed to be spiraling out of control and he was starting to cut off contact with his family, especially with his younger sister with whom I had had a few sessions in the past. When Marty showed up at his mother's for dinner I sensed he was a little bit apprehensive and on high alert. We had the session booked for right after we were finished with dinner. During dinner the conversation went in a spiritual direction and subjects such as possessions, hauntings and such were brought forward. Many questions were directed to me and I answered them as best I could. As the conversation progressed I noticed that Marty was becoming more and more uneasy and somehow I knew that if I did not ask him to go upstairs right away with me he would probably decide to leave.

"Marty, it's time to get started. I see that you are pretty spooked." I smiled trying to allay his tense mood.

"Yeah…" He said slowly his forehead creasing. "Maybe we can move the session to another date?" He tried to wiggle out from his decision to undergo the hypnotherapy.

"I think it would not be very wise to do that. I know as I am reading you if we will not start immediately, something will talk you out of doing it all together. Your headaches and whatever else you are suffering from are not going to go away on their own."

"I think you might be right. OK." he said and began heading towards the staircase leading upstairs to the large guest bedroom where Marty's mother had prepared everything for us. She had put a nice warm blanket for her son to cover up with, and placed the chair onto which I was to sit on the left side of the bed. I had my little tape recorder with me as I was planning to tape the entire session.

The drapes on the windows were drawn and the room was nice and cozy.

There were large double doors leading from the landing to the bedroom and I decided to leave one of the doors open half way in order to keep the bedroom lit enough so that we would not need to turn on any table lamps inside the room for the duration of the session. There was ample light coming from the four wall sconces on the landing which would give the bedroom a soft pleasant glow. It's easier for clients to relax and go deeply into hypnosis when they don't have bright lights on in the rooms.

Marty laid down on the bed and covered himself with the blanket. My chair was at an angle that allowed me to see the doorway over my right shoulder. I turned the tape recorder on at the beginning of the session, since I sometimes forget to do this. He regressed easily and the session began. I'm not able to say why but I often know how deeply into the hypnotic state the client is going in by the time I reach their knees with my relaxation suggestions. With Marty I knew he was going very deep and was ready to go back in time. Where we would began searching for the roots of his devastating migraine headaches.

I took him back in time to his 13th birthday, then to his seventh. He didn't have any bad headaches at this age. He was able to describe in detail his 7th birthday, told me who attended it and what he got for presents that year. He was a very easy subject and was able to retrieve large amounts of detail about the time periods I send him to recall. The next step was to get him to his 5th birthday and we were on the way there when something strange happened. I barely finished my last sentence suggesting to relax his scalp, when both Marty's hands lifted up and grabbed his head. At the very moment he did that, a deep, guttural voice came out of his mouth. The moaning got louder and the voice I heard was definitely not Marty's voice. It was very creepy and almost non human. As this was happening the partially opened double door started to close on its own. I was alarmed at the amount of light seeping into the room, which is why I glanced over my right shoulder to see why somebody (thinking perhaps Marty's mother) was trying to close the door. I thought we had agreed that the girls would stay downstairs and wait until the session was over. There was no one at the door. It was moving slowly on its own, squeaking a little and stopped when only a narrow slit of light was left. Not wanting to lose momentum I turned my attention back to Marty who was till moaning in that low, strange voice.

"Marty, what is happening?" What came next shook me even more than the door closing.

"Who are you?" I needed to get a hold of myself and hide any signs of fear for my own sake and safety.

"Guess, ha ha ha!" Creepy laughter followed.

"If you are so smart, you should know!"

The voice became even lower and more ominous "You have no idea, bitch do you."

"Listen, whoever you are, I don't have to talk to you. It is in your best interests to talk to *me*... This is your only chance before you go back to your darkness." My voice grew stronger and more defiant.

"What is your name?' I asked again, sternly.

"Call me Daryl," it answered.

"What are you doing inside Marty?"

"I live here, bitch!" I am used to being called different names and never take any of this personally, but this particular entity was very abusive and continued trying to intimidate me.

"How long have you been with Marty?"

"Almost as long as he has been alive. Since he was 5 years old."

"You have no right to force yourself into someone else's body…"

"I have used him for long enough to claim it as my own residence… what's it to you and why are you bothering me…?"

"Daryl, let's stop playing this game and get to the real reason why are you here, and also, what happened to your own physical body?"

"I do not have to talk to you, bitch." Another insult.

"Yes, you do, since I am the only one that is able to drag you out of the darkness you are stuck in. If I decide to leave, you are back in your black hole, do you understand that? I might be the only bitch that can hear you." My voice was hard and cold.

"So let's start from the beginning. Who are you and how did you find Marty?"

"I live in the house he moved to when he was five years old." I sensed that the entity started to soften a bit and was willing to open up a little. "I was married and had a daughter, but my cock-sucking wife left me and took my daughter with her!"

"I want you to be honest and tell me the truth of why your wife decided to run away from you? It's not because you were a sweet and loving husband, was it?"

"She could make me angry then I would smack her." I was not sensing any guilt at all in the voice.

"I would like to know more about your daughter." I asked, sensing that this was the root subject that needed to be explored.

"What about her? I love her, she was my beautiful girl. She was 5 years old and already so pretty.I loved her a lot…" The voice died down for a moment and I was getting a strong premonition of what was coming next.

"Did you love her the way father should or in some other way?"

"Why are you asking me this question?" The entity recoiled defensively.

"Because these questions are the ones that are keeping you stuck. Did you love her the way fathers should *not* love their daughters?" I was relentless and wouldn't back down until I got a straight answer.

"I… touched her… Sometimes I thought of her as my little woman."

"You molested your daughter! That was the real reason your wife left you, isn't that the truth?" I sounded like a prosecutor.

A long period of silence lingered in the air before it answered.

"Yeah, she told me I was a sick pervert and that I would never see my daughter again. The bitch took my little girl and I got a court order to never try to look for them. I was ordered never to approach her again."

"What happened next?" I wanted to move the session forward.

"I stayed by myself in the house but started having headaches which got worse and worse. I was diagnosed with a brain tumor and my life turned to pure hell. The pain was so terrible that sometimes I wanted to kill myself."

"How long did you live with this tumor?"

"20 years."

"Did you die here or in the hospital?"

"In the hospital."

"Why did you come back here?" Shrug of the clients' shoulders.

"Tell me how you entered Marty's body."

"They moved into my house and one day he came to fetch his ball that had bounced downstairs to the basement. This was when I jumped in."

"Is it you causing Marty to have these horrible migraine headaches?"

"Yes, it's me. This pain is always with me."

"It was also you who caused Marty's behavior to change after he would drink even the smallest amount of alcohol?

"Yes."

"Why did you stay around, why did you come back to your house?"

"This was my home, where was I supposed to go?

"You were supposed to go towards the light, that beautiful bright light."

"There is no light… there is only darkness."

"Do you want me to help you to see the light?"

"You can try. I have never seen it."

"I want you to think about your daughter. Think about the love you felt in your heart for her… can you do that?" Small nod of his head.

"Concentrate on this feeling in your chest right where your heart resides. It's a ball of bright light shining from the center of your chest. Can you see it?"

"Yes, yes. I can! Oh my God it feels so light! ."

"Let this light become even brighter and let it expand from your chest all around you further and further."

"Yes… I can!" Marty's face brightened and a little smile crossed his lips, "I can go now. I must go. I don't want this beautiful light to disappear. Can I go?" The voice was softer now.

"Yes, go now and allow the beings of light that are now surrounding you take you to a better place. They come with love and without judgment. Go now!"

Marty's chest rose and then sunk back onto the bed and he became still. I then slowly brought him back into the conscious world.

He laid motionless on the bed after opening his eyes and took quite awhile before speaking.

"That was so weird. I'm so sorry I did not mean to let him call you names, but he was so powerful, I couldn't stop him. It was as if I sat alone in a dark movie theatre and there was only a white screen in front of me. Then I saw him on that screen. He was a tall bald man with a square face, chiseled jaw, sunken brown cold eyes and hardly any eyebrows. He wore a dark tweed jacket and pants. He walked into me in the theatre and started to use my voice to say these terrible things."

"Marty don't worry, I never take these things personally. He was a lonely, lonely man with a load of guilt and carried dark secrets… let's talk about you. How are you feeling now?"

"I feel great! And that ever present soreness in my head is gone. I don't remember feeling this good- ever!"

"Well, then let's go downstairs and have some tea," I suggested, and we walked downstairs to the family room where everybody was waiting patiently for our arrival. The women were talking in hushed voices as if making sure we weren't disturbed.

"Hi girls, we are back." I announced, to let them know we were there. "Let me ask: Did anyone try to close the bedroom doors when we were in the session?" That quite honestly spooked me more than I was willing to admit.

"No, we were all just sitting here, making sure nobody disturbed you. Why?"

"Nothing." I shrugged my shoulders feeling another tremour run down my spine. "Must have been a draft."

I learned several weeks later from Marty's mother that her son had not experienced any more migraine headaches since that session and his personality was becoming more gentle, the way she remembered him in his younger years. At that time she also told me her side of the story about purchasing the house when Marty was barely 5 years old. She said that when they arrived at the house for the first time, he stood on the sidewalk, looked at the house and started to scream that he didn't like the house and was not going inside. After they moved in, Marty would never go downstairs. He said that there was a mean old man there that would hurt him. All was dismissed as a young child's vivid imagination. One day, maybe two months after they moved in, Marty was playing with a ball and it bounced down the stairs to the basement. Marty followed the ball downstairs.

Shortly after, Geraldine heard him screaming at the top of his lungs. She rushed downstairs thinking that he maybe had fallen and hurt himself. She found him standing in the middle of the basement, both hands holding his head. He was stiff and his face was dark purple from screaming. He wouldn't respond. His body went stiff and rigid like a piece of wood. Terrified, she rushed him upstairs, packed him into the car and drove to the nearest hospital. He screamed all the way there and once in emergency, lost consciousness. Doctors performed every possible test but they could find no medical reason for the incident. It was from that day forward that Marty began suffering from debilitating migraine headaches which got worse in puberty and when he started to party with his friends later, and began drinking.

In the end I want to mention that the full session was captured on the two tapes that I still have, but I have never listened to them for some reason.

### Cornelia

Besides Marty I also had a few sessions with Geraldine's daughter, Cornelia, who was depressed after losing her favorite dog and couldn't stop crying. During the session we learned that she had the same dog in her past life and that the dog on one occasion died while saving her from drowning in a river. This brought forward the impression of feeling safe with the dog in her present lifetime and that she needed to take good care of him. The dog eventually developed a tumor in his chest and sadly had to be put down within two months of getting sick. The session brought about an understanding, amazingly, that souls, even if they are animals, tend to reincarnate and search for their previous life time masters as happened in this case. I was able to show her that the soul of the dog was already reborn and wanted to find her. The little pup showed up in her hypnosis session, telling her which animal shelter it was waiting for her to pick him up. To my bewilderment the address given through this session was a *real* address and Gloria managed to find the puppy that she saw during the hypnosis. The little pup was of the same breed as her other dog and had almost identical markings on the side of its neck. Needless to say Gloria could not have been happier.

In my experience it is the first of only two cases which hypothesizes that reincarnation also occurs in animals. I have always believed that every living being from the smallest animal to plants have souls and can return to life within the *same* species.

The only thing I did not believe was that we don't cross species-reincarnate and yet one of my Native American clients proved me very wrong by recollecting a life in the body of a gray wolf. He vividly remembered hunting deer and described the taste of blood and the thrill of crushing the windpipe of his prey. During this session he would make growling and snarling sounds the way a wild animal would bare its fangs. It was quite an astounding event, since as I mentioned I had never before encountered this anomalous type of case.

Ronald was my best friend's husband so I agreed to take his case and see if I would be able to help this man heal his wounded and abused childhood.

*Men can only be happy when they do not assume that the object of life is happiness.*

— George Orwell —

## CHAPTER TEN: LARISA AND RONALD

Ronald was one of many native children placed in the care of the Canadian Government Residential School for Native[1] children. During this period of time he suffered severe verbal, psychological, sexual and physical abuse that left him scarred for life. Since early adolescence he had been involved in alcohol and drug abuse. Then he met my friend Larisa who looked as fair as any white woman I have ever known. By her heritage she was a mixture of Native and French backgrounds. We met at one of many sweat lodges I attended in Northern Alberta during seven years of my fastings and spiritual search. We immediately became fast friends and our friendship continues to this day. We have supported each other through thick and thin over the past 22 years. As I conducted a series of hypnotherapy sessions with my friend, we uncovered a chain of life -altering events including her childhood rape and such that did extensive damage to her self esteem, trust and confidence. Through that process we managed to remove and clear Larisa's psyche from the aftermath effects of her horrific early life that also helped cause her to put on extra weight after her two boys were born.

1 see: http://www.vice.com/en_ca/read/the-wildly-depressing-history-of-canadian-residential-schools

Larisa is the most upbeat, positive person I have ever met in my life, non judgmental and always trying to see the positive side of any situation. Compassion and a kind nature were reasons for which Larisa chose to undertake social studies which would allow her to work with the Native Community and help the damaged ones heal and move towards better lives.

After completing University she was hired by the City of Edmonton as a social worker where she works to this day. During these hypnotherapy sessions we discovered lives that have interconnected our two paths. We have been both North American Natives, during which I was a Cheyenne Warrior and she was a female belonging to different tribe. Destiny connected our lives as lovers and she became pregnant. Our relationship remained secret since the warrior society of Larisa's tribe didn't accept me, as a former enemy. As a couple we tried to prove that old hatreds and feuds could be put to rest and peace can be built on the love and respect we had for each other. We wanted our tribes to stop fighting and become allies. This never happened, as Larisa's tribe continued treating me as a sworn and feared enemy. When our relationship was finally discovered Larisa's tribesman attacked her causing her to lose our baby and permanently separating us from each other. My woman died shortly after this. Losing the love of my life, I never settled down with another woman or started a family. I spent the rest of my life lonely and seeking revenge on Larisa's tribesmen. They paid the ultimate price with their blood, but that never brought rest or peace to my tormented soul, and only left me in a darker and more alienated and empty place in life. As a couple all we wanted was to live in peace to raise our children and help our tribes unite and bury their hatchets. (pardon the play on words) We hoped for peace but instead were dealt sorrow, pain and loneliness.

When we met in our first sweat lodge we had such a powerful connection. We are still the closest of friends even though we have lived in different provinces for a number of years. Interestingly enough, if there is something going on in one of our lives, the other can sense that and the phone call or text message comes right when most needed.

Now lets get back to Larisa and her husband Ronald. After they married, Larisa agreed to move to the reserve, and that was, as she put it, her biggest mistake. Her husband remained involved with substance abuse and in and out of treatment centers more or less throughout their marriage. He did try to reform, had numerous treatments, and counseling but nothing lasted longer than a year or so. At the time I met Larisa her husband had remained clean for the longest time, or so she thought. He was working in a Native Treatment Center as a youth counselor. I'm not sure how effective his work was with young Native youths trying to help them to conquer their addictions, when he himself was not healed and better.

I remember one of the sweats which Ronald attended. It was the only time that I actually had to lie down trying to overcome an incredible feeling of nausea and dizziness. I truly thought that I was going to die. Later, the medicine man who conducted the sweat lodge told us that he himself got quite sick and said that someone in the sacred circle had a dark heart and evil intentions.

After a sweat lodge it is customary to have a feast and socialize, and I invited Larisa to my home which was on her way back to town. She agreed and shortly after I arrived home I heard the van engine and sound of the door slamming. Standing in the doorway I watched her and Ronald approaching. I had a beautiful border collie/Australian shepherd mix dog that poked its head next to me and immediately began growling, showing its snarling white fangs. He had never done this to anyone before. The closer Larisa and Ronald got to my front door the more viciously Bear snarled. Larisa continued walking and started talking to the dog for a moment. He stopped showing his teeth and let her enter the house, but what happened next was absolutely confusing. My dog stepped forward, lowered his head towards the ground, his teeth glistened ominously, growling. What happened was absolutely mind numbing to everybody who witnessed this.

Ronald stopped abruptly, turned around and walked back to the van, opened the back door and the next thing we saw he was holding a big axe in his hands. With his head pulled forward and a challenging dark expression on his face, he was heading toward our front door. I froze in horror, realizing what was happening. The only one to react was Larisa.

"Ronald stop right there!" she screamed. "Don't you dare take one more step!" Her voice was sharp and strong. "What the hell do you think you are planning to do with the axe?"

"The dog was trying to attack me," he responded through clenched teeth "I have the right to defend myself!"

"The dog is on a leash and he is not going to hurt anyone. I just passed and it didn't touch me..."

Ronald just stood there with a mixture of confusion and anger on his dark swarthy face, and all of a sudden turned back and headed towards the van parked on the street.

He opened the driver's door and got in. He didn't bother closing the door and it stayed gaping wide open to the street.

Larisa turned to me and I saw the shock on her face, "I'm so sorry. I am not sure what got into him… He was acting very weird in the sweat lodge. I am so sorry I talked him into participating. I think he was the one who made us so sick during the second round…"

"I know," I answered, "there was something really evil at work in today's sweat, even the medicine man felt sick and had to perform a cleansing on himself after we were done."

"I will not be staying," she said, "I better take him home… I am so tired of his bullshit. I am so tired of all his acting up…" She felt defeated, which was not usual for a strong woman like Larisa.

"Are you sure it's safe to go home with him?" All of a sudden I felt a cold needle of fear settling in the pit of my stomach. "Let me talk to him before you go," I decided.

"Ok," she agreed," I'll wait inside"

Walking towards the van, I watched Ronald sitting behind the steering wheel staring vacantly into space.

"Hey, Ronald can I talk to you for a moment?…" I asked, approaching the wide opened van door. I noticed that the axe was sitting on the floor on the passenger side.

He nodded, without making a sound. He looked tired and drained.

"I was afraid your dog would attack me...", was all he managed to say.

"Bear never attacked anybody in his life. He is not an aggressive dog, you know that. What in the world made you act the way you did? You were around our dog before..."

"I am not sure. I really don't remember how this happened. I just remember Larisa's angry voice..."

He appeared genuinely confused and lost.

I looked straight at him.

"Would you agree to hypnotherapy with me so maybe we can clear some of the past from your psyche and help you?" I offered.

"I am not sure what we can afford..."

"That's Ok, I will work with you gratis. I will do that for Larisa as she is my best friend."

"When?" He asked immediately.

"I'd like to do it as soon as possible..."

"I want to do this as quickly as you can see me. It's time for me to look into my past and see what is still holding me on a tight leash." I smiled, amazed at the metaphor he chose to use in the face of this most recent incident.

"How about on Tuesday after you are done with your work?"

"I am going to town and we can do it in your home. You will probably will feel more comfortable there?" I suggested.

"Could we do it in the morning around 9 AM, then I can go to work after that. I have a client that I need to do an assessment on..." he replied.

"If that's better for you then I am OK with it." I accepted this though deep down I did not think the explanation he gave me was the real reason he wanted to have the session that early in the morning. I must admit that the arrangement made me a bit uncomfortable and I promised myself later on that day to meditate to tap into the real reason that stood behind Ronald's decision to have his first session in the morning when his wife Larisa would be at work.

I did so during my evening prayer asking a higher force to help me understand Ronald's reasons. What came to me was a total surprise. His decision had nothing to do with me, but was tightly connected to Larisa. How tightly and why was uncovered during not the first but second session I had with Ronald.

## Ronald's Case

Not surprisingly, Ronald, being Native American went into a deep hypnotic state within three minutes and I could focus and spent most of the two hours of our first session on exploring his troubled childhood and bring forth several incidents of sexual and physical abuse he had suffered throughout his early years. The abuse started right in his own family. Being born into a family of alcoholics living on the reserve he was witness to his grandmother's murder that took place right in her own home. He was barely three-years-old and was hiding under a pile of dirty clothes in the bedroom closet. She was stabbed to death by her own brother-in-law during one of their many drinking parties. Needless to say few arrests were made, and the longest sentence served was three years for manslaughter given to two persons involved in this incident.

As we went through the panoply of Ronald's life I learned that there were more than 5 suicides, and a supposedly accidental drowning in Cold Lake. As the picture of Ronald's life was shaping in front of my mind's eye I was starting to understand more and more exactly how sad and tragic his life was. Under the circumstances I was quite impressed with how well he was doing, holding his job as a counselor and lasting 16 years married to one woman, fathering two beautiful sons. Little did I know this was on the surface. Much of what was bubbling under that semi-calm exterior was coming from Ronald's own cruel nature.

One would say in Ronald's defense that he was a victim of unfortunate circumstances, and the abuse he suffered could damage anyone, maybe even to a worse extent, however through the experience gathered in long years of working with people, in the end it is a person's own decisions that make all the difference in the world.

It was the next session that not just stunned me but also caused me to worry about Larisa's safety.

### Ronald's case session number 2

As previously, Ronald set his next session for early morning wanting to make sure that Larisa was at work. This again puzzled me, but I tried to remain professional and calm.

Again, he went under very quickly and in less than three minutes his journey into the past began anew. I directed him towards lifetimes which would explain the reasons for the extensive abuse and suffering he was exposed to throughout his early childhood and adolescence.

"I would like you to find the roots that began your journey into this life with so much sorrow, suffering and pain" I directed him gently, noticing his eyes start to move rapidly under their lids. As they fluttered even more rapidly I knew he was at the right place and at the right time and we needed go exploring.

"What is happening?" I asked quietly not wanting to startle him. "Where are you and who are you?" Two first basic questions following one after the other. Then I sunk back into the chair and waited for what was coming.

"I am a man..." He started furrowing his brows as if attempting to see more detail.

"What is your name?"

"My name is Alphonzo, but nobody knows me under this name... they all know me as Ben Thomas."

"Who are you referring to as 'all'?" I asked to clarify.

"The people who rob banks." His answer surprised me.

"Tell me where in the world are you located?"

"I am in a Territory called Texas..." came the answer that led me to believe that he was *recreating*, not creating the events.

"What year it is?"

"1879." Another immediate answer. Wow.

"Tell me more about yourself." I encouraged Ronald to elaborate on the life he was revisiting.

"I was born in 1852 not far where I am now. I had one sister and she died of pneumonia at the age of 6. My parents were farmers. My father had some money and bought a patch of land where he raised some cattle. He did very well until my mother was stricken with some mysterious illness they could not cure. She died when I was 7 years old. My father started to drink extensively and I was no longer welcome at home. He beat me when he would get drunk. He told me I was useless and he was not going to feed me for free. He threw me out with nothing. I was adopted by a group of missionaries. Who were passing by with a wagon train."

"Did your life improve with the missionaries?"

His answer did not come right away.

"No… I was better off at my father's home even if he beat me up twice a day…" there was a bitter tone in his voice.

"What do you mean… what can be worse than beatings?" I must admit I was nonplussed by his answer.

"The missionaries raped and beat me. I had to steal bread to eat. In their holy minds I was a devil and I brought all this punishment upon myself, . There was a time when I started to believe in what they were saying."

"How do you mean that?"

"Strange things were happening to me at night…" His voice was lower and hesitant.

"Tell me about these strange things…" I encouraged him.

"I would go into these trances where I would speak different voices and they were saying terrible things about me. I had scratches on my back, my arms and legs that would appear out of nowhere and wouldn't heal." As Ronald began explaining what was happening to him I came to the conclusion that he had become possessed by some entity.

"How long did you spend with the missionaries?" I wanted to move him further forward feeling that some very important information was to be revealed during the session.

"After 7 years I ran away. I was 14. I was adopted by a group of bank robbers, and they taught me how to get money without working for it. I learned very fast and after two years decided to go on my own. I did not want to share my money."

"Did your previous symptoms disappear?"

"After I ran away from the missionaries I never got any more scratches…'

"Now, I want you to take me forward in time to some important event that has changed something in your life." He thought for awhile.

"I met my wife…" A tiny smirk flashed over his lips and soon vanished.

"What is her name and how old are you when this happens?"

"I am twenty-three…Her name is Luisa Marie Lafountain," came this unreal, precise information.

"Is she French?"

"Yes, the same as she is now."

"What do you mean?" I was puzzled with his answer.

"It is Larisa…" he explained and again, a pale glint of a smile flashed across his swarthy face.

"Do you know her from before?"

"Yes, she was my woman in a previous life." He seemed annoyed.

"Are you talking about the life in which her name was Salima?" I was recalling from our first session.

"Yes, that was Larisa, she was not a good woman so I had to send her to Sultan's Court. They punish women like her."

"She was not unfaithful to you. She just did not want to have anything to do with you after she caught you with another man..." I recalled.

"If she told the Sultan about me they would have impaled me. I could not let that happen..." He furrowed his brows again and his jaw clenched with determination to defend his position.

"Let's go back to Luisa Marie..." I wanted to push the session towards the life of Ben Thomas. "Did you marry her because you loved her, or you had other reasons?"

"No, I could not love her, she was one of these religious fanatics. I met so many of them in the missionary camp."

"So why would you decide to marry her if you did not love her at all?"

"So I could hide behind her and do what I wanted to do to get rich."

"You mean getting rich by robbing banks?"

"Yes..." he answered with no hesitation."

My alertness was increasing since I considered Larisa one of my best friends and I felt there was something unhealthy about Ronald's relationship with her.

"Please tell me how long you stayed married to Luisa?" I asked, wanting to learn more about the patterns this man was carrying through his lifetimes and I also knew that unless these patterns were broken they were bound to be repeated.

"Six years. We had two sons, they were twins."

“Did you learn to love your wife and sons?” I asked hoping for an answer that would reduce my suspicion that something was not at all right.

“No, they were my burden and I had to feed them,” came the answer that chased away my hope that Ronald’s soul was here in this lifetime to correct and repair the past mistakes.

“Tell me what happened.”

“I robbed the bank in town and buried the money in our backyard. I was waiting until everything quieted down. I was planning to take the money and go to California. I heard that there was lots of gold. I could become a prospector.”

“Then what happened?”

“Luisa Marie found the money and threatened to take it to the sheriff. I could not let her do that “

“How were you planning to stop her from doing that?’

“I bought a shotgun and I blew her head off…” he said as casually as if this was just another thing to do.

“You murdered your wife?” I felt my skin crawl. “What did you do with your two boys?”

“I left them in the house, they were small and I was sure they would die before anybody would find them in the house.” He said all of this without a hint of remorse. I was flabbergasted.

“Then what happened, did you manage to go to California?”

“No, I was digging my money from under the tree where it was buried when the sheriff showed up with his men and they captured me.”

“They saw blood on the ground and found Luisa Marie’s body laying close to where the money was buried.”

“What happened to your sons?”

"They took them, ."

"What happened to you?

"They hung me in town." Fascinating.

"I want you to take me to the last moment of this lifetime when they hung you, just before the stool is kicked from underneath your feet, and tell me what are your last thoughts." As I was instructing Ronald, I hoped that even though Ben Thomas went through his life committing these atrocities and other ruthless acts, at the moment of death he would have a change of heart to see the truth of what he has done and feel bad about it. To my disappointment he not only did not have any remorse he felt he had justification to do what he had done.

"She was a stupid woman and she deserved to die," he hissed through clenched teeth, but what he said next made my blood run cold, "I blew her head off once, I am planning to do it again."

After hearing that I was unable to continue the session. My thoughts ran towards my friend and I could not stop thinking that her life was in danger. I brought the session to an end and programmed Ronald with some positive affirmations.

## Conclusion of Ronald's Sessions

Later on that day, I asked Larisa to sit and talk with me for a moment. I had to tell her what had transpired in the session and warn her to be very careful with her husband. In my mind he was as capable in this life to perpetrate evil acts as he had done in his past existences.

My friend listened to me very carefully, her face serious and drawn.

"I knew he was an evil bastard, but never realized how truly evil until now. Did I do something to him that caused him to hate me and the boys that much?"

"No, Larisa it never was about you..." I answered her question. "He had always had the tendency to attract evil, and instead of letting go and forgiving his oppressors he turned it around and became one of them. His soul is dwarfed and stinted in its progress. He has a dark soul... I can now see that some people are born iniquitous and meant to kill or hurt others."

A few months later after an incident when Ronald took Larisa's car, was drunk and rolled it into a ditch, my friend decided to ask for a divorce and end her marriage. I welcomed the news when she told me. I could rest peacefully knowing she was no longer in the direct presence of a man that had taken her life twice and would willingly be glad to do it again.

Larisa filed for divorce and moved to Edmonton where she landed a great job with the City and raised her two sons by herself. Both boys are doing well.

One more interesting thing before Ronald's case is put to rest. During their marriage Larisa and Ronald purchased 2 life policies, which she continued paying after their divorce. I recall our conversation on that subject. I agreed with my friend's decision to continue paying for Ronald's policy, we both thought that one day the boys might have some funds to use for their education.

Many years later after Larisa was just about to marry a very lovely, quiet man from Europe she got news from the Police that the body of her ex -husband was found charred in the torched house on the reserve where he lived after their divorce. He had turned again to the heavy use of drugs and alcohol. His death was ruled accidental, however Larisa thinks that her ex was murdered by one of his own family members in a drunken stupor and the fire was set afterward to destroy the evidence. The investigation into Ronald's death was eventually closed due to lack of evidence of foul play. After the policies was paid out in full, Larisa's boys finally had the money that their father had refused to pay for all their young lives. If Karma exists, this would be a good example.

*He who is not contented with what he has, would not be contented with what he would like to have.*

— Socrates —

## CHAPTER ELEVEN: DOROTHY'S CASE

Dorothy was the daughter of one of my clients. I saw her several times to help her heal early childhood issues that were mainly but not exclusively connected to the life on the Indian Reserve.

It was early in March when I received a call from Sandra, Dorothy's mother.

"Hi Ursula." The voice was familiar to me even before she introduced herself to me. "This is Sandra… Maybe you don't remember me…" she continued before I interrupted her.

"Hi Sandra, I do remember you very well. I remember each and every one of my clients…" I assured her.

"Are you feeling OK?" I asked, concerned that maybe the issues we worked out during our sessions were not all cleared up and there was still more work she wanted to do.

"I am OK." She explained, "it's about my youngest daughter Dorothy."

"What is wrong with your daughter?" I asked, concerned.

"Can I bring her over to your place so you can tell me?" She seemed distraught. "Do you have any openings today?" she asked anxiously.

"You want to bring her today?" I was surprised at her rush.

"Yes, she is not doing well…" she said.

"OK, let me see if I can change one of my appointments to a later hour and you can bring her right away."

"Thank you, I really appreciate that!"

"Let me call my client and see if she will be OK to move her appointment. I will call you right back. Just in case, please give me your telephone number."

We were in luck and my morning appointment answered the phone on the second ring.

"Corrin?"

"Yes it is Ula?" She recognized my voice.

"I have an emergency that I need to assist right away, and I was wondering if you would mind moving your appointment to a later hour today or tomorrow morning?"

"You know it's funny, I was just about to call you and change my appointment for tomorrow. I was called to work today since one of my coworkers called in sick and I have to fill her spot," she explained.

"Oh my God it was meant to be then. Thank you so much. I will see you tomorrow then at 10 AM," I confirmed before hanging up.

Sandra was sitting by the phone and waiting for my call. She answered even before I heard her phone ring.

"Hi Sandra, it's all worked out, so please bring your daughter over right away."

"We will be right there."

It took 20 minutes for my client and her daughter to arrive at my house.

"Please come in!" I welcomed them in. I looked outside, the sky was blue and sunny but the temperature was low and the air crisp.

The girl was moving like an effigy, there was no expression on her face, her eyes appeared to be void of light and unfocused as if dead from the inside.

Sandra asked Dorothy to sit in the Living room and wait, which the child did without uttering a single sound.

I was surprised, since I vaguely remembered Sandra complaining about her youngest daughter being hyperactive and frequently disturbing other children during her classes.

I sat Sandra in my kitchen and offered her cup of coffee, but she politely refused.

"So, please tell me what happened," I asked her then sat quietly.

"It all happened before Christmas," she began "She had invited her best friend to stay over the weekend. We were upstairs preparing dishes for Christmas Day. You know that my husband and I are Catholics…? The girls decided to get out of our sight and went to play in the basement of our home. They were gone for hours, so we were not concerned about what they were doing down there. I was just about to call them up for supper when the most horrifying screams came from downstairs. Both girls were screaming as if they were cut to pieces. I have never heard these kind of terrifying screams in my life except for horror movies which I hate watching anyway. I ran downstairs as quickly as possible. My sister and my husband followed me. When we got downstairs I saw my daughter's friend lying unconscious on the floor, while my daughter looked like she was changed into a pillar of salt with the most terrified look on her face. She was still screaming at the top of her lungs. I noticed a large broken vase that used to stand on the mantle of our basement fireplace. And on the coffee table I noticed a ouija board! I know I would never allow my daughter to use such a thing. It must have been her friend who snuck it into our house. This was what the girls were doing all afternoon!"

She tried to calm herself by breathing deeply, her face was flushed with anger and embarrassment.

"I really thought that my daughter knew better... we called an ambulance right away because even though we were trying to help Gina, my daughter's friend was not regaining consciousness. We managed to calm Dorothy down trying to find out what had happened in the basement but she wouldn't say anything. She has not spoken a single word since then."

"She has not spoken for three months?" I gasped, having a hard time believing what I had just heard.

"She responds to instructions like a robot but something has been locked inside her and I am really worried that whatever they evoked is holding her prisoner and is getting more and more access to her soul..."

"What happened to Gina. How is she now?" I asked uneasily.

"She is still in the Psychiatric Hospital where she was taken by ambulance. Her mother told me that she regained consciousness but doesn't recognize anyone. She is not talking. She is in a frozen state similar to my daughter. She also admitted to me later that it was she who bought that damn ouija board as a present for Gina for Christmas. I could not believe she did that..." She was seething. "That stupid woman caused all this..."

"Ok, let's calm down and see how I can help Dorothy. But first I have to do my prayer and smudge myself, you and your daughter. This is not something we can play with lightly."

After we conducted the smudging and I prayed for protection I asked the girl to follow me to the office, sat her in the chair then sat on the other chair in front of her.

I asked her to close her eyes which she did and began relaxing her as I do in every hypnosis session. Luckily she followed my instructions and was regressing beautifully.

When I sensed the girl was fully relaxed I asked her to go back to the day when she and her friend decided to use the ouija board. I was prepared to wait for awhile for this to unfold.

"I don't want to. I am too scared." She whispered so softly that I almost missed what she said.

"Don't be afraid. I will be there with you and nothing will happen to you. I need to know what you did that day and what happened that caused you and your friend to get so scared and caused yourself to stop talking and landed her in a psychiatric ward."

I'm going to ask you to move out of your body and watch everything as if you are floating in the air and barely observing what is happening in the basement of your house. This way you will be untouchable and safe."

"Are you sure?"

"Yes, I do this all the time when someone is too afraid to go further in the session."

She nodded her head in agreement.

"Are you downstairs now?" She nodded again. "What are you doing right now?"

"Gina just took the ouija board out of her backpack. She sneaked it to the house because she knew my mom wouldn't let her bring it."

"What do you think about that?"

"I think it's a stupid board from Walmart… how would that hurt anyone?" she said without much conviction.

"What is happening next?" I asked.

"We put the board on the coffee table and decided to watch some TV."

How long have you been watching TV?"

"Maybe half an hour. Gina really wants to play with the ouija board. She is excited. I think I am getting starting to get excited too. We left the TV on so my mom wouldn't be suspicious and come downstairs to check on what we are doing. She would be very angry with me if she saw a ouija board. She told me never to touch things like that."

"So what is happening now once you have decided to play with this ouija board?

"We're sitting on the floor by the coffee table and we have the tips of our fingers touching the pointer. We're starting to ask questions…"

"What questions?"

"If we are going to pass English next semester. Gina had a hard time with English the past semester and she wanted to know if she was going to do better this year."

"The pointer started to move on the board towards different letters spelling the words."

"What words is it spelling?"

"You gonna fail, you gonna fail. It is repeating this over and over again."

I think Gina is moving it, but why would she say she is going to fail English?"

"What is happening now?"

"Gina asking if there was a spirit moving the pointer or me?"

"Stupid, stupid, stupid!" the pointer spelled the words quickly "It is me, can't you see that?"

"Who are you? Are you a good spirit or bad?" Gina asked.

"Bad, very bad!" The ouija board spelled it out. The pointer was moving very rapidly now and I felt neither of us was doing anything to make it slide over the board. I am starting to be afraid." Dorothy's voice was tense.

"What is happening now?" I prompt the girl to tell me more.

"I started to smell something bad, Gina is excited, not scared. I think we are doing something very wrong. I tell Gina I want to stop."

"What does she say?"

"She said this is fun and that I am spoiling her fun… she is asking the spirit to prove to us it was there by doing something we can see."

"Does the spirit do something to respond?"

"Yes…" there is a sudden movement underneath her closed eyes, "Oh, my God, the TV just started to flip through the channels on it's own!" Laboured breathing. "I want to stop! I am scared, really scared," she whimpered and I notice that she is wringing her hands now.

"Gina continued challenging the spirit!"

"How does she do it?"

"She says: 'Is this all you can do, change channels on the TV?' "She is laughing. Right after that Dorothy tells me that the TV turned off by itself."

"Was that good enough for Gina?" I probed.

"No, this stupid girl is not happy with what this spirit is showing her. She said for it to do something more impressive… I don't know what's wrong with her." There was more and more distress in the girl's voice.

"I want to stop! I said to Gina stop it right now. Tell him to leave!"

"Are your hands still on the ouija board?

"No, no! My hands are not. I stood up to leave…"

"Gina is laughing at the spirit… she challenges the spirit to show itself to us."

"Stop it Gina! I'm shouting at her."

"Tell me what is happening?"

"The vase flies off the mantle and crashes by Gina's feet. It is a big vase and it flew right across the room. My mom is going to be very angry at me when she finds the vase broken…"

"Dorothy, please continue." I pulled her back and directed her to continue.

"Gina is still laughing. I don't know what is wrong with her, she looks mad and crazed." I am walking towards the stairs. I want to get out from the basement. I want to call my mom…" Dorothy started to sob. "This is wrong, so wrong."

"Stop it, Gina! Stop it! I screamed at her but things are crazy now…"

"'Show yourself you coward!' Gina screamed at the spirit…"

"I feel the basement suddenly become freezing cold like somebody opened a window and then I see this thing…" the girl's voice trailed off and she was silent for awhile.

"Please describe this thing you see…" I instructed her.

"It's a huge dark shadow with fuzzy edges that comes from the corner of the basement. It starts to grow bigger and bigger and there are these red glowing eyes. I start to scream at the top of my lungs when the shadow rolls over Gina and starts to move towards me. This is all I remember. Next thing I see my mom and aunt shaking me. Gina was laying unconscious on the floor. The black form was no longer there."

"Could you tell me what caused you to stop communicating?" I ask her.

"Since that day the shadow would sit at the edge of my bed and it growls in a low voice to keep my mouth shut. It said that if I tell anybody what I saw it would hurt me and that my friend would never leave the psychiatric hospital…I believed this thing would really hurt me so I decided not to speak at all."

"Do you still feel it could hurt you?" I probed

"I feel much safer with you. You can make this thing go away?"

"Yes, I think can." I confirmed to increase her confidence. "These type of entities," (I started, not wanting to use the word Demons, replacing it with 'Entities'), "always try to convince you that they can hurt you to keep you under their control and this way isolate you from other people who can convince you otherwise."

"Am I going to be OK?" Dorothy asked.

"You are already better." I assured her "After the session is finished I will ask you to smudge and I will put light around you for protection. You will have to make sure that you will pray everyday and strengthen this light every day for at least two weeks. It would be better if you retain this habit for good. It is important to always make sure that you are within protection of the white light. Promise me that you are never going to touch a ouija board ever again!"

"I promise, I will never try to play with it. I've learned my lesson." As she said this I believed she would keep her promise.

Dorothy's mother was awaiting for the session to end. When we returned to the livingroom where she sat waiting for us I could see how nervous she was.

"We are finished," I said as we entered the livingroom "She is going to be OK," I added to assuage her fear. "We need to do a smudging ceremony before you leave," I said and grabbed my sacred pipe carrying bag where I always keep all my sacred herbs. The Ceremony took 15 minutes and I asked Sandra to prepare the smudging every day for a minimum of two weeks. I also asked if she could bring a Medicine Man to her house and have him smudge and cleanse her entire house especially the basement. She said she would do it right away. I could sense that she was afraid that if she did not do this something that was having hold on her daughter would come back and cause more problems for the entire family.

"I don't know how I can thank you enough," she sighed, relieved. "You do such a great job for us." By 'us' I assumed she meant the Native community.

"You are most welcome. Native people deserve healing." I gave her one more hug and they were gone.

After they left I did what I normally always do after any of my readings or hypnotherapy clients. I would take a bowl filled with sacred smudge and cleanse my entire place. I know the consequences of not doing this, for a few times in the past I neglected to purify my home after working with a client. They would go home feeling so much better and happier and I would have all hell break loose in my own place.

*It is dismal coming home, when there is nobody to welcome one!*

— Ann Radcliffe (1764 - 1823), *The Mysteries of Udolpho*, 1764 —

## CHAPTER TWELVE: ROMAN

It was in our rental home in Calgary. I had a young man come to see me for a reading. Right away, I sensed that he came to find out about his brother who had died nine years earlier in a freak car accident early one April morning on his way to work. The police were not able to explain how he went off the road, rolling his car and dying instantly. The day the accident happened on that sunny April day, the roads were clear and dry. He was not speeding as was reported by other drivers who passed him. Unfortunately nobody was close enough to see, how it happened.

"I loved my older brother very much, he had always looked after me and protected me from the bullies in our neighborhood. There was an 8 year difference in age between us but he never treated me like a stupid kid. I missed him when he moved out. He got married two years later and they had a little baby girl. They lived not too far from us so I saw my brother almost everyday. We remained very close until the awful day the police came to inform my parents that there had been an accident and that they needed to go to the hospital morgue to identify the body. I thought my world had collapsed in on me and I never accepted the fact that my brother was gone forever. I sometimes feel he is with me but I am not sure. I think it only may be my imagination and wishful thinking."

The reading brought up the subject of his brother right off the bat. I sensed the spirit of the deceased man right away when my client walked into my house for the reading. After the session my client, I will call Roman to keep his privacy, asked me if I thought he should have an hypnosis session with me and if this would help him to clear his brother issue and help him to move on. I thought it was an excellent way to reconnect Roman with his brother's spirit and help him understand what caused the accident and through this help him to go through and complete the process of his grieving. And help him to deal with his pain. My client was very happy with the results of his reading because now he learned that he was not the only person aware of the presence of his brother's spirit and through the reading I brought to the surface his sorrow and released some of the pain that was bottled inside him. He felt lighter and happier. Less depressed.

These were my client's own words 'I feel you can help to let go of this heaviness that I have been carrying inside me since the accident.'

I did not want to tell him that the heaviness was caused by the presence of his brother's disembodied spirit right inside him. The depression that Roman felt was not his own. It was his brother's sorrow, and the sense of loss that he felt. Not being a part of his daughter's life and witnessing his wife's ongoing struggle trying to get her life back.

We set our next appointment for four days later which was a Thursday at 6 PM in my house. I must mention here that to my husband's great annoyment I do not have an appointment book so every appointment I make was strictly in my head. This was the reason how this funny situation happened on the day of our scheduled appointment. As I had a day job at the time I totally forgot to open 'my mental appointment book' to remind myself that I only had an hour to get home from work, grab something to eat and be ready for our 6 PM appointment. On a last minute suggestion of my husband who was unaware of the set appointment, we went for dinner at our favorite Chinese Restaurant. When we were done and my husband was clearing the bill, my cell phone rang. I managed to look at the time and noticed that it was already 6:45 PM. It was Roman's wife trying to find out where I was and to tell me that her husband had been sitting in his car in front of our house for the past 45 minutes. I felt terribly embarrassed and asked her to promise her husband that I was on my way and should be there in the next ten minutes or so (luckily the restaurant was very close to our place). All the way home my husband was chastising me for forgetting about my appointment. This wasn't a new thing for us. He will gladly tell you about the night I had (apparently) made three different appointments with clients at the exact same hour and he ended up playing host and entertaining two of these when I was working with the first one. And each session is usually between 1-2 hours long for each client!

As we pulled up to the house, I saw Roman getting out of his vehicle carrying a beautiful bouquet of flowers. To my great surprise he brought these flowers to thank me for the way I made him feel after our previous reading. As one can only imagine this made me feel even worse for making him wait the extra hour in front of my house.

We started the session without further delay. As I predicted his brother's spirit sensing this only opportunity to make Roman aware of his presence, came forward right away as I managed to put Roman under.

"Ok. Let's start. Roman do you feel you are not alone?" I asked him gently.

"That's right. That is exactly how I feel." He appeared a little surprised that I would know that he wasn't alone.

"Who is there with you?" Right after I asked this question a gap-jawed look spread over Roman's face. The shock was so great that it took him awhile before he responded.

"Daniel?" he whispered "It's Daniel!"

"Who is Daniel?"

"He is my brother," he explained trying to shake off his amazement.

"Can you ask Daniel why he is with you and ask him what happened the day he died?" I directed.

"He said he that didn't know where to go and that I pulled him towards me." Roman was reporting an internal dialogue taking place between the two brothers. Normally I would take the lead and address the spirit directly, but in this case I felt that the brothers needed to have a more intimate conversation.

"Can you ask Daniel to tell you what happened that day when he was on his way to work and had the car accident? Please repeat to me what Daniel is telling you about the accident." I asked.

"He is telling me that he had just got up. He is in the kitchen looking out through the window. The sun is just rising, he says it was going to be a beautiful April day. He had his coffee and toast. He did not want to wake his wife so he made himself a sandwich to take with him for work. He is walking to the car."

"Ask him how he is feeling that morning."

"He said he feels sad, he feels that he shouldn't have forgotten to go to the bedroom to give his wife and daughter a kiss before leaving. He said it was the first time he had ever done that."

"What did he do next?"

"He almost turned around and went back to the house, but figured he might be late for work, so decided not to."

"Please go with your brother so you can see for yourself what happened that morning… What is happening?"

"I feel I am sitting next to Daniel on the passenger seat…" As he said that I sensed that he was surprised at his statement. "How could that possibly be? I wasn't there in the car when the accident happened?"

"It's possible to do that. It's your brother's way of showing how his accident happened. You are going to be safe, nothing will happen to you," I explained to him.

"Can you look at the speedometer and tell me what speed your brother is driving."

"He is going 80 Km/hr. That's the speed limit on this road," Roman continued reporting.

"So, Daniel is not speeding?"

"No, not this morning."

"Tell me, what are the road conditions?"

"It' s a beautiful sunny morning, the road looks good."

"Please continue." I prompted.

"We are going into a curve to the left. Oh, my God! Slow down Daniel! The road looks dark like it is wet... Oh no, no!!!" came Roman's distressed voice. "There's a patch of black ice, this area is in shadow so the morning sun hasn't thawed this section of ice. The car goes into a spin. It starts turning and sliding into the ditch and then starts rolling and ends up on it's wheels. The engine stops and it's deathly silent now. Daniel's head is crushed on his left side, he is bleeding and the window on his side is smashed. Blood is all over the car."

"Look at your brother," I told him. "Roman, is your brother still alive?"

"No...!" Roman gasped and his eyes were welling up. He died on impact."

"He did not suffer. He didn't even have time to realize he passed on. That's the reason he never knew he was gone and he found his way to you. You gave him comfort. He has been with you ever since the day of the accident. He missed the moment when he was called towards the light. Your grieving held him stuck the past nine years."

"Daniel, my brother, I am so sorry I held you back!" Roman was very emotional.

"Are you ready to let your brother depart to the light where he can finally find peace and move to the spirit world where he belongs?"

"Yes, I want him to be happy, he deserves better."

"Tell him one more time how much you love him and how much he has taught you. Tell Daniel that he is free to go and that you are going to be OK."

It took a while after I brought Roman back out of hypnosis to calm him. He cried for quite awhile, then he finally stopped and I sensed a great deal of peace filling his heart.

Before he left my place, he gave me a warm hug and said something that forever will stay with me.

"Even if I was to wait in front of your house for you to come back for another 10 hours, it was well worth it. Thank you so much for helping me."

"You are most welcome!" I smiled at him, still slightly embarrassed at missing his appointment.

## Conclusion of Roman's Case

Roman was a classic case of shadowing and partial possession. It shows that violent and unexpected deaths are much of the time caught between life and death by the simple unawareness that a transition has taken place and that they no longer belong to the land of the living. On the other hand uncompleted grieving can be one of the strongest hooks that can prevent the deceased person to transition into the light. Unfinished business, unspoken words, unexpressed feelings can be our entrapment on both sides of the thin line in life that separates two distinctly different yet similar planes of existence. Our awareness locks in one split second and time stops meaning anything anymore, we no longer exist in a linear way. One part of us perishes and the other gets stuck sometimes for eternity in a place where nothing moves in any direction and we view existence from behind a "thick glass wall." We can see and hear loved ones, but they cannot see or hear us. We can try to touch them and sometimes they can feel us, but we cannot be touched back…the 'thick glass wall' doesn't allow us to participate in life events, we can barely be observers.

*You have it easily in your power to increase the sum total of this world's happiness now. How? By giving a few words of sincere appreciation to someone who is lonely or discouraged. Perhaps you will forget tomorrow the kind words you say today, but the recipient may cherish them over a lifetime.*

— Dale Carnegie (1888-1955) American writer —

## CHAPTER THIRTEEN: LORETTA

I got to meet Loretta though my husband. When I met her for the first time she appeared unsettled and unsure of anything. A woman with very pleasant manners, which indicated to me that she had learned how to hide her real emotions from everybody in her life. At the time she had been divorced for many years with adult children that had moved out of her house. She felt empty and often depressed and just recently was diagnosed with lung cancer. Her illness was the main reason for which she wanted to see me. My husband talks to many people, often strangers, about me and what I do. I suppose, what I do will never cease to impress and amaze him. He believes in what I do since on many occasions he has seen changes that were almost immediate in many of my client's personalities and lives.

Within the first 20 minutes of my meeting with Loretta I knew that she needed hypnotherapy since I sensed she locked many heavy feelings and emotions in her 4th Chakra which was the biggest culprit in her lung cancer fight, followed by the fact that for much of her life she was a heavy replacement smoker. Which again confirmed her strong self distracting tendencies.

"When can we start our sessions?" She was very upset and terrified of dying.

We set our first session for the next day. She showed up at my door half and hour early.

We started.

As soon as I reached her knees in the process of hypnotic relaxation I knew that she was going into a very deep, hypnotic condition.

"Loretta, I will count from 20 down to 1 and with every number you will sink into a deeper and deeper trance state. And as you do so, you will go back in time to the beginning of what is causing you to develop lung cancer. At the count of one you will in the right space and time realize what happened that started this process to Cancer."

I wasn't afraid to call it what it is.

I watched Loretta's face and noticed that her eyes began the hypnotic subjects' normal REM (Rapid Eye Movement) as she started to see into the distant past.

"What are you seeing? Where are you?"

"I am at home…" She grimaced somewhat and her forehead frowned as if attempting to understand what she was seeing.

"Who are you?"

"I am Loretta. I am me." she said.

"How old are you?"

"I am four. I am in my home… but I'm not feeling good."

"What do you mean?"

"I'm scared…"

"Are you by yourself? Where are your parents?"

"They are not home. My uncle is with me. I don't like my uncle."

"What is the reason you do not like him."

"He is mean to me and he does things to me… I don't like…" Little girl voice.

"Tell me please about the things he is doing to you." I encouraged her.

"I don't want to, they made me a bad person!"

"Loretta, you are four years old and you are not a bad person. It sounds like your uncle is the bad person."

"He is touching me on my bottom…" she said, her voice low and harsh. "He tells me that I need to listen to him since my mom asked him to look after me. He says if I will not do what he tells me he is going to tell my mom that I am a very bad girl and my mom will punish me and send me to an orphan's home."

"Do you believe him?"

"Yes, when my mom is angry with me, she says the same thing." My heart sank hearing this. This made me realize how vulnerable children are and how literally they take the words of the adults in their lives. Even if adults do not mean harm, how it is processed and interpreted by the child can be totally devastating. I thought at that moment that one should write a book devoted to what to say and what not to say to his/her child. Adults often unwittingly create chaos in their kids minds by making statements that the subconscious mind is not able to interpret other that negative and offensive.

"Did you tell your mom what your uncle is doing to you when she is not around to see it?"

"No, I don't want my mom think that I am a bad girl."

"How long has your uncle been doing these bad things to you?"

"Until I was six years old…"

"Then what happened? What made him stop?"

"He got sick and had to go to the hospital."

"What was his problem?" I asked sensing what might be the answer.

"He got lung cancer…" the last word was stretched out and her brows knitted her forehead.' "Oh my God, he had the same illness I have."

"Tell me how long was your uncle sick?"

"He died in three months."

Then a male spirit became apparent to me, and to Loretta, standing kind of in front of her pronate body and melding through the bed.

"Loretta, … could you let me talk to your uncle directly? Tell me what is your uncle's name?"

"Fritz…he says he has wanted to talk to somebody for a long time but no one could hear him."

"Hello Fritz," I started, "How long have you been with Loretta?"

"50 years." The voice was lower than Loretta's so I knew right away that I was communicating now with the Fritz entity inside Loretta.

"Why have you been possessing her for such a long, long time?"

"I felt I needed to look after her since I did some terrible things to her when she was a young child." It sounded shamed.

"Was that you who pushed Loretta to start smoking at the age of 12?" I had asked Loretta before we started our session when she had her first cigarette. Smoking was one of many factors that led inexorably to Loretta's health issues.

"Yes."

"I want you to understand that even though you might feel guilty for sexually assaulting your niece, you have not stopped hurting her."

"What do you mean, I'm trying to look after her!" The entity became defensive.

"Being inside Loretta's body, you continue harming her. It is the nicotine habit you pushed on her as well as the residue of your own cancer that killed you that is resonating inside Loretta."

"I am so sorry. I don't want to hurt her more than I have already in the past when she was a little girl."

"Then it's time for you to go to the light and allow Loretta to fight for her own life and health."

"She is angry at me and I don't know how to beg her forgiveness… I don't want to go to hell."

"Loretta, can you hear this? Do you want your uncle to leave?"

"Yes." She said in a stern, hard voice. "I don't want him around, he has done enough…"

"Loretta your uncle's spirit will not leave until you release him."

"I want him to go!"

"He will not leave until you can let go and forgive him." I told her.

"He does not deserve forgiveness…!" she shouted out.

"I know but without forgiveness you will never be free of what he did to you and this process of getting sick," I explained to her "Can you look inside your heart and find enough love to let go?"

"Why did he do this to me?" She was sobbing now. "He really screwed me up."

"I will help you to see. I will now count from 5 to 1 and you will move back in time with me to see the reasons your uncle did to you what he did when you were a little girl. On the count of one you will see his life unfolding backwards toward his childhood and perhaps beyond," I explained, then started the count down.

Loretta was still for a while after she heard the number 1, but I could see her eyes moving under her eyelids as if following the pictures in her head.

"What do you see?" I prompted her. She took her time.

"I see Fritz as a little boy, he is 9 and my mom is 10. I see them playing in the barn. They play hide and seek." she explained. "They are having fun, but there is someone else coming into the barn…" Loretta's face became still, not a muscle moving.

"Loretta… tell me who came into the barn?"

"My grandfather…" He is mean to my uncle."

"Tell me what happens."

"He grabs my mom and is dragging her to the corner to the pile of hay".

"What is your uncle doing?"

"He is trying to pull his sister by her hand away from his father's grip…"

"Then what happens?"

"My grandfather slaps him hard across the face so strongly that he hits the dirt floor. There is blood coming from his cut lip. He says: "Stand there and watch you little shit, maybe you can learn something useful!"

"Then what happens?" My quiet voice prompted Loretta to continue. I was starting to perspire now, dreading what was coming. From the expression on her face I knew that what she was viewing was very disturbing.

"My grandfather raped my mom…! She is laying in the pile of hay and her brother is sitting on the floor, crying. My grandfather is gone now…"

"Can you at least see now how your uncle got prepped for what he later did to you? Did your uncle ever get married?" I asked her.

"No, that is why he was living with us when I was young…"

"Can you see how your grandfather singlehandedly destroyed at least two lives with what he did to your mom? Your uncle never married, never wanted to be close to any woman because of what happened to his sister and he was made to witness it. He was an angry man with an empty heart that was twisted by the criminal acts of his own father. The anger had eaten up his lungs, because his fourth chakra was clogged and never allowed love to flow through it."

"I forgive him!" Loretta said suddenly "I forgive him, and he can go now! I understand now why he was the way he was."

"I want you to say something to your uncle's spirit before he departs to the light." I told her.

"I am sorry that my grandfather made you watch the terrible things he did to my mother. I see now that you were predestined to be who you were. I am not angry at you any more, go now."

I knew that Loretta meant what she said and that her forgiveness was genuine. Sometimes all it takes is to see the vicious circle of abuse to understand the mechanisms of the events that shatter our lives and to be able to generate enough love to bring about forgiveness and let go of the past.

"As I count from 5 to 1 we are now going to move forward again in time to your present life to find other reasons that are contributing to your lung problems."

"Where does your mind take you?"

"I am on my wedding day," she informed me. Smiles, sort of.

"How do you feel? Are you happy?"

"No, not really. I think it is time for me to move on."

"What do you mean? Tell me about your husband."

"He is OK. I think we'll be OK together." I didn't feel that was a good enough reason to get married but I did not point it out to Loretta. I assumed she had her own reasons for marrying this man.

She took me through 15 years of her marriage with nothing spectacular unfolding, with the exception of a daughter who made her real happy since from that point she had an outlet to unleash her emotions without the fear of getting hurt. The marriage was slowly unraveling as the years passed. Loretta's husband began drifting further and further from her. Then the years of fierce arguments and fights started. On one fateful (and probably inevitable) day she caught her husband with another man and this lead to a bitter, contentious divorce and a tremendous amount of resentment, anger and disappointment. Her already clogged chakra 4 was made even more deadly, as she had been harboring this anger for the past 10 years.

"Do you still feel angry today?" I asked

"Yes, he betrayed me. This is unforgivable." Bottled up anger.

"Do you realize that this resentment and anger are really instrumental and a causal factor in creating your cancer?"

"No!" She said "How could that be?"

"Your Chakra 4 is completely locked. There is no vital energy flowing through. No vital organ can remain well when a person harbors so much anger. This anger is no longer hurting your ex-husband, he doesn't feel it. It's become your enemy."

"Oh my God, I'm doing it to myself." She suddenly came to this realization. "Am I killing myself?" she whispered.

"Yes, you are, but you have power to change it and since we have the power to destroy our health we also have the same power to heal our bodies and minds. I just need to know that you are ready to use this power to begin the healing process."

"Yes!" There was so much determination in her voice that I had to believe she was going to fight for her life. "I want to see my daughter graduating…" I saw an image in my head of Loretta sitting in a large auditorium and could feel the excitement and pride to see her *granddaughter* receiving her High School Diploma.

"If you clear your heart of anger and negative feelings you will not only see your daughter's graduation but also your granddaughter's." I assured her.

"Really? Please help me to clear what I must. I don't want to die!" she entreated.

"I want you to take a deep, deep breath, hold it for the count of 1, 2, 3 then I want you to exhale. As you exhale, press gently on your diaphragm to push all the used air out of your lungs. Let's do it again… and then again…" I instructed her. "With every breath you inhale you are bringing into your body a vital wave of healing energy, hope, optimism, joy, faith…and with every breath you exhale you are removing from your system and from every cell of your body, mind and spirit: illness, anger, darkness, resentment and all other negative emotions and beliefs. The emotions you don't need that never belonged to you." She was following my instructions exactly. Her chest would rise, she would hold her breath and on the count of three would exhale through her mouth until empty of all stale and used air.

"For every breath you take in more and more brilliant light is entering and spreading throughout your body, every cell is touched by this wonderful healing light. Your lungs are filled with this radiant, healing light. I want you to see the dark matter zooming out of your body leaving behind the most pure and clear, healthy and vibrant organs. I want you feel your heart void all the heavy feelings you kept there when you came to see me. Now they are all gone and your heart feels light and happy."

"It feels wonderful. I feel so peaceful."

After that I gently brought her out of hypnosis. When she opened her eyes, she laid there still staring at the ceiling. I remained quiet giving her space to gather her thoughts.

"I have never felt so peaceful and good." She smiled, and and sat up on the bed. "How can I ever thank you?"

"Just get better." I said, "And never let go of that vision of the large auditorium where you are watching your granddaughter graduate!"

"You are my angel." With that, she gave me a big hug.

## Conclusion of Loretta's Case

I was ecstatic to learn that Loretta's lung surgery went well and she was recovering. She told me later that she continues hearing my voice replaying in her head telling her to visualize her granddaughter she did not have yet, graduating and her being there to be part of it. Before surgery, she closed her eyes when the general anesthetic hit her veins and with these pictures locked in her mind.

Ten years later when I last heard from her, she was still doing well and just told me about her granddaughter who was turning three that very year.

As I look at this case from the prospective of time and in conjunction with other cancer cases I worked in my practice, I have a straight-forward explanation and proof that we are the makers of our destinies including our own wellness. As I look at today's society of detached individuals and families, I contend that we are enablers of a disease of anger called cancer. I am an even firmer believer of the adage that "*Disease of mind creates disease in the body.*"

*A strong positive mental attitude will create more miracles than any wonder drug.*

— Patricia Neal —

## CHAPTER FOURTEEN: ANGELS

I always like go back to the time when for the first time in my life I was given a chance to have a glimpse of what the Bible presents as angels. Maybe before I get to the subject I should give the reader some introduction to my ideas of these biblical beings. Even though born in a heavily Catholic country and family that followed a very regular schedule of participating in religious events such as Sunday mass-like most Poles- I started drifting away from this way of life as early as the age of fourteen, when in my young mind I could not embrace the image of God as a punishing force that has nothing better to do but watch and wait for our smallest mistakes so it can pounce on us and punish us for being human beings. I never read the Bible on a regular basis. I knew some of it from our religion classes as a curriculum subject. I saw images and visages of Biblical angels and demons from sculptures in churches, in Discovery programs and such. So the image of a winged creature with heavenly, porcelain perfect features would be the last iteration my mind would admit seeing.

One memorable winter's Christmas Eve of 2001 the phantom of an angel appeared to me standing next to the piano as my husband was playing traditional Christmas Carols. As it happened, that evening he played them so beautifully as if his fingers were guided by some magic power. We were both pretty emotional that evening. We felt sad and lonely, but grateful for at least having each other, because we understood that for many people in our situation they have nobody and were *truly* alone and lonely. We at least had each other. Our relationship was at a young stage at this point but I felt it had great potential going forward with our mutual attraction, respect, admiration and love of each other, bringing us closer every day that we spent with one another. I must admit that this was the first Christmas Holiday for each of us out of our previous marriages. A Christmas that left us all alone without the presence of our young 9 and 12 year old daughters who were spending this holiday with our soon-to-be ex-spouses. My husband has a soft and melancholic nature and he was suffering bad. It was around 11:30 PM. The house we were renting had a sunken living room, soft blue decor, and Michael's Baldwin Baby Grand piano sitting proudly in the Bay Window. It was a cold, crisp evening and I noticed beautiful shimmering and glittering tiny icicles, illuminated by a solitary streetlight, drifting elegantly past the window, settling down on the Charles Dickens-like deep snow drifts in the yard and street. I was sitting on a low stool by the piano listening to my husband play. We were both wearing new robes and drinking some kind (forget what)of Christmas libation. At one point I became slowly aware of a presence that appeared at the end of the piano. What I was seeing absolutely took my breath away and left me in a state of shock and wonder. I didn't know what to think about this vision. The figure that I saw stood 7-feet tall, it had a powder blue long dress or gown with long pointed, white feathery wings flowing down below the level of the top of the piano to the floor. Was it the face of a male or female… I could not and still cannot say. This being had very long wavy soft brown hair cascading over its shoulders and chest. The features of this winged presence appeared as clear to me as if the face was made of the highest quality porcelain and yet it was so much alive and animated. It is amazing that it is so hard sometimes to focus on one feature when one sees everything at once and the image we see has the most perfection we have ever been exposed to. The softness and gentleness of this face I was looking at, at the same time, had much graceful power and firmness in its expression. One would never think these features could meld together so perfectly, as did this beautiful being which was surrounded by a soft glowing halo.

Its long fingered white hands were resting, propped one over the other the way one would see them portrayed on Rembrandt's or Ruben's paintings of beautiful women of their time.

I could not tell how much time passed since I first saw the angel behind the piano, but as my husband told me later I was staring at it without blinking. He noticed this, stopped playing and asked me what was going on. He could not see this angel but felt that something in the atmosphere in the room had noticeably changed. What happened next was even more perplexing.

I am not sure how I heard what I heard; was it in my mind or did I actually hear a voice that was as clear and melodious as the sound of a bell? The voice said, 'Do not dust your paths; walk the pathways that are dusted for you.' Right after that the angel vanished and the whole room filled with sparkling silver dust. It looked like the flakes of snow sparkling in the light of the street light outside our window. It took a while for the silver dust to disappear then I recall a stream of deep emotion washing over me like a tidal wave. It was the most beautiful sight and experience I have ever seen and been privy to. Tears streamed down my face and I could not and did not want to control or hide them. They felt good and at that moment I knew everything was going to be OK. I know there is a high, loving energy, you may call it Divinity, the Lord, God, the Creator or so many other names. He is watching over us and we were going to be OK.

I talked for hours afterward with my husband and even today he often brings up the subject of what had happened that Christmas Eve.

Interestingly, this event was monumental in effect for both of us. Being Catholics, it seemed important and useful that we share what I experienced with other believers and Michael decided a week later that it would be remiss of him (us) not to let the Church know what happened that beautiful night. Having a majestic angel visit us and pass on the guiding message it conveyed, especially at just a few minutes before Christmas Day, must have special relevance and we took it to mean we had a responsibility to act. Especially with all the turmoil and angst going on in the world.

He called up the Calgary Catholic diocese office and asked for the Bishop's office. He was transferred to the Bishop's assistant priest, or representative, and proudly and carefully explained in full detail what had transpired.

Here is the answer given him by the Priest: "Well, that is a private matter." And then basically hung up. Unbelievable.

Needless to say shortly after that my ex-husband brought my daughter back to live with me. I must mention that in October of the previous year I drove my daughter to live with her dad. After our separation she cried and became depressed, missing her father so much that I had to put my feelings aside and act in her best interest. I love my daughter and I wanted the best for her, so after a conversation I had with my 9 year old she told me that she wanted to live with her dad. It was the hardest thing I have ever done but I knew that the only good I was interested in was my child's welfare. She was not going to be a pawn in our divorce, she was not to ever be a tool of manipulation, that unfortunately is so frequently used by divorcing parents. I hope that if you, my readers, are going through a divorce please do what I did; do what is the best for your children and put your selfish and controlling actions away and prove that you truly love your children. Allow them to have both parents as much as they can because this is what guards their wellness and assures their development to be unhampered by the take-no-prisoners battles that occur in many divorces. Give them the gift of growing with confidence and support and surrounded with love. Which we all need so desperately in our lives, at any age.

## More Angel Stories.

The second time I had an experience with Angels was during my session with a nice woman of German background, who had been diagnosed with one of the most malignant breast cancers a woman could contract. She was told that Medical Science had very little knowledge about this type of cancer. It was one of the rarest cancers and one of most deadly, according to what I learned about it.

At around the time she was scheduled for mastectomy surgery she found our number from one of my former clients who told her about my line of work and she called for an appointment. Obviously there was great urgency to set this appointment as quickly as possible thus I saw Gertrude within the same week. When I arrived at her quaint, little doll-like house in southwest Calgary she gave me a big hug and thanked me for seeing her right away.

She was living alone and said that she had never married and 15 years earlier she emigrated to Canada. The rest of her family was still living in Germany. Gertrude, in her early sixties, was of a very positive and happy nature so it was puzzling to me that such a gentle woman who appeared not to harbour much anger or resentment in her life could have the unfortunate luck to develop such a rare and vicious type of cancer. Accordingly, I wanted to try to help her as much as possible.

She was scared and lonely and my heart felt for her.

I counseled that before we began the hypnotherapy session, I wanted to perform some energy healing on her. She agreed since she was ready to do anything that could help her beat this cancer, and so we began my hand's-on energy session. She sat on a chair and I stood behind her. When I do hands -on healing my hands don't actually touch the person. I hold them 2-3 inches away from the body. I didn't know which one of her breasts had developed the tumor. As I was moving my hands in front of her chest, I zeroed in on a spot with a very cold area centered around the top of her left breast. Energy was not flowing through that area at all. The spot had no energetic vibrations. I call it a dead zone. I asked her if this was the area where the tumor was located. She was surprised how precisely I was able to pinpoint where the cancer was located.

"Yes, that is the exact spot." she confirmed and closed her eyes. I held my hand over this spot, moving it gently trying to push more energy through the blockage. Breathing deeply and slowly, I closed my eyes and began praying. What happened next was nothing short of a miracle. I felt a sharp poking pain in my left breast in the very exact spot I was trying to open up to accept the healing energy. Suddenly I became aware of a presence standing right behind me. The presence was so close that I felt a gentle push along my entire back, shoulders and arms. The presence behind me was the *same* blue angel I saw in our home standing behind our piano that Christmas Eve! Two beautiful, translucent hands were placed over mine and I could feel heat coming from the back of my hands through my palms and penetrating onto the woman's breast. Then I felt the cold spot gradually start to heat up and it began pulsating.

"This was what her body needed, now see what her soul needs…" A quiet whisper and then the presence suddenly disappeared leaving a soft scent of Vanilla lingering in the air. I opened my eyes and put my hands on Gertrude's shoulders. She was quietly sobbing.

"I felt the power of your hands!" She said "They were so hot that I thought they were going to burn my skin." As she said this

I turned my hands to look at my palms and was shocked to see them beet red as if had I burned them in very hot water."

"It was not me." I said.

"Was there someone standing right behind you?" she asked me quietly as if afraid to bring up the subject.

"Yes. I had a beautiful Blue Angel standing right behind me. Its hands covered mine and that was its energy passing through my hands to your body."

"I felt it was not just you and me," she said solemnly.

"He/she told me that we need to see what is in your heart."

"I am ready, I will do whatever I need to do." I believed her without a shadow of doubt and I also knew that she was in this Angel's care. She had a great chance to survive this malicious tumor.

I also felt we had to find other internal/spiritual reasons for her illness and remove them before the physical healing could find a clear route to success.

We proceeded to her living room where she rested comfortably on the sofa, her head on a soft pillow. I began to relax her and very shortly she fell into a deep hypnotic state. I then began to be aware of the presence of the apparition of a young man in a German soldier's uniform, standing off to the right side of the room. He was a very good looking young man that carried some physical resemblance to Gertrude. When I see these spirits, the vision is one wherein the spirit seems very lifelike and almost solid, save for the holographic specter which would be the nearest way I can describe the manifestation.

"Gertrude, I want you now to take me back in time to the period where your cancer started" I instructed her softly.

"I am in the doctors office." Her eyes closed, she began slowly moving her head from side to side as if trying to see what was around her.

"Whos' office is this?

"It is Gunter's office," she answered without hesitation.

"Who is Gunter?

"He is my long time friend who practices psychiatry in Berlin."

"Are you in Berlin right now? Are you seeing your friend for some counseling?" I was not sure what was she describing to me.

"No, I am in Canada…"

"What year is it?

"It is June, 2000." It was a date taking us a year-and-a-half back in time. Now I was even more confused.

"If you are in Canada in June, 2000 how can you describe to me the psychiatric office in Berlin at the same time? And it dawned on me that I might be talking to somebody else. That revelation prompted me to ask next question, "What is your name?"

"Gunter Klautz," came the immediate response

"What is happening, Gunter?" I wasn't that surprised at this sudden turn of personalities as in my work, this phenomenon is a common occurrence, as strange as this may sound.

The voice coming from my client had a strong Germanic accent. The entity started to speak German, and I asked my client to translate into English so that I could understand, as I don't speak that tongue. I don't know how this peculiarity operates.

"I am at work. It is early morning and I am getting ready to see my first client. My secretary is not in yet so I have to grab the file on my first patient to quickly review the case," the voice explained.

"Tell me what is happening next."

"All of sudden the door blasts open and a man barges into my office. He is very agitated and holding a gun…Oh, my God he is going to shoot me." The voice was tinged with real fear.

"Who is this man? Can you recognize him?"

"Yes, it is Helmut Glinzer a patient that I had to hospitalize a few years ago. He went psychotic and almost killed his entire family. They must have let him leave the psychiatric hospital." Breathing hard. Scared.

"Continue Gunter… Tell me what happens next!"

"He is screaming that it was all my fault and that I did it to him on purpose…Oh my God he shot me, "the voice trailed off.

"Where did he shoot you?" I asked, even though I already knew the answer. I knew that he was shot through the upper part of his left chest.

"He shot me though the left side of my chest," the entity confirmed. "There is blood everywhere over my desk. I feel weak and am collapsing on the desk. Then I hear another shot."

"Did he shoot you a second time?"

"I don't think so…" Gertrude kept turning her face from side to side. "He shot himself," the voice said.

"Do you die that day, Gunter?"

"Yes." Almost entertaining if it wasn't so tragic.

"What are you doing inside your friend Gertrude? When did you enter her body?"

"When she came to my funeral (in Germany). She cried so hard and she was so heart broken that I wanted to console her."

"By entering her body you have brought her this problem with cancer in her left breast…"

"Oh no!" the voice cried out. "She is my best friend. I would never want to hurt her."

"Then it is time for you to leave to the light where you can find peace and solace and allow Gertrude to heal her body and recover from this cancer."

"Can she forgive me, I never meant for this to happen to her?" There was great distress in the entity's voice.

"You can ask her directly… she can hear you," I explained.

"Yes, Gunter." Gertrude said in a soft voice "You are my friend, how could I hold anything against you?"

"I never meant to cause you any distress or pain. I love you. I always have loved you…"

"Why didn't you tell me?" She was bewildered. "I loved you too and we could have had a good life together."

"I wasn't sure if this would have destroyed our friendship…"

"Well it's too late to talk about it." Gertrude said. "I want you to go to the light where you belong…" she said gently. "Gunter, I will miss you my friend but now you have to go. Please."

After the entity left, my client became still and quiet for quite awhile and I allowed her this time so she could embrace and absorb what she had just discovered.

"I feel so peaceful!" she said smiling. "I don't remember when I felt so good and calm."

"That is very, very good. You need to regain your confidence and strength to beat the odds and to come out of this better, stronger, healthier and happier."

We both waited. Now, I had to tell her about the German soldier's spirit I noticed when I came to her house.

"There is one more shadow I see around you. It is a very good looking young man in a soldier's uniform. Can you tell me who he is?

"This is my baby brother Hans…" She was flabbergasted.

"What has been holding him here for this length of time?"

"When he was drafted into the army he became depressed and took his own life," she explained "I could never let go and forgive him for taking his own life."

"Can you let me talk to him directly?"

"I have to translate what he has to say." she said "Is that OK?"

"Of course it's OK." (She spoke first in German and then in English)

"Ask Hans why he decided to take his life." It took awhile before I heard her answer. I waited since I knew that there was an internal conversation going on between the siblings.

"He said when he became a soldier he could not bear to become a killing tool again in the hands of the government. He said he was a Nazi soldier during the Second World War. He did lots of killing and he did not want to be forced to repeat such a horrible life."

"Tell him that taking his own life was not the right way to do it, but now it doesn't matter. Tell him that you love him and never thought ill about him being a soldier and you want him to be happy and in a good place where he does not have to feel guilt and shame. God loves him just the same."

"Hans, I love you and you have to let go of feeling guilty of taking your own life. I now understand why you did what you did. It's OK, I forgive you. Go to the light and find your peace"

Gertrude's closed eyes were once again moving from side to side as she watched her brother's spirit departing and disappearing into the light.

"He is gone."

"How do you feel?'

"A little bit sad but good."

I slowly brought Gertrude out of her deep hypnotic state.

She looked much younger as she sat on the sofa looking at me.

"Thank you so much," she whispered and I noticed a single tear sliding down her cheek. "I am *so* grateful that you agreed to see me and help me to get rid of things. I know now that even if I am not meant to survive the cancer I am OK with that." This was a very profound statement that showed me that one of her clouds (fear of death) was cleared and chased away. Carrying fear is detrimental to our well being, as it sends the wrong vibration into the Universe, inviting to us exactly what we are afraid of.

"I know that you are going to be OK!" I said to her, stepping out of her house into the bright afternoon sunshine.

"Just remember to do what I told you to do and you will be OK. The Blue Angel told me so."

## Conclusion of Gertrude's Case

I will never forget that feeling of the Angel standing behind me with its hands covering mine. The potency of the energy that flowed through me at that moment was so amazing that I will never stop feeling it as long as I'm alive. What was also imprinted onto my mind was a feeling of immeasurable peace and serenity.

This is very similar to that which I experienced one morning during my seven years of fasting.

It was my fourth and last day of fasting. The sun was just lifting it's fiery face over the Eastern horizon when I crawled out of my primitive shelter which had been built out of branches over which a few tarps were stretched for protection from the rain and the coolness of the late May nights. I sat on a little piece of foam and began my morning prayer. It was so quiet and peaceful that beautiful morning. Even the birds had not yet started their morning chirping. The silence was so enthralling and overpowering that you could feel nothing but the greatest respect. A silence that was louder than any sound I have ever heard. A silence that made you hold your breath and strain your ears because you just knew something would speak to you and for that special moment you were prepped but not really prepared. No one can be prepared for the moment when that silence is what one needs to hear. The voice that comes from everywhere and nowhere at the same time. A voice that is all around you and yet there is no discernible source for it. Words said but not spoken in any human way. Their meaning unfolding in your mind in some magical way and a feeling of knowing that this may be the first and only time you have been chosen to hear that voice, that will make you shrink, feeling insignificant and then allow your heart to raise up in joy, feeling appreciated and loved. A special feeling that no matter what is awaiting for you tomorrow, all is OK and always will be. That everything is where it is supposed to be. Everything that was wrong will be righted and everything will be as it is to be.

That morning I sobbed so hard it hurt with a good pain, my crying could not come from the deep recesses of my heart and soul, and yet I wanted to cry forever, because it felt so good. The rapture that I felt from this shedding of tears allowed the gates of my heart and my soul to be unhinged letting out all the pain, resentment, anger, sadness, sorrow, negativities and fears, leaving me submerged in harmony, serenity, peace and hope.

At any time in my life, when I have reached the point of breaking I take my heart and thoughts to that very day to recall and bring back the same feelings and memory. This is what continues to keep me sane and balanced.

### Caroline's Case: My Third Encounter With Angels

I want to bring this book much closer to home since this next case is about my own family member, one whom I love and respect very much. Why is this so important? It is because it is referring to my third encounter with angels. Caroline is my mother-in-law, a very sweet old lady who calmly took all that life had to throw at her yet invariably never complained. Sometimes, what appears on the surface to be simple becomes tremendously complex when seen up close.

One evening in 2003 we received a phone call informing us that my mother-in-law was taken to hospital with a very severe attack of neuralgic pain on the left side of her face. I was aware that she had had prior issues with this and was actually on some potent painkillers to keep the discomfort under control. We were worried but not alarmed since neuralgia is a painful, but not life threatening, condition.

It was almost one o'clock in the morning when we arrived at the emergency ward in the Rocky View Hospital in Southwest Calgary. My husband who was always very protective over his mother, was very upset and unsettled about his mother's condition, and became even more worried when he saw her in the hospital bed, pale and shrunken under the hospital sheets. She was laying still and motionless, moaning quietly with her hand pressed against her cheek, where the most excruciating pain was located. She had received huge doses of various pain killers but nothing appeared to work or make even a slight difference. I became aware of the specter of a male spirit who wore all the signs of high blood pressure and heart conditions, that appeared out of the blue behind the headboard of her hospital bed next to the rolling hanger used for suspending intravenous medications, saline bags etc. I was standing on the left side of the bed and my husband was on the opposite, touching gently his mother's wrinkled and grayish hand. All of a sudden the spirit of the man behind the bed hit the bag and suspended plastic tubes attached to it causing it to swing quite visibly from one side to the other. I felt that he had no right to be there and understanding *why* he was there, made me angry and I hissed through my clenched teeth.

"Stop it!" my words caught my husband by surprise.

"Stop what?" he asked.

"Not you…" I corrected, "I am talking to him." I pointed behind the bed. Even before I finished I could see surprise giving way to dismay as I knew my husband could see the swaying of the saline bag but couldn't see what had put it in motion. He did not respond, just looked down at his mother's face.

Standing there in the hospital I became so aware, remembering how dangerous hospitals can be when it comes to psychic attacks, possessions and such and immediately began saying a quiet mental prayer for protection from anything that was dwelling in this place of unrest wandering the corridors and rooms of the hospital. This doesn't include the idea and empirical fact that hospitals often are incubators for infection, disease and physician caused deaths and mortality. Quite an unfortunate combination.

In the next few days, each time we would come to visit my mother-in-law I became more and more aware of how quickly her condition had begun to deteriorate and worsen as more and more toxic medications were poured into her veins. According to her physician, she also had three 'specialists' assigned to her. In a week's time she became so incapacitated that she stopped eating, going to the bathroom or even opening her eyes. During one of our visits I became so emotionally overwhelmed that I had to step out of the room to hide my tears. My husband followed me outside and tried to calm me down not understanding what was happening.

"Why are you crying?"

"She is going to die," I whispered.

"She is going to die if we don't take her out of this hospital!" I chose to stay out of her room rather than show my anxiety and signs that I'd been crying, so she would not be able to see my despair and get more upset and worried. We left that day and decided to come back the next day when I was calmer and more focused.

We came back to visit the next day around 4:30 PM. Caroline's condition had not changed; in spite of vials of painkillers pumped into her body, the pain was barely dulled but never gone. She lost quite a bit of weight since she had not touched food for almost a week. I decided to do a 'hand's on' healing session with her to see if I could direct vital energy into her body and help her fight the battle she was in the middle of. I went into a deep meditative state during that time, trying to breathe deeply to support the transfer of the Universal Energy (Jung?) . I went inside her head and traveled along the inflamed swollen red nerve, knowing exactly where every curve and angle was located. Remember, I am not a doctor and am not at all familiar with detailed human physiology. I could see the reddish steam surrounding the nerve and was aware of it's pulsating and throbbing motion. Mentally I began to pour cold ice water over the engorged and swollen nerves and watched more steam rising from them and heard inside my head a hissing sound similar to the one made by a burning log of wood when water is spilled over it. I continued doing this until the nerve color began to change from fiery red into light purple and eventually into a ice-crystal-like-blue, with its size shrinking rapidly. Next, I received an image of the gauge on a bold pressure apparatus with the Mercury inside the tube reaching 260, which indicated her blood pressure was really going through the roof and posing more than a serious danger of a stroke. Using mental focus and deep breathing during this process I began to push the mercury inside the tiny tube down to 130. It moved slowly at first then dropped even below 130. During the entire process my eyes were tightly shut so that I could go inwards and draw upon as much strength as possible. This took me about 7 to 10 minutes. When I was finished and had opened my eyes, the first thing I noticed was my mother-in-law laying quietly, her hand for the first time not on her cheek but gently resting on her chest. Her regular breathing betrayed that she had fallen asleep during the healing session. Wanting her to rest, we quietly left the room and decided to go home to grab something to eat, before we would pop back again to see her that evening. After we ate and at about 5:45 PM I went to our home office and began meditation and prayer for Caroline to see what was causing her condition to deteriorate so rapidly. What was revealed to me was so disturbing and unsettling, but knowing what it was gave me a chance to act and attempt to help Caroline overcome what was causing her condition to become so grave and serious.

I slowly became aware that there were 5 possessing entities siphoning the life force out of Caroline's body. One of the spirits was the man that I had seen behind the hospital bed (not explained before, but the apparition was partly embedded in the wall behind the bed). He was solely responsible for Caroline's skyrocketing blood pressure that was posing a serious threat of stroke. I performed a ceremony to release the entities which left without resistance or a fight. I knew that these entities were spirits of people who had died in that hospital. I was finished around 6:15 PM and we decided to return to the hospital to see how Caroline was doing. On our way, I told my husband what I had learned during my meditation in our office. He was stunned and listened without making a sound. Talkative and inquisitive almost all the time, he surprised me with his silence. When we walked into my mother-in-laws room, to our great surprise she was sitting up on the bed with her feet down on the floor, her face clear and she wanted somebody to help her to the bathroom. After the nurse brought her back from the washroom, she asked for food for the first time during the 8 days of her stay in this facility.

What brought my husband to be absolutely blown away was the report by the nurse who told us that at exactly 6:20 PM Caroline buzzed her and when she walked into the room she saw her patient sitting up on the bed, trying to get up but unable to do so, being attached to the intravenous drip. She commented that my mother-in-law was very vocal and bossy in her demands of visiting the bathroom as well as expressing her hunger.

"Oh, my God," he said trying to wrap his mind around what he just heard and comparing notes on the exact timing of what I did in the house and the subsequent reaction of his mother in the hospital. Even today he is still trying to put it all in perspective. Whenever he tells this story he always says at the end that 'I saved his mother's life.' I say that it was not me, I was merely the tool that delivers this healing from a much more powerful source. Familiar refrain.

That evening I also became aware of the presence of three Angelic beings that were in the room. One of these angels was the very same blue angel that visited our house the previous Christmas Eve. Surrounding her bed, they made the hospital smell not of Lysol but of sweet Vanilla. The angels were put there by the Divine, I would surmise, to protect her from further possessions. My mother-in-law was released from the hospital three days later (I must say once she felt better she was quite thrilled to be served and catered to by the nursing staff, so she was not so anxious to go home).

The day she left, two of the three angels were gone but the blue one remained, and remains with her to this day. She is now 94 and her sister just turned 102 years old. A few years ago, feeling somewhat awkward she said to me:

"I don't what you did, but I know you saved my life." It would be more than a great understatement to say that I treasure these words like precious jewels. I love my mother-in-law and know that the day she will decide to depart from this mortal sphere and plane of existence, will be a very sad day for me.

*The hour of departure has arrived, and we go our ways - I to die, and you to live. Which is better God only knows.*

— Socrates, *in Plato*, Dialogues, *Apology* —

## CHAPTER FIFTEEN: ERNIE

Whenever I am writing about cases which involve close family members it becomes more difficult for me to stay objective. However, in my father-in-law's case it has been different. Ernie was from the old school, a product of an English bred father, and an Irish background mother, both of whom had come from unstable family trees, and both his parents had many personality defects, including alcohol abuse, domestic violence as well as mental issues, which actually resulted in his mom being in a mental hospital three times in her life. This information was not known to the extended family including his children until well into the twenty-first century. He had a tough upbringing as the oldest of 7 children, and had to bear the yoke of leading the way for the others, which also included going off to war in the Canadian Navy in World War 2, as a 17-year-old adolescent.

As such, Ernie had a dichotomy of problems in his outlook with his family, which resulted in a juxtaposition of good and bad personality characteristics. The repressed anger that he often felt, sometimes erupted rather violently with his family, with unfortunate results, in particular with his wife. At heart, I feel that he had deeply rooted causes for his attitude and behavior. On balance, he had resurrecting good qualities including his generosity, a lively sense of humor, and his passion in the field of natural healing, folk remedies, vitamins, herbs and others. Which became our common ground between us, and gave the two of us hours of interesting, uplifting and learning experiences. This fascination with natural healing, I feel, helped extend his life 10-15 years, at a minimum.

On our way back to the Coast, in 2003, I told Michael that his father had cancer. When he asked how I knew this, I told him that I smelled it. Which brought the inevitable question:

"What do you mean, you smelled it?!" Up to this day, I don't really know if this is akin to what animals physically smell in the chemical changes in the body when one of their kind, in particular, has death approaching. Perhaps so. Maybe one day science will also discover the secret behind this biological mechanism.

Six months later we were being married on March 30, 2004 in Las Vegas and I had a chance to monitor Ernie's health further. It had deteriorated alarmingly. He looked weak, and when I tapped into his energy fields I noticed that his aura was shrunken and low, with grey areas around his abdomen and waist. A month later, we got the news that in fact he had both Kidney and Colon cancer.

In my husbands desperation to help his father, and remembering what I had accomplished with his mother in 2002, Michael asked me to fly to Calgary and try to save Ernie's life.

In the next few months I flew back to work with him by myself in his home.

The first time I arrived there, on a deep level I knew that he was beyond help. Though I never gave up trying to help him as much as I was able to. And help him understand how we create our own illnesses and downfall. *Dis Ease in the mind equates to Disease in the Body.*

I also wanted to help him unload his childhood experiences and empty his emotional baggage that had him pay the ultimate price. In the process, he learned what triggered his increased violence towards his wife, that the weakness of her asking for mercy transported him back in time to his mother who he considered weak for not protecting the family from the violence of his own drunken father.

He felt ashamed and wished there was something he could do to change the past and atone for all the harm he had done.

In this process, the anger was extricated from his psyche and he became more melancholy and peaceful. It also allowed him to handle his cancer with such grace and without self pity. I - and the family - were very impressed by this, and showed how much growth as a spiritual being Michael's father accomplished in such a short period of time.

He was very brave, and handled this terrible death sentence better than the grieving souls around him.

The most important part of this story is yet to unfold.

One day we had a phone call that Ernie had decided to undergo surgery. I had a dreadful overpowering premonition come over me and I knew that if he went ahead with this, that his fate was sealed. Very quickly after the surgery, as I predicted, his condition worsened and he became hospitalized.

It was around October of that year that the doctors contended that he wouldn't survive through Christmas. Again, the words to my husband were that not only was he going to make it to Christmas, indeed he would make it to his birthday on January 19, 2005.

We spent that Christmas in the hospital with him, and indeed he did have his Christmas dinner in the hospital, courtesy of Michael's sister Theresa. The next day we flew back to the Coast as we had spent almost the previous month with him in Calgary.

On the night of the 20th of January, 2005, as we went to bed, we left the door to our bedroom ajar so that the room wasn't totally in darkness. I had just managed to fall asleep when all of a sudden, through my eyelids I became aware of a source of light that was much brighter than the room held. Surprised and sure that it was Michael who had for some reason turned on a light, I sat up in bed and was amazed to find him sleeping soundly beside me.

My focus then went to the ball of bright light that seemed to be coming from the open doorway to the hall. To my amazement I saw the figure of my father-in-law standing right in the middle of this bright light, which filled the entire doorway. Thinking that I was still asleep, I asked him how he had possibly come to our home, even though he had never been there before. Michael was right out of it and completely unresponsive when I shook him and exclaimed: 'Michael, your Dad's here!'

For a heart-pounding second I thought Michael had died, and only his breathing assuaged my fear.

His father looked calm and healthy. He wore a long, white linen tunic which was another strange element that brought me completely out of the illusion that I was looking at a real person.

And then I heard him say, or it could have been telepathically delivered:

"I just came to tell you that I will be going home soon."

After this he vanished and the room became dark and silent again. It took quite some time before I was able to fall back asleep.

I told Michael the next morning what I had experienced.

When he asked me what I thought it meant, I responded that I didn't know, even though deep down I knew what 'Going Home' really meant. Michael seemed anxious.

That very morning, not long after this exchange, Michael's brother called from Calgary and said that our father had taken a serious turn for the worse, and when asked if we should get on a plane and fly there, he replied that 'it was up to us.'

When Michael asked me what we should do, I said to book the flights right now if we want to see Ernie alive. So we did.

We arrived at the hospital that cold Friday night.

When we walked down the hallway towards the room Ernie was in, I acknowledged a crowd of six spirits standing outside the room. They were (later verified by Michael by the descriptions I gave him) Pamela, Ernie's youngest sister who died in the early 2000's, his brother Bob, who passed away from a heart attack in 1993, both his parents, his grandfather, who died in 1957 at the age of 87, and another woman, who we can't identify.

What was unnerving and peculiar was the strange presence that I encountered when I walked in the room. It was a little man wearing a double breasted black suit, wearing a black bowler hat, standing on the right side of the head side of the bed. He looked like one of those morticians from an old Wild West movie. He was kind of hovering there. He informed me somehow that he was a 'Soul Collector', and then I knew that time was short for my father-in-law. What I noted as the day passed, this specter would smoothly and imperceptibly slide down the length of the bed towards Ernie's feet as the day went on.

So, on that weekend I felt that he was mentally calling me into his room. And without a word of explanation to Michael I got up and walked toward the room. As I came into the room, my sister-in-law got up and without saying anything to me, nodded and left, as if she knew we needed to be alone with each other, as I knew that he wanted to ask me something important.

Dad was partially turned towards the window, staring at me. He looked very tired and worn out. After a long moment of silence, I finally had to say it to him.

I said, "Dad, you want to ask me a question, don't you?"

He only nodded.

"You want to ask me how it is to die, don't you?"

Another nod from Ernie.

"OK, I'll tell you how it is to die," I said softly, "Imagine that you had a good day at work. Lots of clients came that day, and very good sales and business. You come home after this great day, you are tired, but it's a good tired and you have a nice dinner. You sit back and watch some TV until your eyes become heavy. You have a nice warm shower, you crawl into your comfortable bed. You feel very calm and relaxed. As soon as you put your head on the soft pillow, you close your eyes and drift into a deep peaceful sleep"

I paused for awhile so my words could be absorbed.

"That is how you die."

He nodded his head, and said in a quiet voice, while a single tear ran down his cheek, "I think I can do that." And then I knew that he finally released his tremendous fear of dying that was holding him hostage and disallowing himself the freedom from pain and misery.

After he fell asleep, I left the room.

On the Monday morning, we were to leave for a few hours to help Michael's sister at her store but something told me that I needed to stay in the hospital. When I came into his room about 9:30 AM again, Theresa left once more as before.

In the first 5 minutes the nurses came to rub his back and change his position as by this time he was unconscious and couldn't move by himself, and totally unresponsive. They moved him from a side position to laying on his back. There was a big clock on the wall on the left side of his bed, and the specter of the Soul Collector was by now hovering at the foot of the bed by his feet.

Right behind the center part of the bed, between the bed and the wall in that small space, I noticed a silhouette of a blue angel, with long swooping wings, almost to the ceiling.

He was turning around slowly to face me. The same peaceful feeling I had with my Mother-in-Law, Carol, swept over me.

At 9:47 I got mental instructions to start counting Ernie's small, shallow breaths.

It was exactly seventeen breaths, and on the last one, his eyes fluttered suddenly, and a soft smile lightened up his emaciated face, and I heard a soft, gentle child like sigh. His chest rose, and at that moment I saw a thin whitish cloud forming on the top of this chest.

I knew he was gone. A short moment later, he materialized at the foot of the bed next to this Soul Collector. I heard him say, "You didn't lie to me Kiddo!" At that moment I was no longer aware of either one of them.

What was bewildering, was the temperature in the hospital room plummeted so suddenly that the room became like a freezer. I could actually see my breath. It was then that I got up, and more like a robot than a live person, walked across the hallway to the nurses' station to inform the Doctor. When I told her that Ernie had died, she asked me how I knew. I told her that I watched him die. She followed me into the room and commented as soon as she entered, "Oh my, it's freezing in here!"

That gave me confirmation that it was not my imagination, but a physical occurrence, verified by others.

After checking his vital signs, she said that I was right, he was gone.

I said, "But he's not gone yet. He's still in the room."

The doctor said to me, "Yes, I can feel him too."

At that moment the six spirits that had been patiently waiting in the hallway slipped into the room, while the doctor, who wanted to give me some time with my deceased father-in-law, left the room. Interestingly, at the very same time, the Soul Collector was no longer there. Then I said aloud: "Dad, don't stay. Go with them. Go to the light." When I said this, I felt my skin cover with goosebumps, even though the temperature quickly rose to the point that the room became stuffy and hot.

As I looked at Michael's fathers' body in the bed I realized that I could not even recognize his likeness as Ernie, but only an empty shell. This happened to me before with a Medicine Man with whom I used to attend Sweat Lodges for quite a few years. At this mans' funeral (He had died in a freak car accident), at the social hall where the funeral was conducted, I remember looking down at his body in the casket. He looked to me as a wax figure, with no likeness to the real man, or his soul. But at that funeral I saw him leaning on his coffin, and he said to me, as he knew I could see him:

"Why are they crying? I am OK. I am not there anymore."

It was then that I really realized that the body is merely a vehicle, that our souls continue on. And I want to say right here the greatest thanks to Ernie, Michael's father, that he gave me the honor and privilege of being there with him and showing me that death is as powerful, peaceful, joyful event as is our birth. And therefore the two create the perfect balance in the cycle of life. And took away from me, for good, the unreasonable and unfounded fear of dying that so many of us -and Society-carry to the last moment, and beyond.

It took about 10 minutes, between the time that I saw Ernie emerging from his corpse and the moment he was gone to the light, along with the other spirits in the room. A few hours after Dad died, Michael and I were sitting in the family visiting room down the hallway from his room in the hospital. Of course we were in pain and grieving as was everyone in the family. The Catholic priest who had been looking in on Ernie for several months with him, and who helped with the Sacrament of Extreme Unction while Dad was ailing badly, came into the room to sit with us. Michael said that this fellow had gone to High School with him in the mid sixties and had turned to the Priesthood after graduating. They were the same age.

Knowing him well, Michael thought it a good time to relate what had happened spiritually in that room when Ernie passed away. As I listened, he told the priest everything in detail. To both of our surprise, his friend just stood up and walked out of the room, without a word. I think he actually left the hospital, as we never saw him again after that episode.

I have no clue what he thought or why he did that.

During the beautiful times I was able to work with Dad in the hospital, and he was kind of accepting that he wasn't going to survive this terrible cancer, we came to an understanding. Whenever he wanted to communicate with me, he would let me smell his cigar smoke. Ernie loved his cigars and was known for often being seen with a proverbial stogie in his mouth. I don't approve of smoking but this was a habit that more or less 'defined' his personality when people thought of him. In the last 10 years, on at least 6 occasions, his spirit came to me by warning me he was there with the unmistakable scent of his favorite cigar Brand: La Palina.

And he hasn't been too far from Michael's mom either. On a few occasions, when we were visiting her in their condo in Calgary, he could be seen(me) sitting in his favorite green leather recliner, or sitting at the kitchen table. Carol would sometimes say to me that she felt him laying next to her in the bed at night. I don't disbelieve her.

*True wisdom comes to each of us when we realize how little we understand about life, ourselves, and the world around us.*

— Socrates —

# CHAPTER SIXTEEN: MORE CASES

## Malcolm

I met Malcolm during a time when I lived in Northern Alberta. One of my clients recommended for him to come and see me. The first time I saw Malcolm he presented himself as a man who always had everything under control and that not many things could rock his world too easily. As is my normal practice I had a short conversation/reading with him to sense what his problem was and how he could be helped.

"What is it that troubles you?" I asked, not sensing anything external that could be contributing to his reasons for seeking my help.

"Well, I don't know how to put this,"... he was wringing his hands, . "for at least a year since I turned 40 I feel that there is no purpose for anything I do. I have no drive, no goals, no reason to do anything...". More hand wringing.

"I sense that you are exhibiting some of the symptoms of mild depression?" I intonated, my statement being more of a question than anything else.

"It was mild depression until a month ago..."

"What happened a month ago?"

"It was my 41th birthday," he explained, but since then my depression started to get worse. I'm more than sure that there is no purpose for me doing anything anymore, since I just know I will die by the time I'm 42."

His blatant statement shocked me, but what upset me more was the force of his conviction that it was an ultimate truth and that nothing could be done to change it.

"Wow!..." was all I could say in response. "Can I take a look at your hands?" I asked.

"Of course." He pulled his chair slightly closer and gave me his hands. I turned his palms upward so could began the study of the lines and marks on both of his hands. As I looked carefully at his palms, I was stricken by what I discovered.

"You have one of the longest and most solid life lines I have seen in a long time. I see you reaching the age of 92-94 at the minimum. Honestly, that you could have the idea about not making it to your 42nd birthday really puzzles me."

"I don't know. But I feel sure that something is going to happen to me, maybe an accident or something like that."

"I think having a short session would let me go into your past and we can try to uncover the reasons you feel this way. I really don't see anything in the state of your health or life line that would make me envision an unpredicted event such as what you just mentioned."

"Can we do it today?" He asked.

"Yes, fortunately I do happen to have about two hours available before my next appointment."

I asked my client to recline his chair and get real comfortable. As we were proceeding with general relaxation it became clear that Malcolm was a person who had strong controlling needs, and would have a problem letting go and going under without resisting. During the time I was trying to relax him, we needed to come up with a different way to approach the session to bypass his resistance.

"Malcolm, tell me what is your favorite activity?" I asked him.

"Hunting." he said immediately.

"Can you take us back in time to the last time you went hunting?" I instructed him. "Tell me where you are and what is the date?"

"It is December, 1997, very early morning," he said confidently. My client was taking us three months back.

"Are you by yourself or there is someone else with you?" I was anchoring Malcolm to the time he was recollecting.

"I am by myself. I never hunt with anybody else."

"Please take me slowly to that day and tell me all the events."

"It is a beautiful morning, cold but sunny…It is very quiet and I can smell the pine trees and moss. There is not much snow on the ground," he explained

"Continue." I directed him gently.

"I hear some thrashing around, not far from where I am standing. I'm leaning against a tree."

"What is it?"

"I see it now…" his voice fell into a whisper as if he was afraid that the animal might see him and bolt.

"What do you see?"

"Oh! It's a gorgeous buck. Nice antlers on him!"

"Does he know that you are near by?"

"Yes!" came the surprising answer. "Now he is looking straight at me..."

"He knows you are there yet he is not running away? I want you to look the deer in its eyes and go inside his head. I want you to become him."

Follow me with what happens next.

"I dare him to shoot me." Malcolm's face brightened with a mischievous smile.

"Aren't you afraid that you might be wrong and he might pull his trigger finger and fire his gun?'

"I'm daring him to shoot me...but I know he's not going to." Something like a giggle came from Malcolm's throat.(?)

"Malcolm..." I addressed my client.

"Yes?" he answered after a brief silence.

"Are you going to pull the trigger?"

"No." He answered curtly" He told me not to dare. I cannot kill him!"

"Has anything like this happened to you before?"

"Never. I always brought the bucks back from my hunting trips.

At this point, my client was very deeply under, because he was comfortable in recollecting something he is passionate about.

I took Malcolm back in time through five of his most recent existences. In each of these he ended dying in a violent and untimely manner, either through murder or accidents, the most recent one being just before his present lifetime in which he was shot on a hunting trip by his friend. He could not figure out if this was accidental or a premeditated act.

Interestingly, Malcolm was an incredibly great subject after all, who would recall a great many specific details including the full names, dates, a description of places and times during which his lives were lived.

One of the facts he provided to me, and which I later cross referenced and verified later, was most impressive. During his most recent lifetime he had started a company in Innisfail, a town located north of Calgary. He stated that he started this company in 1910 which would make the company 87 years old at the time of this hypnosis session. The Company is still in business(1997) and remains in the hands of the family who holds the same last name as the one that Malcolm provided during his regression. I have to make it clear that my client's last name was not the same as the one he had in this past life and he had never heard of this company that he (spirit) had founded in 1910.

It became apparent that in each of his five recollected consecutive lifetimes, he died untimely and sudden deaths. All of which took place between the 42nd-45th years of his life. After bringing my client out of hypnosis I asked him if he knew anybody by the name he claimed he had in 1910. And he had also told me that had never been to Innisfail, yet under hypnosis he provided extremely detailed and precise descriptions of the town which included names of the streets and descriptions of the buildings that still stand today.

Before bringing Malcolm out I proceeded with deprogramming him and then put new data in his mind and re framed what was causing my client to be so convinced that he wouldn't live much longer.

It was such a classic case of patterns at work that we often bring with us into our present lives. If not corrected, such patterns can lead to very self destructive behaviors, that in the end can unfortunately lead to the fruition of our fears and have us act in ways that can bring about the expected and preset patterns of early departure. Malcolm has never experienced any more of the nagging thoughts that made him so convinced he was going to die an early death.

## Roberta's Case

I received a call one day from Henry, Roberta's husband, and he stated that he was really worried about his wife who upon learning she was pregnant with the couple's third child, had started to act strangely. The couple lived on an Indian Reserve not far from my home at the time. Henry explained to me that he was worried about his two children's safety. He did not elaborate on many details, he just asked how quickly I could see her. I agreed to have an appointment with Roberta right away, since his concerns about his children's safety gave me an uneasy feeling in the pit of my stomach which I thought should not be treated lightly.

Roberta was a very pretty native woman in her early thirties, educated and well spoken. When she came into my home, she had a heavy, troubled air about her.

We began.

"So Roberta, tell me what is happening? When did it start?"

"I love my children very, very much but I am afraid that I might hurt them. I have this voice in my head and it's becoming stronger and stronger." Her dark brown eyes held a deep expression of fear and guilt.

"Tell me more about the voice," I asked her.

"Please don't think that I am a bad person…" she pleaded, before relentlessly going on about the voice in her head.

"I am not here to judge you. I am here to try to help you." I assured her. "Tell me when you started to hear the voice and what is it telling you to do."

"OK. I hear it for awhile but it has never been so strong as it is now."

"When did you start hearing this voice?"

"The first time I heard it was after my first child was born."

"What is this voice telling you to do?"

"Different things. One evening when I was giving a bath to my 8-month-old, this voice was telling me that I should put my baby's head under the water and hold it there until it's no longer moving. It said that the little bugger will not suffer for long."

"Is this a female or male voice?"

"Male."

"What else would this voice ask you to do to harm your children?"

"Last Monday when I was driving back from Saint Paul it shouted in my head to grab my baby and toss it through the window. End it for him so he would not have to suffer later…" She started to cry.

"I am so scared that it will get to be so strong that it will make me do something terrible!"

"Well you are here so please don't think about this right now. We will make this voice go away and never bother you again. How does that sound?"

"My husband told me that you helped many people who live on the Reserve. He said that if anybody could help me it would be you."

"Have I ever met your husband?" I inquired.

"No, I don't think so, but he seems to know you well." She was puzzled. "I don't know how he could have never met you?"

"I can ask him later. Let's get started." I asked her to recline comfortably in the chair and close her eyes. As I have already experienced with other Native people, they need little guidance to go into a very deep hypnotic state and that always leaves me ample time to explore everything we need to find out.

"Roberta, take me back to the day when you were bathing your baby and you heard the voice that wanted you to drown him. When you hear that voice please let me know right away."

"It's already here, it tells me to tell you to leave me alone. That you have no idea about what I need to do to help my children not suffer."

"Can you step back and let me speak directly to this voice?" I asked knowing all too well what I needed to do and how to proceed.

She nodded and became still as if her own personality had stepped aside to allow something else inside her to come to the surface.

"What is your name?" I asked. Not fooling around here.

"Larry."

"How long have you been with Roberta?

"20 years."

"Did you know Roberta when you were in your physical body?"

"Yes, she lives with her family two houses away from where I live."

"Larry, you are telling me all this in the present tense which leads me to believe that you think you are still alive and dwelling in your own body."

"Of course I'm alive, otherwise how would I be able to talk to you?..." The entity became aggravated, which was exactly what I wanted to achieve. This line of questioning generally proves to be a good way to entice a disembodied spirit to be more compelled to leave if given a chance to do so.

"I want you to take me back in your life and tell me something about yourself," I encouraged. "Go back as far as the age of five."

"No, I don't want to do that,"

"What is your reason that you do not want to do that? What is your reason for refusing to go back to revisit your earlier life?"

"There were bad things that people did to me, very bad."

"I want to help you so I need to learn what happened..."

The entity did not need more encouragement. What I heard next made me physically ill. The excesses of abuse Larry suffered since the age of 8 months in his lifetime was overwhelming and would be hard to repeat out loud, to save my readers the horrific graphic details of Larry's sexual, physical, and mental abuse. Suffering to this extent would drive most of us to the same obsession of trying to numb this pain. He tried everything from alcohol, drugs, even suicide attempts.

"Larry, I want you to go through the last day you had on Earth that took away your physical form and left you trapped in the limbo where you are now."

"I don't understand what you are saying to me!" The entity became agitated and confused.

"I will help you to understand what had happened, but I need your help to do so. Go to the last day you are aware of being in your own male body, where everybody knew you as Larry." The entity paused for a moment.

"I am with my friends at a party."

"How old are you?"

"I am eighteen… this is my birthday." The voice was showing strong emotion.

"What are you doing?"

"We are drinking and we did some crack before that. We are really drunk and I told them I had to go and get some more booze."

"Then what happens next?"

"I am on the road in my friend's car. It's really dark and I am drunk. I can hardly see the road."

"Tell me exactly how you feel."

"I am cold inside, I don't feel anything. It is crazy that I have lived that long. Nobody cares about me, they won't even notice that I am gone."

"What are you saying?"

"I think if somebody tossed me into the traffic when I was a baby, I would not suffer…"

"Larry tell me what is happening next!"

"I see bright headlights coming towards me. They are getting closer, but I decide not to steer away. I don't care… I hope it does not hurt too much.

I hear the terrible scraping of crushed metal and everything goes quiet. I am not in the car anymore. I am floating like an eagle…" There was awe in the entity's voice.

"What do you see as you're looking down?"

"There are two cars on the side of the road. There are people shouting something but I can't hear anything."

"Can you describe to me the scene you are looking at?"

"My car rolled over and was wrapped around a tree on the side of the road."

"Is anyone else hurt? Was another vehicle involved in this crash?"

"No, they are OK, they are just upset that they can't get my body out of the twisted car…I am not there, they can't see that. I see Roberta, she was driving with her father. She is scared and crying. I want to console her and let her know that I am OK now. I should have died a long time ago, it would have saved me so much pain." The voice trailed off and there was silence for a long while, which I decided to honor and wait for the rest of it.

"Larry… did you come inside Roberta that night on the side of the road?"

"Yes."

"Is that your voice that Roberta hears, that tells her to hurt her babies?"

"Yes, but I just want to help them…" The entity became defensive. "I love babies…"

"So if you love them, then what is the reason you want to make their mother hurt them?"

"If they die now, they will not have to suffer the way I did!" A soberingly simple statement that explained the motives why Larry felt compelled to cause her children to die.

"Larry, I am so sorry for what adults did to you as a child, inflicting all that horrible suffering on you. "

"I was a bad kid. Nobody wanted me. Nobody cared."

"It wasn't you Larry, you were a good child and good in your adult life, you just happened to be born and raised by people who had no ability to love you and take responsibility, for whatever reason. It wasn't your fault. None of it was your fault. You deserve a better place to be than stuck inside Roberta. She loves her children and she wants them to be safe. You are trying to confuse her and push her to do something terrible, and even criminal. I know you do not mean that. You are a good person."

"Why would you say this, you don't even know me?"

"Yes, I do. And I am so sorry that you had to go through so much pain in your short life. I want to help you to change all that and I want you to cross over to the light... It is the place where you will feel loved and needed. You will be finally free of your darkness and pain. Do you want to go?" I suspended my voice and waited for the entity to respond, even though I knew what the answer would be. I have released hundreds and hundreds of these lost souls and have yet to encounter one that did not want to move toward the light to set itself free from the dark netherworld.

"I want to go. I want to go..." It was convinced it needed to do this now.

"You are now free to cross. If there is anything you want to say to Roberta before you go now is a good time to say it."

"I didn't mean to hurt your babies. I just didn't want them to suffer the way I did. I am sorry. I have to go now…" After Larry's spirit departed, Roberta lay still and quiet. She had been crying. Of course.

"Oh my God, I felt so sorry for Larry." she said in a stunned voice. He was always good to me, used to bring me candies and take me on his bike. I am so glad he left."

After that I brought Roberta out of the hypnosis, programming her with positive confirmations and statements.

She sat on the bed deeply submerged in her thoughts. It took awhile before she finally spoke.

"I feel so light and peaceful. Almost serene." She said, her voice low and careful. "Thank you so much for helping me."

"You are more than welcome, you need to stay healthy and strong for your children."

As I reflected on this case after Roberta left my home a thought struck me like a bolt of lightning. That whether in the world of the living or that of the dead, the best intentions might not be enough to bring about goodness and a good life. Often quite the opposite. I expect the expression "The Road to Hell is strewn with good intentions"[1] rings with more truth than we wish to think.

---

1 Samuel Johnson said "The road to hell is paved with good intentions"

## Luisa's Case

Luisa was a native or should I rather say Metis woman quite involved in Native ceremonies. This was where I met her and she learned about my abilities from a friend. Not long after we got to know each other she asked me if I would be willing to do a hypnotherapy session or two with her.

As Luisa was involved in prayers and sweat lodges as many spiritual people are, she was an easy hypnotic subject. She went under within three minutes and we went on a two hour exploratory journey into her subconscious. Several of Luisa's problems were a depressed state of mind that would come and go, a feeling of being submerged in a fog, and severe pain in the big toe of her right foot.

I decided to address her big toe issue first, sensing that this might be one of the easiest to clear.

"Luisa, I want you to take me to the root of your big toe pain."

"Yes." she said quietly.

"Tell me where you are."

"I am sitting alone on the bench close to my father's grave."

"Could you tell the date that this takes place?"

It's Father's Day in 1995. I went to the grave to visit my dad."

"When did he die?"

"On father's day exactly a year ago." she said, the corners of her mouth frowning as if tears were coming next.

"How do you feel?" I probed.

"I feel very sad. I miss my father so much. I want him to come back to me," she explained with the simplicity of a child.

"I am sitting there and crying, asking my dad not to be gone."

"What happens next, what do you do next?"

"I am back home getting ready for bed. I feel somehow funny inside. I went to sleep around midnight but something woke me up. I am not sure what, but I felt my father's presence. It was probably just my wishful thinking." She paused. Then the grimace of pain swept over her face.

"Oh, my God, my big toe hurts so bad. It feels like somebody is twisting it off my foot… Oh, my God, the pain is so terrible!" She moaned.

"Who is there that is causing this pain, come forward and talk to me…" I demanded.

"I am here." A low masculine voice.

"Who are you, what is your name?"

"Anthony. I am Lissy's father."

"Why are you possessing your daughter's body?"

"Lissy called me, she cried so hard and asked me to return, so… I couldn't listen to her crying any more. She is my little doll, I don't like seeing her sad and so heartbroken."

"Dad, it's you!" Luisa's surprised voice joined the conversation. "Dad I miss you so much. I felt so lonely on father's day…"

"Anthony, do you love your daughter?" I asked, breaking the internal dialogue between my client and her deceased father.

"Then you will have to leave your daughter's body, because she is not well and she has a terrible pain in her big toe. She is more depressed and unhappy than ever," I explained to the spirit.

"I am so sorry Lissy. I came because you were sad and you asked me to. I don't want to cause you any pain. I will go, Lissy and you must stop being sad and I know you can take care of yourself."

"Luisa I want you to tell your dad that you want him to go to the light and that you want him to be happy and in peace. Can you do that?"

"I want you to go daddy. I'm going to be OK now. I am so sorry that my despair pulled you back. It' s not a good place for you to be."

"I go now Lissy, be a good girl." As these words were voiced, I watched my client's chest rise up, relax and then she sank back into the chair.

"The pain in my big toe is gone…" she marveled, "I feel no more pain, dad took it with him." She told me after the session that her dad suffered from a severe case of gout that had settled in the big toe of his right foot when he was alive.

But we weren't finished as I then found out.

"I feel very anxious!" I heard my client's say suddenly as her head started to move from side to side, her face beginning to twitch.

"Who is there with Luisa?" I demanded. At first there was no answer, so I addressed my question to my client." Luisa, I want you to become aware who besides your own spirit is inside you now?"

"John." I wasn't sure who was speaking.

"John… how long have you been with Luisa?"

"Since she was 6 years old." I quickly did the math.

"You have been possessing Luisa for 46 years? Tell me when did you attach yourself to her? Did you know Luisa before you died?"

"Yes, her family lived in the same settlement."

"Tell me your age the day you died."

"38. And my brother was 32."

"Did he die with you? At the same time?"

"Yes, I tried to save him, but I couldn't. It was all my fault!"

"Tell me about yourself."

"I'm an awfully bad person, even my mother left me behind. She ran off and left me and my brother in the hands of my father. He beat us every day, he drank and the more he drank the more beatings we would get. There was never any food in the house for us. He bought food for himself and made sure he had enough money for alcohol. By 7 I had to go out and steal food for my brother and me. My father told me that our mother didn't want me and that I was a useless mouth to feed."

I listened carefully without interrupting.

"I started to drink a lot and everybody thought I was worthless. I must have been, even my own mother thought so." A heavy sigh emanated from this entity." People like me don't deserve anything."

"Why would you say that, you weren't bad, you simply were born to the wrong people who didn't offer the good things that parents should give to their children."

I switched the conversation around.

"Luisa, do you remember John? "I asked her.

"Yes," she answered. "I was six years old and John used to bring me candy." Her face brightened with a shy smile.

"You see, John, a person who would feel compelled to bring candy to a little child can't be all that bad. You cared enough to do that! You are a good and kind man. You just had no luck and nobody stood by you and protected you from a heartless world and these selfish people. You deserve better John, I know you do."

"I never thought that about myself. The way my life went I was sure that it was my doing and that I deserved all the things that had happened to me. I don't have to be afraid that I am so deserving of retribution that I will be going to hell?"

"No, you are a good man, with a big heart, who was unlucky enough to have all these unfortunate things happen to you. You were just born to people who could not heal from their own past wounds and they only passed it all to you and your brother. You are free to go to a better place now John." I addressed the spirit as gently as I could.

"Go to the light, John! Go now and don't look back. There is nothing left behind worth giving a second thought. You need to go the place that will welcome you and make you feel loved and happy about yourself. You will find the peace you never managed to find in your earthly existence."

"If there is anything you want to say to Luisa, you can do it now before you leave."

"Yes, I want to say I am so sorry for causing you any hardships and pain, Luisa. I never meant to. You were such a good girl and somethings that happened to you bothered me a great deal. I hope you can forgive me."

"I already did that John, a long time ago. I have always liked you and was sad when you and your brother drowned. I want you to go, as Ula tells you, and be happy. You deserve it. Good bye John. I'll see you again one day when it's my turn to leave this earth."

I watched Luisa's chest rise for a moment and a smoke-like cloud formed over her chest as John's spirit left her.

"Is he gone?" I asked after a prolonged moment of silence.

"Yes, he is gone." she said finally with susurration. "He was such a good man."

"Don't feel the sorrow that can pull him back to you. He is in a better place now and you can start your healing from here." I told her to be aware about the possibility of repossession or inviting another wandering lost soul in by just being in the wrong zone, state of mind or mood.

My clients often ask me if an entity that was released can return. My answer is: yes it is possible but unlikely since these spirits want to be set free and they want to be in place of light and peace. But on rare occasions when the connection is very tight to a living person such as a lost parent, child or lover it *can* happen, simply because the dead feel pulled back (to the living) by unfinished grieving, anger, unforgiveness or a sense of loss that is not fully dealt with. It's safer for both the living and the dead for both sides to let go of the past and set themselves free.

*When you relinquish the desire to control your future, you can have more happiness.*

— Nicole Kidman, in *The Scotsman* —

## CHAPTER SEVENTEEN: CLOSE TO HOME

In this part of this book I will review some of my close encounters with death, the dead and the unseen. I will look at experiences and incidents that induced me to be open and know that there is an inexplicable, secret and sometimes frightening side of life. Which many of us will never admit.

The first time I can recall an encounter with ghosts or astral entities happened when I was about 5½ to six years old. Eight months after we moved into my parents' new apartment building in Poland, in December of 1963. It was a hard winter and for some reason I remember it extremely well, perhaps because it was exciting to move into a building that had an in-suite bathroom and I wouldn't have to go into the dark staircase outside of our old place anymore, where the common washroom shared by three other tenants was located. Traumatizing is a tame word to describe my thoughts in those days.

There were always two things that would really scare me out of my mind: darkness and (the)spiders that were always crawling around in that washroom.

One September evening in 1964 I was returning with my mother from visiting one of her friends. It was a cool evening, but there was still plenty of light from the sun setting behind the forest covered hill on the west side of the street fronting our home. We were perhaps 10 meters or so from the entry to our apartment building when I noticed a young Gypsy woman standing with a 4-year-old girl, not far from the entry door. They both were facing the building as if they were waiting for someone to emerge. The little girl look quite sad standing there, holding her mother's hand. I felt sorry for them. So I looked up at my mother and said:

"Mommy, you can give this Gypsy woman some of my clothing that we just put away because they are too small for me to wear anyway? She can have them for her daughter, they look so poor."[1]

I will never forget the shocked look on my mother's face when she asked me, "What Gypsy woman?"

"The one who is standing there by the door looking at our building," I explained, unfazed by my mother's (silly) question. "Can't you see them?" I was almost angry that I had to point out the two figures with my index finger. "They're standing right there!"

"Dear, I can't see anybody there!" my mother said, not-so-calmly, but I felt her fingers squeezing more tightly around my small hand, as if she felt suddenly nervous and unsettled.

"Can't you see them?" I asked, still not believing that my mother couldn't see what I could see so clearly. It was as real as she was to me at that moment.

---

1 Translation (to Polish) to make this even more real and in the moment: "Mamusiu, możemy dać tej Cygance niektóre z moich ubrań, które sa juz na mnie zamale. Jej corka moglaby ich uzywac. One wygladaja na bardzo biedne."

"There is nobody standing in front of our building." she said, pointing towards the spot that I had indicated to her. I looked again, following her hand and indeed there was no one there.

"Where did they go?" I felt shocked and somewhat disheartened to be proven wrong, but it also struck me as odd and creepy. We passed the spot quickly, entered the building and rather hurriedly walked up to the third floor apartment.

As a young child I would incite no amount of frustration for my parents because I had absolutely no fear and, when the family went on walks, would often walk alone way ahead of everybody else. Often it was a country road leading through the woods or a lonely street in town that harbored anybody or anything that would lurk in the darkness. On one occasion, going through poorly lit streets I was stopped by a police car, the officers perplexed by a 5-year-old child walking alone at 2 AM.

"Where are you going?" I heard his voice as the car pulled over to the side of the road."

"I am going home!" I answered, in a cocky voice, looking right up at him.

"Where is your home?" he asked, a little taken aback with my answer.

"There." I pointed down the dark road, "It is far." At that age I didn't have any idea how to describe distance.

"Where are your parents?" was his next question.

"Back there." I pivoted on my heels and pointed along the dark road behind me.

"What are they doing back there?" he asked, obviously not impressed.

"They are walking home." This should have been obvious (to my young mind.)

"Why aren't you walking with them?" He bent down to take a closer look at my face.

"They are too slow!" I shrugged.

"I'll stay with you here and wait for them." It was not a question but a statement that didn't sit well with my stubborn nature.

"I'm not afraid" I challenged him. "I am big enough, I can walk all by myself!"

"You should be afraid even if you are an adult. There are places that even adults should not go into alone," he said in an instructive voice that I have never forgotten to this day. For some reason it sent shivers down my spine.

"You should never walk alone in the night at your age, or even during the day. There are plenty of bad people who could hurt you." His explanation caught my attention.

The Policeman waited with me until my parents and my brother approached.

"Is this your little girl?" the Policeman asked.

"Our stubborn little girl?" my father answered.

"She does this all the time…" my mother added shaking her head, disapprovingly.

"She will not be doing this again." the policeman looked right into my eyes.

"Will you do this again?" His eyes bore into my face like sharp blades. He waited for my answer before he started to walk towards his car.

I knew, then, that I would not dare again to walk alone in the dark, though for slightly different reasons.

This time when I saw the apparition of the Gypsy woman with her little girl, I realized then that I had an ability to see what others could not, but it took a very long time before I was able to learn to live with this ability (disability?) and even longer to fully embrace it.

My younger and early teenage years were plagued with night terrors, nightmares and night visits that I was too afraid to reveal to anyone, not even my closest friends.

I often dreaded going to sleep for fear that I would suddenly without explanation, wake up and sense that there was someone standing or leaning over my head as if trying to whisper something(what?) into my ear.

What was even more unsettling was that even though I had my eyes open, I was really unable to move even the smallest muscle in my body. I couldn't utter a sound or even less scream in terror for help. Trying to wake up my older brother, who slept in the same room and never seemed to be bothered in the least by nightmares, was fruitless.

One of my most debilitating experiences began and lasted the entire year I turned 14.

It began with a string of nightmares that would repeat themselves night after night, the only difference being that there were more illuminating details revealed every subsequent night dreamt.

This, my fourteenth year, was also plagued with health problems that were either centered in my throat or down lower in my lungs, leading to breathing difficulties which were diagnosed later as asthma.

The first recurring Stephen King like dream had me crawling through a dark, dingy tunnel trying to escape from something or somebody. I could literally assimilate the slimy, dirty tunnel I was crawling through. I could hear and feel the mind numbing squeaking of the giant rats trying to bite me. I could sense their little feet on my skin as they ran over my body. I knew that whatever or whoever was chasing me through this tunnel was very close even though it made no sound. I could sense the ominous presence with every fiber of my body. Some nights I could feel cold claws wrapping around my ankles, trying to drag me back where I was running from.

This recurring nightmare lasted for three long months and later was replaced with one that would start from hearing *The Blue Danube* by Johannes Strauss, for the first time. The music would grow louder and I would find myself in a beautiful garden with flowers, where tall cedar bushes would fence off the place from the outside world.

It was a gorgeous sunny day with not a cloud in the sky. In the center of this large garden there was a rectangular swimming pool, maybe 25 meters long and filled with sparkling clean water reflecting the azure cobalt blue sky. The landscaped area around the pool was made of black and white tiles, thus creating a chess-like appearance. The tiles were sparkling clean and shiny as though never touched by human hands.

I then become aware that I was standing outside a large, white house which is right behind me and I am looking down at the pool. I am perhaps 20 years old, and have beautiful dark black, curly hair which I can feel draping down my bare back.

I am wearing a chiffon snow -white dress, richly gathered around my narrow waist, draping a bit above my ankles. I have on a pair of ballerina -white satin shoes.

It appears that I am waiting for something or somebody.

I can hear the beating of my heart in rumbling silence, drowned out in the sound of the beautiful Waltz and what shocks me is that the silence and music have nothing to do with each other as if they do not blend or mix, like oil and water. I hear them both and this is what makes me feel strange inside. Everything seems motionless and in some sort of eerie suspended form almost as if painted on a canvas.

This acute awareness of my body and my every thought and emotion feels almost uncanny, yet exciting. I am not sure why my heart is beating so hard, is it from excitement or just fear? I couldn't tell. Then I see the figure of a tall man appearing at the far end of the swimming pool.

He is very tall, dressed in an elegant black tuxedo with a snow white shirt and black bowtie and I notice his shiny black patent dress shoes and white gloves. I can't see his face since he is wearing a wide brimmed hat which shrouds his face in shadow. I feel my hands tremble in strange uncontrolled excitement which pushes me to start walking towards the man. Somehow even though no words are exchanged, I know he has invited me to dance the waltz with him. I feel a high wave of anxiety flooding through my mind. It seems like one part of me tells me that I should not be wanting to be anywhere near this strange man, while the other urges me to walk yet faster. It seems that I have no control over my body and that what I do is programmed and absolutely beyond my ability to change.

This is when the dream stopped the first night I dreamt it. It continued for another month, moving forward in small steps. Every night I was almost anxious to go to bed so that I could get closer to this mysterious figure. It was almost like this dream for whatever reason, was taunting me and playing with my emotions, trying to get them as strungout as possible. Every detail of the dream would be identical with only the difference being that there were a few more steps allowed that would get me closer to the phantom man.

More thoughts came into my head. I imagined how handsome he would turn out to be. How charming and charismatic. Every step that brought me closer to this man would manifest itself in even more powerful and potent emotions.

Even only a short few steps from the man I still couldn't see his face.

The man appears to be so much taller than I am, so that even standing on my tiptoes doesn't bring me up high enough to see his face.

In the third week of this nebulous, tenuous dream replaying night after night I finally feel one of his white gloved hands wrap around my waist with the other hand taking my own hand when he leads me to dance. We are dancing now on the black and white chess tiles around the pool. All I can see is the white ruffle of his shirt in front of me. As we pivot around the pool I am trying to dance on my tiptoes to lift myself higher to see his anticipated handsome, masculine face with those beautiful, brown eyes.

It took another three nights of this raptured dancing until I was able to look into and penetrate the shadows that hid his face. This is what triggered the loud screams that brought me out of my slumber and caused my parents to rush to our bedroom to find out what was happening. What I saw will forever stay in my memory. It was not the handsome face of a man, after all... It was a whitish skull with huge, black holes where the brown eyes, I imagined, should have been.

Even without this face, whatever it was, an ethereal voice made the message very clear, "You are mine and you will come to me whenever I call." I woke up covered with a cold sweat.

Interestingly, this was the last night that I had the same dream, and even though some forty plus years have passed since then, this dream still stays in my memory as vividly and clearly as something that I saw an hour ago. Many times I have tried to understand and explain to myself what it was that I saw. I could never come up with a plausible explanation sound enough to put it away once and for all. Was it pure evil that, through my dreams, tried to entice me and exhibit to me the unprovoked power that can be exerted on the human mind? Or maybe it was the will of God trying to warn me of the ways evil works and how one must be prepared and wary of it at the same time.

What appears to be beautiful on the surface may be deeply deceiving and if one is not aware and on their guard, can be put in stark danger of being possessed and consumed by dark forces.

Besides these otherworldly dreams, I have been witness to events and situations that I did not and still don't have rational explanations for. These events many of us don't care to speak of, for fear of being ridiculed and laughed at, even today.

Right or wrong, believed or not, they exist and eventually will demand resolution.

Looking back on years of my work, and the countless entities that I have managed to help to move to the light there are those special cases that I choose to leave alone and advise my clients to move rather that try to challenge and anger.

*If there were in the world today any large number of people who desired their own happiness more than they desired the unhappiness of others, we could have paradise in a few years.*

— Bertrand Russell (1872 - 1970) —

# CHAPTER EIGHTEEN: OTTAWA CASES

## Ottawa Case #1: Stephen

During my visit to Ottawa in 1993, I had a male client who was a trained and educated psychiatrist and who, due to some health and mental issues was forced to suspend his private practice.

It was one of my first morning appointments that were booked that day.

I felt rested and ready for the 12 hours of readings and hypnosis that were on my schedule that day.

I was sitting at a desk in the room that was designated for my appointments when the door quietly opened and a man's head popped in.

"Is it my time?" He whispered so quietly that I almost missed what he was saying.

"Are you Stephen? I looked at him.

"Yes," he nodded, his eyes sweeping the room suspiciously.

"Then, yes." I smiled trying to make him feel welcome. "Please, come in." I invited him inside. I must say his somewhat weird behavior sent a strange, unpleasant shiver down my spine, as normally I would have left the door to the room open until my friend returned home from work.

"Is it safe?" Stephen asked in a tight, low voice. This again inexplicably, shot spears of cold fear through my scalp.

"Are we alone?" came another odd, disturbing question.

He slid inside the room and closed the door behind him. As an immediate reaction to this I had a stupid question pop into my mind: "Why is he shutting the door on his tail?" which I immediately dismissed as a ridiculous, if not crazed, thought.

The man dragged behind him a long shadow that looked bizarrely like a crocodile tail. I immediately then realized that this was a crowd of discarnate spirits that dragged behind him the way fire trails behind a falling meteor.

"Please sit down." I hurriedly pointed to the chair on the other side of the small desk I was sitting at. I felt relieved that it happened to act as a barrier between us.

The man took the chair and sat with his shoulders pulled forward and his head sloping downward. He looked about 45 however I felt he may look older to some with the dark circles penciled under his eyes (A good indicator of poor sleeping habits) and the grayish tinge of his skin indicating not the best health.

My friend, who had known this man for a number of years, said that he was a psychiatrist who had had a private practice in Ottawa for 16 years, which he was forced to close due to health issues, about two years ago.

The mans' hands were clasped together and it was a little disquieting to see him wring them together for no apparent reason.

"Relax, Stephen, I'm not going to bite you…" I tried to put him at ease. "It's going to be OK. We will try to find what the problem is and help you resolve whatever it is."

"Do you think we are alone?" His voice was barely audible.

"There is no one else in the house." I said. But what do I do with this fact: (to myself) *You know they came with him, don't you?*

"Let's talk," I encouraged him.

"They can hear me!"

"I know but you really came to see me to help you get rid of them, didn't you?"

"When did your problems start?"

"About four years ago," he said allowing me to lead the conversation. "It started one night just before Christmas…"

"How long have you lived in your house?"

"Over sixteen years, since shortly before I opened my psychiatric practice."

"Was your office in your house?"

"The whole main floor was allocated for my clients. We lived…well, we still do, upstairs"

"Are you married?"

"Yes, and we have two children, both are now studying and away from home." There was a note of pride in his voice. I noticed that a lighter subject like his family made him feel proud.

"So tell me how this started," I asked gently, knowing the hour we had booked for this appointment was ticking away and I needed to get to the bottom of this man's problems.

"I was finishing paperwork in my office. It was in December, very close to Christmas and I wanted to catch up with all my reports before the office closed for two weeks for the holidays. It was dark outside and I thought my wife had gone Christmas shopping that evening. The kids went with her, so when I heard knocking on the office door, I thought they had come back and I hadn't heard them. I got up from my chair and opened the door to tell them that I would be finished in a half an hour, but there was no one there.

This repeated itself five times and every time I opened that door there was nobody there! Since my wife and kids were still out shopping, I continued organizing my files when all of a sudden my Professional Diploma which was hanging to my left by the window flew across the room and smashed against the opposite wall. It just flew like somebody threw it with great force..."

"Do you believe in the paranormal?"

"No, I am a psychiatrist." He gave me a reprimanding glance as if trying to tell me that my question was completely out of line.

"Well, you are here..."I said with just a hint of a smile.

"There is no other place I can go to ask for help. I have tried everything... I saw other psychiatrists, a psychologist. I had all the tests done...They found nothing wrong with me! ... I tried to commit suicide three times."

This type of statement I have heard so often that I am no longer stunned by the admission.

"Tell me more of what happened."

I tried to divert his attention to something else before he would lock up and hide inside. There was a crowd of entities that followed him into my temporary office. This was exemplified and apparent to me as a gray mass of disparate entities- maybe as many as 60- crowded around us into this little temporary office space, and I also somehow knew that there were many more right inside him. What I did not know was that there was something else much more menacing hiding in the crowd that was not there just to confuse him or to use his body to catch glimpses of their own expired physicality.

But really meant him serious harm.

He said:

"I want you to see this, but please don't tell me that I did this to myself like every doctor I have seen. With these words he stood up, and pulled up his shirt from his trousers.

My eyes shot right open, seeing the skin on his stomach, and later as he showed me, on his back, arms and neck which were covered with the countless welts of scratches that appeared in sets of three. Some were whitish and healed, some showed a raw redness that was in the process of healing.

It was the first time I had a close encounter with the physical symptoms of spirit attacks. Some of the scratches appeared to be very deep. The healed welts of the older ones looked like yellowish snakes crawling all over his skin. There were so many of them that I had to conclude that these attacks had to have been happening to Stephen for a long time.

"How often do these scratches happen?" I asked, still examining my client's skin.

It was obvious to me that even if Stephen could inflict some of these injuries to himself in places like his arms, chest, and stomach, there were many that he could not possibly have done to himself.

As I sat back behind my desk, I needed some time to take in what I had just seen.

"I know she is doing it to me…" Stephen's voice brought me back out of my thoughts.

"Who is she?" I asked.

"My wife. I know she can do this to me even if she's not at home…" He kept staring into the space on the wall behind me.

"You know it's not your wife doing this to you. She was the one asking me to get you an appointment, so you could get some help. Your wife worries about you and she loves you."

"Then who is doing this to me?" His eyes were still glued to the wall behind me, staring into empty space.

"I want you to tell me about one of your male client's who committed suicide three years ago?" My words jolted him out of his catatonic state and his eyes focused on my face. His brows knitted so much that they almost touched each other over his nose.

"I see a very angry and confused male spirit standing right behind you," I said not realizing that my words would startle my client to the extent that they did.

Stephen jumped up from his chair, panic all over his face, looking frantically around trying to locate the spot where the spirit was standing.

"Calm down Stephen, he is not going to hurt you! !" I reassured him.

"How do you know?" My client's eyes were crazed and darkened. What does he want with me…?"

"Please sit down, and I will explain it to you."

After a while, after pacing around the small office for awhile he sat back down in his chair and his head dropped dejectedly.

"He was a client of mine for two years," Stephen begin to tell me. "I was confident I could help him. He told me he had been hearing voices and that he saw people in his house, that his family wasn't able to see. He started to act more erratically and this depression worsened in spite of all the meds I prescribed. They only seemed to make it worse for him. He had the same scratches on him as I have now. I thought he was becoming a danger to himself, so I committed him to a psychiatric hospital for observation."

During his stay there he got better, there were no more new scratches and he was much calmer. After two weeks he was released and went home.

From that point, everything got so much worse. He would lock himself in his room and refused to come out and see me anymore. I went to his house on his wife's request, but he wouldn't open his door. He just screamed that it was all my fault that I made them angry and that they said they would hurt him real bad.

His wife was worried sick, so we decided to call an ambulance so they could take him back to the hospital. He was screaming as if he was fighting with something or somebody in the room. There were other strange voices we all could hear but none could explain what they were. Then suddenly everything went quiet and no more noise was coming from the room.

When the ambulance arrived the paramedics had a very hard time getting into the bedroom. He had shoved a huge dresser against the door. It was a heavy piece of furniture so we were all shocked how this small framed man could even manage to budge this large and heavy dresser. By the time the paramedics managed to get into the room, my client was dead…"

Stephen's voice died off completely and his head hung even lower than before, with his chin pressing against his chest. "He had hung himself from the closet bar rod with a bed sheet he used as a rope. It must have been a terrible death since his knees were on the floor."

A long period of silence after his last sentence.

"I failed him. I made it all worse." he said through clenched teeth. He blamed himself.

"Stephen, listen to me…" I started, "Your patient needed a priest not a psychiatrist…"

"He was not mentally sick, he was possessed!" I decided to be honest with him and not sweet-coat what my client needed to know.

"What is that?"

He looked at me carefully, and there, in the blink of an eye, the hard skepticism of a hardcore man and doctor flickered in his eyes. "You want me to believe that?"

He chuckled.

"You do whatever you decide is right for you after I explain to you how it all works…You came here knowing that the line of work I do is very different from your mainstream science, didn't you?"

He was going to listen to me now.

"Are you doing the scratching to yourself?" I asked slowly.

"Of course not!" He appeared insulted with the insinuation. "Why would I do that?"

"So, how do they appear?" I was using a method of deduction that works very frequently with skeptical and strong willed people.

"I would wake up in the middle of the night and my skin would burn as if somebody was putting burning matches to it…"

"What else besides the scratches would you feel?'

"The atmosphere would be tense. Usually the room even in summer seem very cold and I would feel something or somebody standing in the dark…"

"Was your wife seeing or feeling the same things?"

"After the first few times it happened I accused her of doing it to me, so she decided to move to a separate bedroom. I would start locking my bedroom, so no one could come in during my sleep."

"Did the scratching stop?"

"No…it actually got worse and more frequent," he answered and there was a hint of the 'Aha' that flashed in his eyes as if at this very moment he finally realized that his wife had nothing to do with this.

"I want you to see that what is happening to you is exactly the same as what happened to your patient."

"What is happening!?"

"What probably started shortly after your client committed suicide, the banging, the knocking, the files being moved or misplaced…everything you told me today is an indication of a haunting."

"You must realize that no one is totally secure and safe but people in yours or my line of work are in greater jeopardy to be affected since we deal with people who when seeking help, bring to us everything that is molesting and bothering them. As we help these people feel better- maybe even cure them- what we removed from by therapy, conversation or simply having them in our house or office can make their baggage and problems become ours."

"So, how come you are OK, you have no scratches?"

"I learned the hard way, so now I make sure I protect myself. And after my clients are gone I purify my home or office. There can never be too much caution."

"I am man of science…" I was surprised to hear that after explaining all this to my client logically, including showing the analogousness relevance, this was all he could say.

Also, I knew that whatever had a stranglehold on him, was becoming more and more secure in its place.

"If you think that putting yourself on antidepressants will solve your problems then there is not much more I can do to convince you that you are very wrong and you are in danger. Especially knowing what you now know after today."

"My wife said that you could help me," he said, frustrated, getting up from the chair.

"I can only help you if you want to be helped. I cannot do that against your will. I have to respect whatever choices you make. It is your life and you are the one deciding what you want to do with it."

"So, if I want to use your help, what do we need to do?"

"We need to book a separate appointment to perform a clearing ceremony to release whatever has this hold on you." I explained.

"Do I need to make this appointment now?"

"It would be wise since I am pretty much fully booked and I am only here in Ottawa for another 5 days. It's up to you."

"I'll call you tonight for another appointment," he decided.

I knew then that I would not hear from Stephen again. What put an additional stamp to this conviction, was a quiet growling giggle that I heard come from behind my client.

As soon as Stephen left my friends' home I opened up my sacred pipe and performed a clearing ceremony. Understanding that I needed to purify the place and myself to protect me, my friend and every other client who would that day step inside that small office.

As I predicted Stephen did not set the second appointment, his wife called that evening and asked for a reading for herself. She said she wanted to apologize for her husband but also needed to get a reading. I had an opening and saw her that same evening. She was a slight, dark haired woman with large, somewhat sad but beautiful eyes.

I could sense that she had reached the end of her rope and when she stated she was planning to ask for divorce, I was not at all surprised. She explained that since they stopped sleeping together, after he accused her about scratching him at night, he had become very antisocial, separating himself from their children and friends.

He had become moody and unpredictable. He neglected his practice and was forced to close his office. He would hardly go outside and eventually moved into his home based office.

"I can't tell you what to do. I can only say that from here on it will only get worse. Whatever has a hold on him will make sure he is not going to seek help. It can exercise more power and control and all it wants is total destruction. It might extend its powers outside and try to destroy everything, including you and your children."

I felt it was my responsibility to tell Stephen's family of the dangers that were lurking in her house and the presence controlling her husband.

"I don't want to continue. Especially now when he told me he is never going to go and see some 'ghost hunters.'" Even though she didn't spell it out, I knew he was referring to me.

."Whatever it is that is inside him has now full control over him. Before I called you I read about what you do and I truly hoped you could help, but he doesn't want to be helped anymore. I knew that even before. When he looks at me he is no longer there."

"May I say something?" I interrupted her cogently.

"Of course, please?'

"The same presence that caused his client three years ago to commit suicide is after Stephen now. Please, once you make the decision to separate from your husband, do not stay in the house. Move!"

"Thank you, this was one of the questions I wanted to ask you." She was noticeably shaken.

"Yes, I know. I heard you ask me this question right after you came in." This happens all the time so I always tell my clients not to ask questions. All the questions that need to be asked will be answered during the reading.

After this I never saw Stephen or heard from him again, and through my friend I know that his wife filed for divorce and moved out of the house. I do not know what became of Stephen, but can see the mournful image of an old man, in my minds' eye who is in and out of mental hospitals. When I visualize his face it doesn't even look like him anymore. I know that Stephen departed not long after he came to see me.

### Ottawa Case #2: Regina and Waldemar

Or: *The destructive power of hatred.*

Regina was a Polish woman who had a great sense of humor and appeared to be upbeat and happy all the time the same way as her husband, but in her case it was genuine. Waldemar and Regina came to Canada from Poland in 1981. They had two children and a nice house. They did well and on the surface it appeared that they were one of those couples one could only envy. Waldemar was 42 years old in 1993 that year. I had a last minute rushed appointment with him. Due to the fact that I was fully booked the time Regina called me I had to scrape aside two extra hours from the very little time I had to rest during my trip to Ottawa.

I was booked from 7 AM until 10-11 PM everyday. One of my emergency appointments was set for midnight due to the fact that I was flying back to Calgary the very next day at 8 AM and that was *the* only possibility to see Helga. (I will describe her case in a latter part of my book.)

Regina was very grateful that I had agreed to see her husband on such short notice. I did that because his condition appeared to be very urgent and I felt that the appointment would give him a chance to heal or even to save his life. As this crazy thought flashed through my head I knew that I needed to do what I was asked, or rather begged to do.

When Waldemar came in for his appointment it was the first time I saw him. He was a jovial, soft spoken gentle man with dark brown curly hair and a bushy mountain-man style beard. His blue eyes were two of the gentlest eyes I have ever seen in a man, and the juxtaposition of polarities for this wonderful man was my first ground position to help him. One side would find this happy and healthy looking man; and opposite to it the truth about his physical health challenges that were even too serious to have any part in a 75 -year-old man's life, much less 42.

Waldemar had had three micro strokes, that left one of his eyes slightly drooping, one that led to a quite serious heart attack, blood pressure that was skyrocketing, insomnia, and kidney stones as large as coffee beans produced with a frequency that is unheard of. These were, one could say, barely the tip of the iceberg. I was truly puzzled since all these physical symptoms would be hard to find in such a joyful, easy going personality as Waldemar's.

Yet he had it all.

As is my usual procedure I first sat down with my client for a short conversation to find out more before beginning the session. For interests sake, the session was in Polish, but of course translated here into English.

“Do you know what hypnosis is?” I asked Waldemar.

“No, not really.” There was a soft smile on his face almost all the time, as if his countenance had never become serious. He was one of the friendliest people I have ever met. This only deepened the mystery.

He had a soft, gentle voice that made you feel very comfortable. I learned that he was very successful. His kids were doing well in school and he had just finished renovations on his house. His marriage was a bliss that would make a majority of married people jealous. Yet his physical health was falling apart bit by bit every day as if something inside of him was corroding and eating away at its soul.

“Are you Ok to undergo the hypnosis session?” I asked as I knew it was his wife’s idea.

“Yes, of course if Regina says I need it then I’m all for it.”

The answer blew away the reservations that I often have in cases when the partner or parent is insisting on someone else going through the process rather than the person him/ herself.

“She believes you can help me, so I trust her.” The simplicity of his statement closed the door on any doubts that I had.

“OK, let’s go ahead with this.” We went to another side of the house that had a bed which my client would recline on for the session. Regina asked me if she could be there during the session.

"If your husband is Ok with that, then it is fine with me, but I need total silence, so you will have to be very, very quiet." I answered. After Waldemar agreed to her presence we all walked into the bedroom. I brought a box of Kleenex just in case we might need it.

I had the chair placed about 2 feet away from the single bed where Waldemar was lying down. Regina was sitting on the floor to my right next to the window.

Waldemar was a very responsive subject and I could see that he was relaxing very quickly and responding to my hypnotic suggestions with ease and without resistance, which always makes my job easier and allows me more time to explore the past in the search of the roots to existing problems.

To add an interesting twist that happened during the session, my friend's cat entered the room and refused to be chased away. It settled comfortably under the bed and responded to my hypnotic suggestions as willingly as my client, paradoxically. This was the first and only time in my practice that something like that took place. To this day, it puts a smile on my face to see in my mind's eye, both my client and the cat opening their eyes, stretching and yawning as if one was mimicking the other.

As soon as I knew that Waldemar was in a deep hypnotic state I began my search.

"Waldemar, I want you to take me to the source of your numerous and serious health conditions you are facing in your life." I stirred him in the direction that we needed to go in search of the roots for his troubles. I must say the power of what happened next blew away all that I was secretly hoping to find. This was another reminder that one never knows what could be lurking behind the scene. As a therapist, one should never assume what we might find when searching for the causes of our misery.

As soon as I spoke I noticed my client's jaws clenching and a strong red flush covered his entire face.

"What is going on? Where are you?"

"I am walking…" He no more than breathed the answer.

"Who are you?"

"I am me…" Immediate response. I detected a strong tone of anger in his voice.

"How old are you?"

"I am 18."

"Where are you right now?"

"On the country road leading to our house… I hate him. He killed my mother, that bastard"… The tone of agitation increased and the flush on his cheeks got darker. His face became visibly distorted by pure, undeniable hate.

"Who do you hate?"

"My father…" he hissed in response. "He killed her!"

"How did he kill her?" I tried to understand what he was talking about.

"He was so nasty and violent that she had no other option but to get away from him."

"How did she get away from him? Did she divorce him?"

"No… Nobody would approve of the divorce. Not where they lived."

"Then what happened?"

"She hung herself, that is how she had to get away from him."

"Waldemar, I want you to take a few deep breaths and calm down," I instructed him.

"He is evil. I hate him" It appeared that my instructions went unnoticed so I repeated them. My clients face was beet red and he was breathing heavily, trying to assuage his deep seated fury. I became afraid that this state might cause his blood pressure to spike and create the possibility of a stroke.

"I want you to breathe," I said in a stern, commanding voice "Now, breathe and let go." He finally started to relax and let go. His face grew paler and his breathing became more even and controlled.

"Good, that is much better." To avoid another wave of agitation, I asked him to move out of his body and float above the scene. This technique helped but to a lesser degree than it did in the past with my other clients.

"Tell me about your father, what does he do that is so terrible that makes you hate him so much?"

"He is cold and ruthless. If my mom doesn't do things the way he wants her to, he doesn't let her have any food. He sits by the kitchen table gulping down the dinner she prepared, and then has her sit across the table to watch him eat while not allowing her to touch a morsel of anything." Waldemar's jaws are again tightly clenched. I can see the muscles on his face working under his skin as he speaks.

"What about you?" I probed.

"He tells me that men have to be tough and keep an iron fist to keep order. He tells me to eat with him when my mom is watching us eat…"

"Do you eat?"

“I have to, he is going to punish me if I don’t…I am afraid of him, but my stomach does not want to accept food. I feel sick, I want to throw up.” He was making a gagging sound, so I am again forced to calm him through deep breathing and letting go.

“What does he do when you don’t follow his orders?”

“He locks me up for hours in the dark cellar under the floor.”

“Does he beat you?”

“No, he doesn’t have to. I am terrified enough hearing what he does to my mother upstairs. I hear her moaning in pain…” Tears forced their way between his tightly shut eyelids. I am so useless, I can’t help her! I hate him so much that I want to kill him…I will kill him one day!” He sobs now uncontrollably. I have to calm him down. It is disappointing to me that even the surefire out-of -body technique is not helping much in keeping his emotions at bay.

At some point I look over my right shoulder towards the window where Regina is sitting quietly as she promised, and see her bent forward and holding a fist full of Kleenex in both of her hands, trying as quietly as possible to stem the torrent of tears just pouring out of her eyes. Her shoulders tremble as she struggles very hard not to make the slightest sound. Not that it did not happen before, but I am stricken with a wave of sorrow that settles in the pit of my stomach. A few tears somehow manage to find their way into the corners of my eyes. As discretely as possible I wiped them with the tips of my fingers.

How old are you when your mother takes her life?”

“I am 18, we just buried her. The church we attended all our lives did not agree to perform a burial ceremony because they say she is unworthy because of what she did to herself. They send us to a neighboring diocese where she is buried."

"Continue…tell me what happens next." I probe gently, understanding that it is a very difficult subject to be going back through all these painful memories.

"He stood at her grave site and acted like he was the one that should get all the pity. He says in his speech that she had no right to leave him like that…"

His anger rose to such a level that he had difficulty speaking for a while. I allowed him to struggle with that without tempering his emotions since I needed them as close to the surface as possible from where I was sure it would be easier to let them go. Again, this session proved me wrong, but that will be shown later.

"Did you make a speech at your mother's funeral?"

"No. I knew if I started to say anything I would blow up and tell everybody what he has done to my mother and me…He knows that, so he is making sure no one asks me to speak…I made my decision to leave right after the funeral. I am not going back home with this Hitler…" It speaks for itself to hear him naming his father after the man who will forever be known to mankind as pure evil.

"I am so broken inside and so angry that I think before I leave I will do something terrible to him. I think that I am capable of this. I want to be."

"Waldemar, you are not your father, you have a good and gentle heart," I said in a soft and soothing voice. "Tell me what happened next."

"I stayed with my friend after the funeral and never even went back to get my things. I found a job in town and got my own place." My client's voice was calmer now as he continued to re-live his past. "I met Regina when I went back to school. She was studying law and I went on to study engineering. We decided to get married after dating two years. Her family wants a big wedding. I don't but I want her to be happy, so I agreed."

"Is she from a different part of Poland?"

"No, she is from the small town where my mother is buried. She lived two blocks from the friend with whom I stayed for a month after I left home. They actually knew each other…" a smile crowned his lips and his face lit up for a moment.

"It's a small world." I agreed with him.

"I hadn't seen my father or even spoken to him since the funeral and didn't want to invite him to our wedding…Regina wanted me to have my family and she thought I needed to invite my father and make up. I never told her much about my past and my family…I was embarrassed and afraid that maybe she would think that I was like my father and would leave me…" I heard a gasp after this last sentence was spoken. I quickly looked at Regina and saw her face twisted with such pain and compassion that I couldn't remember ever seeing that emotion on any other face in my life.

"I loved her so much that I couldn't bear the thought of her leaving me because she thought I could be like my father. I would agree to anything just to have her happy so we sent a wedding invitation to him and he responded very quickly and even offered to have us stay in the house after the wedding. I was surprised at how nice he appeared to be and even for a brief moment thought that he maybe had changed, realizing what he had done to my mother and me and wanted to make up for it."

"Then what happened?"

"The wedding was beautiful, we had sixty people and everybody enjoyed the party. We got almost 12,000 Zlotys as gifts so we had plans to invest and buy some new furniture for our apartment. We had it in an envelope that Regina put in her purse when we went that night to stay in my father's house. I felt it was wrong, that it would have been better to rent a room in a hotel, but the wedding did drain much of our savings and we did not want to use the money we got as gifts from our guests, so we accepted his offer anyway.

He was acting very differently when we arrived. I noticed the same smirk on his face when he looked at my wife. The first thing he said when we entered the house was that he hoped that he taught me well enough of how I should set the rules of the house.

"Did Regina know what he meant?"

"No, she thought he was just kidding and that he was simply this old fashioned man that did not adjust his ideas to the new times.I could not bring myself to tell her the truth. We stayed two nights and I had had enough of him so we decided to leave earlier than we planned. We went to the bus stop and as we were waiting for the bus to arrive Regina looked inside her purse after paying for the tickets and said that the envelope with our wedding gifts was gone. I asked her to check again, but she said that it was not in her purse. She told me that she checked the evening before we went to sleep. She had left her open purse in the kitchen."

"Then what happens?"

"I knew my father had stolen our money, and I decided to go back home myself and confront him on that. I asked Regina to wait for me at the bus stop and went back."

"How does he respond?"

"He opened the door and said: 'What do you want, forget something?'"

"I told him that the envelope with our wedding gifts money was gone and that I am sure he took it. I am so furious that I want to hit him."

"He said I was crazy accusing him of stealing the money from my wife's purse and that even if he did then that would hardly pay for all the food he fed me when I was growing up. I knew he would never change, he was evil and would die evil…" Waldemar's cheeks were dark red, his jaws clenched and he stopped speaking for a long while.

"I hate him even more than I did when my mother was buried. I refuse to attend his funeral…I hate him so much…"

"Waldemar" I started in a low and calm voice," I want you to see now that the real roots of all your health problems are attached to this hatred you feel for your father. If you will not let go, this deep hatred will destroy the rest of your health and kill you. You *have* to let go." I pleaded with him.

"Never!"

"Do you love your wife and children?"

I began breaking down one of the hardest rocks of resistance I have ever encountered in my practice. Usually, the subconscious after reviewing all the reasons, would choose objectively the best course of action to protect one's wellness and life, but in this case his subconscious was just as stubborn as his conscious mind and instead of one tall wall I had two to break down to save this man's life. I knew it was that serious and it was his last chance to change things for his sake as well as his family's.

"I love Regina and my children more that I could ever express... But I can' t stop hating my father...I've tried many times..."

"Your father started this destructive process there is no denying, but now he is even in more control over your life than he was when he put you in the cellar and kept you there for hours. He is destroying your life and your family and you are letting him to do that. He is going to win and do the same thing he did to your mom. She maybe did not have a choice but you do. You have to let go of this hatred..."

"I will never stop hating him, not ever!..."

Even after my last reasoning effort I got nowhere. I was beginning to panic trying to figure it out. The system I used always worked until now. I was crushed but then I resorted to the last thing I would ever do if I needed guidance. I asked Walking Bear, my Spirit Guide what I should do, how could I help this man save his life and severe that painful and cancerous growth and hatred that took over his mind and body.

Then the instructions of what I needed to do next were planted in my mind. The words just arrived, now all I needed to do was tap into them.

"Waldemar, I want to show you something so you can understand the power of this most destructive emotion you harbor in your heart."

I took a breath then continued. “You are in a dark, cold dungeon in the basement of a castle. The walls are thick and there is only one tiny window up high that lets just a tiny beam of light enter. There are no bars on this window. There is no one there but you. The door leading to this room is made of heavy metal, thick and rusty. It has not been opened for a very long time. You are sitting on the cold damp floor and both your ankles are encased in heavy metal shackles that are attached to the wall with heavy chains. You are tethered to the wall and there is no one who will come to rescue you. This chain and shackles is your hatred for your father.

“Can you see yourself chained to this wall?” I stopped and asked him.

“Yes.” he said.

“You are going to die unless you pick up that big ax that is laying on the floor not far from you.”

“Yes, its here…” I could see that what I was advising to do was working.

“If you stretch your arms you can grab the handle of the ax and bring it closer to you.”

“I do. I have it,”

“This ax can help you to break those chains on your ankles and set yourself free to escape through that small window I showed you before. There are no bars and you can fit through with no problem.”

“Can you do that?’ My client only nodded to answer. “You have to hit it hard to break the metal chains, but I know this ax is sharp and you can do it. This chain represents the hatred for your father, the ax represents the love for our family and yourself. Hit it as hard as you can."

As I was saying these words there were beads of perspiration forming on my clients forehead and temples. There were more and more of them as the minutes passed. The sweat started to roll down his face as more tiny beads surfaced. He face was distorted, his brows knitted together showing the huge effort he was putting into breaking the chain. It was about three minutes or so when he finally went still and his face became pale and relaxed.

"Have you broken the chains?"

"Yes, Yes…" Broad smile lightened his entire face. "I am going through the small window outside. I see the sun and trees…Oh my God. I am free." Tears started to slide slowly from the outside corners of his eyes and disappeared into the bush of his curly hair.

"Yes, Waldemar, you are free and safe."

As I brought him back I asked him to open his eyes. He laid there for a moment without moving then sat up and looked at his wrist watch.

"What happened? I was gone for two hours?" He had no recollection whatsoever of the entire session, but that was nothing unusual. I felt tired and grabbed a glass of water to quench my thirst.

"I have to run to the bathroom." When Waldemar left the room I had a short moment to talk with Regina.

She was stoned by the entire event. Her eyes were red and swollen. All she managed to say was, "We have been married for 22 years and I never knew how much he hated his father and how disgusting this man was. He has never told me any of this. I am shocked at how much hatred was locked behind his happy face. Thank you so much for taking time to see him. I am so grateful."

"You are welcome, but I must say he was the toughest client to crack." I smiled. As we were conversing, Waldemar walked back into the room and was holding something in his hand wrapped in a white Kleenex.

"I have to show you something." he said, approaching me and opening his hand for me to see what was inside the folded Kleenex.

"It's the biggest kidney stone I have ever passed, and I've passed many. And it came with no blood and no pain…" He was impressed, so was I since I have passed three kidney stones in my life and none of them were as huge as the one that Waldemar was holding in his hand.

"I'm glad I could save you so much pain." I smiled. "I know that pain from my younger years," I added.

"Now, you need to make some changes in your diet as we spoke of and you are going to be OK."

Quietly to myself I expressed my great thanks to Walking Bear for leading the way and helping me to work with this man and push him towards well overdue healing.

Regina would send me updates on what was happening and could never stop thanking me for what I have done for her husband. She reported that his health had improved so much that his family doctor questioned him on what and how it happened. She told me, that she was more than happy to tell him that his methods were not working and how healing the spirit and emotions can bring about incredible physical recovery.

As I say: "dis ease in the mind becomes disease in the body." If I ever had any concerns that this was true, Waldemar's case removed any doubts forever from my mind.

**Ottawa Case #3: Hilda**

Hilda came to see me on a Wednesday as one of my appointments after my short midday break. She was a tall, slim woman of German background and still had a strong German accent when she spoke English. She was a pretty woman in her late thirties with brown eyes, dark wavy hair and olive skin. Although when I met her, her skin was blotchy and had numerous liver spots all over that were out of place for such a young person. I knew that her body was profoundly toxic because she was heavily medicated and her poor liver had a hell of a time processing the harmful chemicals that had been pumped into her system regularly for years.

Her husband of 14 years drove her to the appointment. He was a nice man of Moroccan descent, who had much love for her which was evident to me.

"Thank you for seeing my wife on such short notice. I can not bare to watch her suffer like this any longer The doctors are making her worse and worse and I am afraid if something does not change that I am going to lose her…" he said before leaving the house.

Luckily, one of my customers wanted to reschedule her appointment for that Friday so it worked out perfectly.

"I will be back to pick her up in an hour." He left and we began our reading immediately since I was very busy and my appointments were back to back until 9 PM. I couldn't afford any delays since they would start overlapping with my later appointments.

Right from the get go I sensed that we had a very troubled woman in front of me. As she sat down and I handed her a deck of cards (to garner energy from her person). I noticed that her hands were shaking and she had a hard time to keep herself together.

"Tell me, did your condition get worse after a loss you suffered?"

I said this as I quickly noticed the presence of a baby spirit which had revealed itself to me. It was just a tiny baby and I knew his heart was sick and that is why he died.

She started to cry right away, sadly, confirming the information in front of me.

"Yes. Four years ago I got pregnant. We were so happy to finally conceive. We had wanted to have a child for many years but I couldn't get pregnant. It finally happened. But I was in my 5th month when I started to bleed and ended up in emergency. I lost my little baby! . I don't even know what it was." She was really sobbing now.

"It was a little boy and his heart was damaged. I think some of the medications you were given were the cause for that."

"After that my depression got worse and I tried to take my life. I didn't want to live anymore. I became such a load to Joseph. I didn't want him to walk away from me. I became so useless to him as a woman."

"But he stayed because he loves you and wants you to get better, do you know that?"

"I am not getting better, if anything I'm getting worse."

"Hilda. There are many black holes in your past, meaning you do not remember some of your childhood. Once we uncover them I am pretty sure what troubles you will vanish. There are always reasons for the way we feel and act. Are you ready to find out these reasons?"

"Yes." She said, shifting nervously in the chair. "I better get better or I don't want to live anymore." I knew she was determined to face whatever she had to and that was a good omen.

We began the session.

"I am sensing strong resentment towards the woman that is an authority figure and looks quite a bit like you. I would guess this is your mother?" I asked and waited for her to respond.

"Yes that's my mother, but I don't know why that would be. She tries very hard to do things for me and helps me a lot."

"Could you please put the deck away for now and give me your hands." She did that and as soon as her cold hands were en-clasped in mine, the pictures and images started to unfold as if someone had turned on a TV.

"You are very deficient in minerals," was the first thing I said after touching her hands. "Your liver is struggling to function but there are so many toxins inside that it's starting to give you trouble. I see it on your skin and inside the whites of your eyes. Are you taking any medications?" An obvious question.

"Yes, for many years."

"You are on antidepressants, aren't you?" I closed my eyes to focus more on the images that were playing out on the screen of my mind.

"I see you asking for help in all the wrong places. I see a medical person who is making it worse and worse for you and I know if you continue seeing him, you are going to end up being hospitalized. He is doing you more harm than good."

Hilda was listening intently to me and her brown eyes were smoldering with anger, and I couldn't blame her.

'This is my psychiatrist. I see him once a week and he just gives me more prescriptions, he doesn't even listen to me. I changed seven 'professionals' in the last three years but they are all the same. Their solutions are to give me more pills."

"Hilda, there is much that can be fixed more easily without drugs, but your body needs cleansing and proper fuel to run properly. Your body has incredible powers to heal itself. We need to detoxify your liver, kidneys and blood, then bring back to you what your body needs to rebuild itself."

"Can you tell me what this is and I will do anything to get better? I'll follow your advice."

"Absolutely. I will make a list of what you need to get right away and let's get on it. But there are also issues from your past that we have to revisit and remove so that nothing is holding you back." She was nodding as I spoke. "Maybe when I get back in two months we can set up appointment for an hypnosis? How about that, how does that sound to you?"

"Joseph will set the appointment for me."

The reading continued.

At the time it never occurred to me that her situation would turn to be so desperate that she would not have to wait the two months for her next visit.

She was shocked and impressed at how many topics I managed to hit upon, many with close to perfect accuracy including her husband. I knew right after the reading that this woman was haunted by her past and unless she cleared this up, her health would continue to deteriorate and her depression deepen. Every month before and during menstruation she would become incapacitated and unable to work. The pains and depression would not let her function at all and she would stay in bed, crying and refusing to eat.

The biggest fear she expressed was her husband abandoning her or dying. She was so terrified of him dying in the next two years that it simply became her obsession. She was afraid that he would die right after his 50th birthday (he was 48 at the time).

The appointment ended and we were waiting for her husband to pick her up. The short 5 minute delay sent her into panic mode worried sick that he must have had an accident. I calmed her down and told her that it was simply the traffic as it was 5:15 PM. Observing her in such a state of despair confirmed that she desperately needed regression work more than ever.

As predicted, Joseph arrived a few minutes late due to the tremendous after hour traffic.

Hilda felt much better at the end of our reading as now she had some hope. The very thing her doctors did not. All they would give her was the statement that she would never be able to be off the antidepressants. Her body's chemistry was screwed up beyond repair. And only drugs could keep it under control, of course.

I would inform Joseph when my next trip to Ottawa was going to happen and we would set Hilda's appointment before any other bookings.

I never thought I would see Hilda again on the very last night I was staying in Ottawa, even less never thought of the condition she would be in when it would happen.

After a very intense fully booked week during which I saw 62 people, some for readings, some for hypnosis and 7 kg disappearing from my frame, I was really looking forward to my flight back to Calgary and a little rest and downtime. I must explain to my readers that during such intense times when so much human emotion, despair and sorrow is on the menu every day, I lose my appetite, the adrenaline kicks in and my body seems to go into self preservation mode. I need to be able to use my mental focus and strength to do what must be done to help my clients.

It was late the Sunday night after my last appointment left and I was having dinner with my friend. We were catching up a bit, as she had hardly seen me. Even after she returned from work, she found me still working with clients and when the last ones left I was too tired even to eat, so often I just crashed to catch up with much needed sleep.

As we were chatting the phone rang and my friend answered wondering who could be calling at 11 PM Sunday night.

I saw my friend's face change as she listened to whomever was on the other end of the line.

"Let me ask her..." she said to the phone before moving it away from her ear.

"It's Joseph..." She took in a deep breath. "Hilda has spent two days in the Psychiatric unit in a hospital and he just picked her up. He is begging you to see her."

She handed me the receiver.

"Hi Joseph, tell me what happened."

"She had an appointment on Friday with her psychiatrist. She went into some kind of shock right after he started to write her a new prescription for some medication to battle the side effects of the antidepressants that he prescribed for her just a week ago...Ula..." he pleaded. "Please see my wife, she can't live like this anymore and she doesn't want to be a bigger burden to me than she already is. I know this time she really means it. She tried to take her life three times before." There was silence on the phone for a while, and I felt Joseph's pain.

"I am leaving tomorrow morning at 8... I started, so the only time I could see her would be now or whenever you can get here." In spite of my tiredness I couldn't bring myself to turn him away. I didn't want to be the straw that would break the camel's back.

Well, they arrived within half an hour and when I saw Hilda she scared me. Her eyes were sunken and there was no light in them. Dark circles under her eyes told me that she had not slept for the past few days.

"Joseph, please sit in the living room and wait rather than drive back and forth, so as soon as we are finished you can drive her home and she can rest."

"Thank you so much for doing this." He touched my hand and I could see the pain in his eyes.

"No problem, let's try to fix her up."

The intensity of this session that took 2 hours and 15 minutes was one of the longest ones I've ever allowed. Usually 2 hours is long enough and it puts lots of strain on me both physically and mentally. During my sessions I am at the same mind level as my clients so this takes me to the same places and situations my clients are re-living. It's easier then to understand and help them to process what they are facing and experiencing.

She responded to suggestions very eagerly and went quickly into a deep state of hypnosis.

"Hilda. I want you to take me back in time to your childhood where the reason for your problems with your mother started." There was no response for a few minutes and I was about to repeat what I said, when she stirred…

"Where are you?" I asked.

"I am in the change room after my ballet class." She said in a voice that could only belong to a child.

"How old are You?"

"I am almost seven."

"How long have you been attending Ballet school? Where is your daddy?"

"My mommy said he didn't want me, so he left before I was born."

"Mommy told me that he was not a good man and that it was better that he was gone. She said that I should be happy to have a stepfather who cares to be around me."

These words blew me like a gust of wind. I couldn't believe, being a single mother myself, that a parent would say such a terrible thing to a young child. I had to really keep my anger under control. It disgusted me that an adult could stoop so low, but the unfolding of this session was going to bring even more shocking discoveries.

"Have you ever seen your real daddy?"

"No. I never met him and my mother said to me if I ever wanted to look for him she would send me away to live with him, even if he did not want me around." That was surprising to hear but not shocking since I have dealt in the past with similar cases of parental control and cruelty.

"Hilda, do you have any siblings?"

"No, my mommy did not want to have any more children, she said one of me is more than she can handle."

"Who brings you to and from ballet school?

"Gunter." She said

"Who is Gunter?"

"Mommy's got a new husband."

"How long has he lived with you and your mom?" I asked carefully, sensing that some powerful revelations were just boiling away, to come soon to the surface.

"He was always there as long as I can remember, but they decided to get married two years ago. I still do not like him."

"Is he nice to you?"

"He is nice but I still don't like him."

"So, tell me when you are dressed and ready to leave the school." I shifted the subject trying to lay the groundwork for the bubble to burst.

"He is waiting outside, but I don't want to go outside."

"Can you stay inside?"

"No. It is late and they want to close the school. I have to go outside now and meet Gunter."

"I want you to go and meet him," I encouraged her, "I will be with you when you go, he is not going to see me."

"He came with his van as always. I hate his van." I could feel Hilda become more and more resistant in going through this unfolding event.

"Just tell me what happens when you get into his van. We need to know so we can make the pain you feel go away."

"We are driving now but this is not the road home." She sounded anxious and fearful. "He's stopped now at the park entry. It's getting dark and nobody is around."

"What happens next?" I am relentless to move her through the memory.

"He said he needs to talk to me and takes off his seat belt. He tells me to unbuckle mine." She stops and remains quiet for a short moment. "I don't want to see this, don't show me, no, no!" Hilda moves around and thrashes on the sofa as if trying to push something away.

"Hilda tell me what is happening!"

"He takes off his pants off and is showing me what's inside. It is ugly. I don't want to see it!" She continues fighting, thrashing her arms and feet.

"If it would make you feel better, you can remove yourself from your body and that way you can see everything that is happening from above," I suggested.

"I'll be OK," she said taking a deep breath as one would before going under the water again.

"Please continue telling me the rest of what happened in the van."

"He tells me that I am a big girl and I need to learn about important things and the facts of life." She was saying all this through clenched teeth and an expression of absolute abhorrence.

"He grabs my hand and forces it on his stiff penis..." she continued, "He clasps his fingers around my hand and starts moving it up and down! I close my eyes so that I do not have to see it."

"How long does he do this?"

"Until this sticky stuff spills all over my hand. I want to vomit. I get out of the van and throw up on the grass."

"Then what happens next?"

"He comes out and walks up to me and lifts me up from my knees. He said that it only feels that way the first time, after I will learn to like it. He says that we should keep it quiet and not tell my mother about this little secret."

"Are you going to tell your mother about this incident?"

"Yes, right after we get back home." She said that with her lips drawn into a narrow line.

"What happens when you arrive back home?"

"We are coming into the house and my step father is sending me upstairs right away to my room. When my mother asks him why he tells her that I was a bad girl and I deserve to be punished."

"Does you mother object to this?"

"No, she never even came to my room to check if I got to bed as she always does."

"How do you feel?"

"I feel sad and lonely. She is on his side…but I am going to tell her about what he did to me tomorrow before I go to school."

"Did you have an opportunity to tell your mother about what happened the next morning?"

"Yes. She asked me why I didn't eat my breakfast. I told her that I wasn't feeling well because of my step father. She asked me what he did and I told her…" Another long silence.

"What did your mother answer?" Even though I posed the question I already knew what the answer was going to be.

"She said that I misunderstood my step father's intentions about teaching me 'about the facts of life' then she pushed me out through the door and told me not to miss my bus."

"How do you feel about all this?"

"She doesn't love me at all, she loves him and will let him continue to do what he wants. I am scared…" she whispered, crying softly.

"Now," I started, "Please take three deep breaths and relax. I want you to go deeper inside and I'm going to ask you to search for a lifetime which started this unhealthy relationship between you and your mother and perhaps your stepfather."

The subconscious mind or spirit, or both, always seems to know where (reason, lifetime, entity, past life or other) the root cause of the problem at hand and where it emanates from. I, nor anyone else I know or have read about, fully understands how this mechanism works. It just works this way.

"I will count backwards from 10 to 1 and you will start going back in time to whatever place you need to go to search for the roots of these unhealthy relationships. Ok…on the count of one you will be right there in the place and time that holds the secrets you need to face to let go and set yourself free. For good, from the load and heaviness of your past, 10, 9, 8…"

I counted down slowly, until reaching the number one.

"Who are you?" was my first question. She spoke slowly and carefully.

"I am an Egyptian woman…" Her voice had changed, becoming deeper and calmer. "I hold a high position."

"How old are you?"

"I am eighteen."

"What is your name?"

"My name is Ankarama. I am the daughter of King Takelot II"[1] she said.

"Can you describe yourself?"

---

1 http://www.acaso.ca/takeloth-ii-amazigh-berber-king-egyptian-22nd-(dynasty-850-825-bc/

* Footnote to the novel re the Egyptian princess:
REF: Joshua J. Mark, Ancient History Encyclopedia
Email 13 August, 2016 Joshua.Mark@Ancient.eu.com

*Yes, I definitely believe in past lives/paranormal. I've had a number of interesting experiences in this area over many years.*

*I was intrigued by your question last night and did some searching. I found an Ankarama, daughter of Takelot II of Egypt, mentioned in a text from 1876 CE digitally reproduced online. It's just one line though — that she was Takelot II's daughter. Takelot II was one of the High Priests of Amun who ruled Upper Egypt from Thebes after the priests of Amun had grown powerful enough to take control toward the end of the period of the New Kingdom. His son was Osorkon (later Osorkon III) also a High Priest of Amun who put down a rebellion at Thebes and later ruled from there. The priests of Amun gained enormous power throughout the New Kingdom amassing more wealth and owning more land than the pharaoh until they were strong enough to just take control of the government. I'm relaying all this because Takelot II lived at a time when being heir to the throne of Upper Egypt meant enormous power and Takelot II had more than one wife and so there would have been contenders for succession to that enormous power and the client's claim she was murdered for that reason fits with the history.*

"I am slim and tall, my skin is an olive color. My hair is very long but I always have it hidden under the head dress that is made of gold. I wear lots of gold bracelets and big necklaces. Actually, it is more like a collar," she corrected herself, then continued." There are many symbols and letters engraved on it. Close to my neck are rows of round onyx stones embedded, I have brown eyes and a narrow face."

"Are you considered beautiful?"

"Beauty is not important to me. I want to be educated. I have to be strong. I have to be ready to take over from my father and I know if I am not strong then there are many enemies that will use my weaknesses to destroy me."

"Who are your parents? Do you know the souls who lived in your Egyptian parents and possibly in your present life?"

"Yes!..." there is an element of shock now in her voice." These are the same parents I have in my life now. My father's name is Takelot II, King of Egypt. My mother is his wife."

"Is this your natural father in your present life?"

"Yes. My mother divorced him right after she got pregnant with me, so he never knew that I was born and that I was his

---

*What I find strange is that this girl is not mentioned at all in any of my books. The only daughter of Takelot II is Karomama who was a singer for the god Amun at Thebes. By another wife he had a daughter Isetweret and there may have been another by another wife but none of them are Ankarama. Further, with his Royal Wife — his queen who would provide heirs — he only had sons.*

*None of this would discount the client's claim at all. Egyptian history is full of royalty getting rid of contenders for the throne and I'm sure there are plenty names we don't find in books. But it's odd that Ankarama should turn up in this one line from the 1876 book and nowhere else. I don't find her mentioned in any entry on Takelot II anywhere. It would not have been strange for a daughter to be named heir. That same situation obtained centuries before with Queen Hatshepsut who was heir to Tuthmoses I. Also would not be strange that she was murdered for the throne — there was a lot to be gained. Only strange that I can't find mention of her anywhere. If I ever do, though, I'll let you know.*

*All the best to you and your wife. Really fascinating work.*
*— Josh*

daughter. He lived in the same city, but my mother told him I was my stepfather's child. My mother had an affair for two years with this man. But I know he is not my father."

"How do you know that?" It was quite a complicated set up, so I needed some clarification.

"I obtained my stepfather's blood sample and had it tested and compared it to my blood. They told me this man could not have been my father. "

"I did this after my first miscarriage, trying to find out if there was any genetic reason for this."

"Let's go back to Egypt." I directed her back to her lifetime as an Egyptian princess.

"Tell me about your relationship with both of your parents." I instructed her.

"My father is a very good ruler and people love him. He is hoping for me to take over when it will be his time to depart from this life. He teaches me many things, and he says I am going to have to know them when I take his place."

"Do you have siblings?'

"No, I am the only child. My mother tried to get pregnant to bear him a son but has miscarriaged in three pregnancies, so there will be no son."

"Tell me about your relationship with your mother."

"I never saw her much, I had nannies looking after me. When I saw my mother she was very distant and she never tried to hide her dislike for me. I think that she was always jealous about my father. She never liked the fact that he was preparing me for taking his place."

"Tell me what happened next."

"My mother is trying to make me marry one of the advisers my father has in his council." She knits her brows. "She is insisting that I don't wait, that I should consider to accept his proposal."

"Are you planning to comply with her wishes?"

"No. I consulted with my father and he said that he does not trust the man and that his daughter needs to marry up for the better of Egypt's future."

"Do you agree with him?"

"Yes, my father loves his country and the people. He has been a good King for the past 20 years."

"Now take me forward and tell me what happens next."

"There is a big gathering in the main courtyard. There are some festivities and the man that my mother is trying to make me marry him is publicly proposing to me and asking me to be his wife."

"What is your answer?"

"I reject him and belittled him in front of everybody. I dislike this man and said I did not trust him."

"He left very angry and humiliated. He shouted that I am going to regret this."

"How is you mother taking this rejection?"

"She also left but I know she hates me now. I know now that she always did and I think that by rejecting the suitor she lined up for me, I destroyed her plans."

"What plans?"

"I don't know but I really feel it."

"Please move forward in time and tell me what is happening."

"I am being woken up by my maid. She is very upset and crying. She said that I have to get to my father chambers. She is screaming that he is dead. I can't understand what she is talking about. I am running to where she said my father was found dead. I see him now. He is laying on the floor. There is blood all over. Oh, my God, he was stabbed in the heart with a big knife. He is dead, there is no one here to protect me!"

Hilda is sobbing quietly and I can sense that she is truly distressed. So I take a short break and ask her to do some deep breathing so she can calm herself down. It always helps. We pause for 5 minutes.

"Tell me what happens now?"

"My mother has taken over and she is changing everything Oh my God! I know why she was trying to make me marry this man…When my father was alive and I was married to him, he would have become King after my father died. He and my mother murdered my father so they do not have to wait that long. They were lovers for a long time, and now she is no longer hiding it. She has all the power, she does not have to answer to anybody. This was her plan…"

Hilda's voice trails off and she doesn't speak for awhile. I let her take time to take it all in. "I am afraid that now I will be next, because as long as I am alive the people and my father's council can demand that my mother be taken from her position and her lover would have to killed."

"Take me forward…what is happening? Where are you now?"

"I am in my chambers. It is night. I am asleep. Something wakes me and I hear footsteps." Her voice lowers to a whisper. "Someone is in my room in the dark."

All of a sudden Hilda's hands fly to her throat as if in self defense.

"Tell me what is happening." I urged her on.

"There is a man sitting on my chest and choking me." She had difficulty speaking.

"Who is this man?"

"It is my mother's lover…He is choking me with one hand and ripping my gown with his other. He is going to rape me… Oh my God… nooo!"

Hilda continues squirming and tossing her arms in the air as if fighting off her attacker. "He rapes me and then chokes me with such hatred. I do not understand why?"

To shorten her agony I ask her to take her last breath and move out of her body. I ask her to look down at her lifeless body and at her attacker.

"He is still choking my throat even though he knows I am dead, he is hissing into my ear. That I should never have rejected him and humiliated him in public. He screams into my ear that he is the one in control and that he destroyed me and he is getting what he wanted anyways without waiting. I always get what I want!"

"I want you to look very carefully deep in the eyes of this man, can you tell me if your soul can recognize this man in your present lifetime as Hilda?"

"Yes," Her voice drops and she says nothing for a minute. I wait until she is ready to continue without being prompted.

"It is my step father!"

"Now, Hilda I want you to become aware of the dynamics that followed you from the previous lifetime." She laid there, quietly listening. "Your mother removed your father from your life even before you were born to have total control over you. You said she did not like you in this life, she has never liked you before and that was because she was no longer the center of attention. She continued her affair with the lover from the life you just relived and he wanted to possess you, but you rejected him and to boot, humiliated him. Look now, how from a secret affair he eventually became your step father and gained full control over your life. He said he always gets what he wants and that is what he did. You mother's betrayal proves that she didn't care about you in either of these lifetimes. There was always competition between you two.

"Then why did I choose to be born?" She asked, "Why would I choose another life to suffer more?"

"You came to this life so you could meet the love of your life, your husband, who loves you more than anything. And to resolve and let go of everything that tied you to these two people. If you can forgive, then you can set yourself free once and for all.

"They will never again have an impact on your life now or in the future. You can also try to find your biological father who as you have seen loved you very much. He doesn't even know he has a daughter. You have a second chance in your life and I know that you are going to do well. With proper detox and natural products you can get yourself off the antidepressants and claim your life and health back."

"You are a strong and good woman. You deserve the best things in life. I say go for it girl. I will assist you as much as I can to get your life back." Hilda laid quietly and I knew she was absorbing every word she heard in the deepest places in her soul. I could see her face brighten, her lips start to smile bringing on an expression of peace and joy.

"I will count from 1 to 10 and I will bring you back slowly into the present moment. On the count of one when I ask you to open your eyes, you will feel wonderfully refreshed and calm. You will feel healthy, focused and happy. You will feel as though you had a long, restful, healing sleep. You will feel wonderful in every way and you will carry this light and good feeling through tomorrow, the day after tomorrow and everyday after that."

Then I brought her out of the hypnosis. It was 2:15 AM when we finished. She sat up on the bed and looked at me with eyes as bright as a child. She smiled and said.

"Thank you so much, thank you for taking this awful load from my shoulders."

This all happened in March of 1993. The next time I saw her was in May the same year, two months later. I couldn't believe my eyes when Hilda and her husband entered my friends house where I again had a whole bunch of people booked to see me.

She was wearing a short skirt that was revealing her long shapely legs, a bright tight sweater that outlined her breasts boldly, yet with discrete sex appeal. Her skin was free of the many liver spots she had the first time we worked together. Her eyes no longer had those dark and puffy bags underneath them. Her beautiful brown eyes were bright, clear, focused and no longer had that haunted expression to them. Her hair had grown longer or perhaps she had just let it down.

"Oh my God, is this the same woman I saw in March?" I opened my arms and gave Hilda a great, big hug. "Is that you Hilda?"

"Yes, it is me and yet not me," she answered with a bright smile and for the first time I noticed what nice, even white teeth she had.

"I did everything you told me from detox to minerals and vitamins and I have never felt better. I have not missed a day from work even through my periods I sleep like a baby and Joseph has to pull me out of bed with a crane."

"Is that true Joseph?" I joked, looking at her husband.

"Yes it is, but now she is constantly on my back and she wants me to do the same: detox, vitamins, the whole nine yards...", he laughed.

"Nothing wrong with that!" I said.

"You may be right but she's obsessive and told me that she has this tremendous fear of losing me and can't stand the thought."

I looked back at Hilda with questioning eyes. She nodded and her face grew serious.

"This is what we need to work on today," she said.

"I should be going." Joseph stopped her by placing his hand on her shoulder. "I will be back in two hours." He kissed her cheek and sent me one of his gentle smiles. "Thanks again for helping us." Then he was gone.

I sat down with Hilda to have a short conversation before getting started with the next hypnosis session.

"Tell me, what is happening?"

"It's strange, but as I started to feel better and my mind started to clear, in that dark cloud always there as long as I can remember, for the first time in years I started to really look at everyone around me and notice things which I was unable to see before. I love Joseph so much and now see how much he must love me, putting up all these years with my depression, avoiding intimacy, and me not being what a wife should be.

Not taking care of any of his needs. He cooked, cleaned and held my hand when I was slipping into this ever present darkness that is finally gone now… All of a sudden I realize how much he means to me and how much I fear of losing him. It's become so obsessive that I can't shake the feeling that he is going to die and I am going to lose him. This thought is always there. Louder and clearer than ever."

"I see. Well, let's find out what the real reason is for you to feel this fear."

Without further delay Hilda laid down and quickly went into a deep state as she did the first time. I had almost 1 1/2 hours to explore the hidden reasons behind her obsessive fear of losing her husband.

Joseph and Hilda were in close intimate relationships in 5 other lifetimes and it was not surprising why these two souls were so in love and attracted to each other in the present time. What, however, was surprising and at the same time self-explanatory was that in four former lifetimes Joseph died from various causes between the ages of 50 and 52. What now made sense to me was the fact that as his 50th birthday was just around the corner in the first days of October that year, and subconscious memories started to percolate to the surface, and brought on this ancient fear that could not be explained in any logical way.

Towards the end of our regression session, I removed the old programming that conditioned and validated this otherwise unfounded fear and replaced it with positive affirmations that were to protect her from the re-occurrence of this paranoia.

"Oh my God," she sighed with great relief after I brought her back. "How is it possible to sense yet not remember consciously what had happened in the past?"

"Your mind is to guard and protect you from knowledge that might prove to be too difficult to deal with. During the years you were trying to survive your own troubles, you would not be able to handle the additional load that this turned out to be. After you had gone through your own healing, then this was the next step".

"One thing I have to agree with you is that Joseph needs to start taking care of himself better than he has up to date. I am going to tell him that."

"Thank you so much. You have not only saved my life but you changed it so much that now when I get up in the morning I can't wait to do the things that I want to do. I threw all my antidepressants in the garbage where they belong and canceled my appointments with the psychiatrist who sent me to the looney bin after my last visit in his office in March."

"Tell me what exactly transpired during that appointment with him. I'm very curious."

"I came into his office, he sat me across his desk and without asking me a single question, even how I was feeling he started to fill out a prescription. I asked him what he was doing. He said he had to give me something to lower my elevated liver enzymes. He had received my tests just before I got there for my appointment and they did not look good."

"What happened next shocked even me. All I remembered were your words: "That there was a medical person who was making me feel worse rather than helping me," and I lost it. I jumped from my chair, reached over his desk, grabbed him by the shirt and started to scream: "Are you planning to kill me you SOB, why are you doing it to me!!!?"

"The next thing I know he pushed the panic button and security men were pulling me away from him and putting me in a straight jacket! The SOB!"

I didn't say anything for awhile trying to comprehend what is happening with our Medical System when the only thing that is ever done for us is to push more pills on us to numb and mask the real reasons and roots of our illnesses and pain. We are drugged and removed from the self-preserving place we all have inside us that through the centuries has guided us to find cures and help ourselves heal our bodies, minds and spirits.

The only conclusion that I could arrive at was the astounding and disquieting realization that our value is measured by the amount of money we could generate for our medical and governing systems, and who were behind them. The wealth they continue receiving from us are in the billions of dollars. The ultimate price we pay to them is always in the most precious currency there is: our wellness. And often our lives!

I know about this unfair exchange from my own life which forced me to take what they did not manage to take away from me, and save myself just by believing that God loves me enough and with creation of human life on earth he also created everything we would need to nourish and heal ourselves.

Since my departure from 'conventional medicine', and taking charge of my own health I have never felt better.

After these sessions I remained in touch with Hilda and her husband for a number of years. They were doing very well. What made them very happy, three years later Hilda became pregnant and carried a beautiful baby boy to full term. From that point, due to my frequent international traveling, and Hilda having her hands full looking after this precious gift, we did not stay in close touch for the first several years. But again, she will always remain in my memory and in my heart.

We are teachers and students and as the famous expression states "when the student is ready the teacher comes." We are in each others lives for as short or as long as we need to teach and learn what we must, then it is time for us to go. The lessons we teach and the lessons we have learned will always remain with us. These are the steps that will measure our personal and spiritual growth.

### Ottawa Case #4: Julian

Julian was a nervous tall man who appeared to be 10-15 years older than he was. He told me at the beginning of our session that he was 32 years old, but he felt that he was too tired to continue to go on living.

I saw him for a one hour reading to decide if hypnosis was the right way to go, but there were things he did not reveal that he should have. He failed to mention that he had endured 17 electric shock therapies in the previous 7 years and was on heavy duty antidepressants. His liver toxicity was definitely showing in his yellow/gray complexion and his sunken, expressionless brown eyes revealed a deadness of life. They were empty and lifeless. He had tried many different therapies, he tried counseling, psychologists, psychiatrists and eventually ended up in a mental hospital where he spent almost 7 months. He was admitted after a suicide attempt that almost succeeded. Over the years he had built resistance to most medications and had to be prescribed new drugs in ever higher dosages to be responsive.

Eventually, his psychiatrist decided to put him through electric shock therapy, to which, needless to say, he had not responded to either. The brain damage that ensued from these treatments was evident in his slower speech, sense of loss and even deeper depression. As our reading progressed, an uneasy and disquieting feeling settled in the pit of my stomach. This was always be the case when I would realize that there was not much that I could do to help someone. But I really wanted to understand the process that lead Julian to this point of no return and why no one realized that there was a way he could have been helped and given a chance for life.

Julian's life story was not new since I have worked with many clients who went through many more horrible situations and yet I somehow managed to helped them. What became clear to me that it was not the troubled and painful childhood that did the most damage but rather those who claimed they were capable and trained to bring help, and their methods that lead to this absolute and utter destruction of a human life.

Julian was unlucky to be born into a family that should have been childless. They were people who were so damaged themselves that having a child was just reckless. He was beaten, left abandoned for days without food, and by the age of four was tending to his own needs to avoid asking for basic things in fear of being punished for simply being alive. The only person in his life even today that he has unfettered faith in was his grandfather, who never beat him. In Julian's own mind sexual molestation was a lesser evil.

He did Ok in school, meaning passing his grades. My suspicion was that his teachers, having seen his bruised face and body did not want to add more reasons for their student to be punished. It appeared that this was good enough, so they didn't have to report this horrendous abuse to the authorities, which would require more work and efforts to deal with.

In spite of all the logs and difficulties he completed high school, took courses in Physiotherapy, landed himself a job as a sport physiotherapist and later on managed to find a girlfriend whom he eventually married. As the story moves forward, they had a baby girl born as their only child before his wife decided to terminate intimacy from the marriage. Julian expressed his thoughts that his daughter was his only reason to live. This is where the real litany of abuse came back to haunt him. When his daughter reached the age of three he would begin going to her bedroom at night and start to fondle and touch her in an inappropriate way. His daughter was the only one person, he said that could give him the love no one else could. As the situation spun out of control over the next few years, and his daughter began to show the signs of sexual abuse, the school reported him to authorities. He was charged with the sexual molestation of his daughter. His wife filed for divorce and he was forced out of his house and had a restraining order served to him which forbade him to come anywhere near his child.

Due to his proven mental problems, he was not charged criminally but he did not need to be. It was right after the trial that he attempted to take his life, and landed in a mental hospital for nearly 7 months where the majority out of his 17 electric shock therapies were administered.

I must say that working on a case like this, it is very hard to go through the process or to recollect details of this child abuse, both the one that was inflicted on him and the ones he inflicted on his daughter. The entire process was very hard to handle. The most difficult task is to remain on the outside and not allow yourself the freedom of judgment which comes easily to a mother of two which I was.

When he came to see me he was too damaged to be helped. It was the establishment that had inflicted most of the irreparable damage. The 17 electric shock treatments fried his brain to the point that made even day to day tasks difficult to handle. It affected his speech, co-ordination, deepened his depression, and the best way to put it, turned this man into a zombie. The living dead.

My heart felt heavy that I was unable to bring this man back to life. And by giving him tools of self healing, help him undo what had been to him and to repent and repay his daughter for the damage that he had done to her. I will never forget his face and eyes that in that very brief moment, held their only glow and liveliness when he told me,"I love my daughter more than anything in my life, I just wanted her to love me back."

I believed him beyond a shadow of doubt, that his words were sincere and rang true. The thing that he still could not understand was that the love he took from his little girl was not and should not been asked by any father in the world...but how was he to know that?

By the end of our appointment I gave him a list of natural things he could take in an attempt to salvage what was left of his life to be able to continue on. I felt sad that this was all that I could say to him to fill the silence hanging in the air before he left. Just before he did that, one more time he turned back and said.

"I wish I had met you before they did this to me, as he pointed at his head. Now there is nothing left to fix."

These words echoed in my mind all these years and are still in my memory like a sliver reminding me, that we all could be in a place where 'too little, too late' is all that's left.

*Our prayers should be for blessings in general, for God knows best what is good for us.*

— Socrates —

# CHAPTER NINETEEN: LIDIA

## Session Number One

Lidia, my sister, asked me in desperation to help her to try to stop the destructive habit of squeezing and damaging the skin on her face. She would stay in the bathroom for over an hour and pick away at her skin until it was all blotchy, discolored and damaged. And sometimes I had to drag her out of the bathroom to make her stop. She continued to tell anyone who tried to stop her from doing this, that she had a badly pimpled complexion and she needed to remove them, as if that was an excuse to persist in this habit. She indeed had a little acne, as many do, but her picking was exacerbating the problem.

She would hide from people, avoid gatherings and more because she was so ashamed of her face. And then this morphed into a mild form of depression which was connected to this ailment.

We started our first session with a regular relaxation method as usual, but when she appeared to fall into an hypnotic state, I instructed her to start going through the process of her birth. I asked her to go to the day of her birth and I noticed great distress in her as she found herself at that time and place. I asked why she was so agitated and upset. In response, she said, "I can't breathe, something is choking me!"

I asked her how old she is as a fetus. She told me, seven-and one half months. She says: "I am being told to come out now." And during this time I notice the difficulty she was having to breathe. I asked her who was telling her that.

She says, "I don't know. The voice tells me this."

She was asking for air and her face was becoming red. In order to release her from this discomfort, I asked her to move out of her little body and float above the scene to see what was happening in the hospital room. She said that she sees herself and she is not moving. And her skin is turning purplish and blue. The doctors and nurses are rushing about.

She is saying, "I see the umbilical cord wrapped around my neck!"

"They have removed the cord and did something and now I can breathe." Neither one of us was aware that Lidia was a blue baby, so we asked our mother about this and she confirmed that indeed Lidia was a blue baby after all.

As I continued the session I asked her to relax, breathe deeply, and then move back deeper into her psyche.

I noticed that her face began to contort to the point of becoming grotesquely distorted. Almost unrecognizable to me. This continued in the trance state and made her speech almost incoherent and impossible for me to understand what she was saying. It was almost as if some external force with invisible hands was putting pressure on her cheeks, caving them in, and pulling her jaw so far down that it was wide open, rendering her almost speechless!

It got to the point that it was so horrible, that if I hadn't known this woman since she was a young girl, I had the irresistible urge to bolt from the room and run for my life!

I started to laugh, trying to control myself from making a sound, both my hands clasped over my mouth. It was so grotesque that I actually thought she was playing a practical joke on me. But it was no joke!

I managed to re frame the session and asked her to stand in front of a mirror and look at her face. The first thing she said was: "I have no face!"

I asked her, "What do you mean, you have no face?"

"I don't have a nose, and half the flesh on my cheeks is missing. I see the bones exposed!"

She told me that half of her skull was gone, as was all her hair.

I asked her to become aware of her surroundings and tell me where she was. She responded saying that it was a cave with a small space in the entry, which was covered by a huge boulder. The space was so small that no one could squeeze through it. I asked her to become aware of the circumstances of how she ended up this cave. I asked her to tell me where she was and she responded that it was in India around 1850 or thereabouts.

It was then that she told me it was her family who put her there to isolate her and not allow anybody else to get her disease. It was Leprosy.

They used to bring her food for some time. Then they stopped feeding her until she finally died.

The conclusion of this session was that, due to the past life memories of the Leprosy, and the distress and loneliness she suffered, the stresses of her present lifetime would trigger those memories and bring them back to the cave where she died. She saw her face as ugly and damaged as it was in the prior lifetime.

I reprogrammed her positively and brought her out of the hypnosis.

### Second Session: 2 Years Later

The reason why my sister approached me again and asked for help was her uncontrollable bouts of crying for no apparent reason and I noticed that her chin would shudder as a child might before they start to weep.

Again, we went again under the spell of hypnosis and she was under within 5 minutes.

I again noticed her chin start to quiver as it was before she would start to cry. I asked, "Who or what is causing Lidia's chin to tremble?"

"It's me, the tiny voice answered."

"Who are you?"

"I'm your sister."

"Lidia, is this you who is speaking?" I was very confused, as I was talking *to* my only sister! In response Lidia's head rolled from left to right, meaning 'No'.

Immediately I thought of the sister who we lost when I was 5 years old, the little sister who died when she was only 24 hours old, a premature baby. She would be 5 years younger than I am if she had lived. Well, I was right, and I was wrong.

This same sister tried to come to us again. I was 22, my mother was 42. I didn't know about this second child until the hypnosis with Lidia!

I told the little baby spirit that we both loved her and that she would have another time and place when she could be reborn into the family. I asked for the baby spirit to go to the light and wait for the right time to return.

Shortly after, I noticed that Lidia started to have difficulties in breathing.

Now, a different voice suddenly spoke through her lips. It was saying, "I'm not going anywhere. I've been with her since she was 2 weeks old in the hospital." This was a young man who was killed by a car in 1969, and they brought his body to the morgue at the hospital where Lidia was having surgery for a massive infection on her jaw bone that almost killed her.

I instructed this entity to regress back to his own death. His face was also damaged by the car that had run over him. His head, face and chest got severely damaged and it was this entity that caused my client to have breathing problems and congestion in her chest.

After the entity was regressed to this period, he was free to leave her body since what I painted for him was a place with no pain and no loneliness.

After this, I slowly brought my client back to the waking world.

When Lidia was conscious again, she sat up on the bed and remarked that she no longer had the persistent chest pain that she had felt for much of her life.

*The comic and the tragic lie inseparably close, like light and shadow.*

— Socrates —

## CHAPTER TWENTY: GLORIA AND THE FRANK SLIDE

Gloria was my good friends' oldest daughter. What brought her to me were two major concerns that she had, one, her inability to conceive for the six years of their marriage and she was afraid that she might be infertile and couldn't have children; and the second which appeared to be more embarrassing that wreaked havoc on her life, for many years.

She was happily married to a nice, soft spoken, tall and handsome oil engineer.

When she stayed in hotels, motels or other peoples homes she would rouse from bed in the middle of the night, completely asleep and forcefully drag her husband out of the bed. Then she would shove him against the wall, in a corner usually, and press her back to him as if she was protecting him from something unseen.

She would yell out, "Everything is going to be OK. Its OK. You're not going to die!"

Some of these incidents required intervention from the hotel staff and other guests. It must be said that, in her awakened state, Gloria was a very calm, good natured career woman who would never do anything similar to these purported 'night terrors'.

Frequently they would have to reimburse the hotel for the damage done to the room, like broken lamps etc.

Of course, they were lucky that more drastic measures didn't occur such as the Police being summoned. Part of her job requirement was for her to travel, and due to this odd problem, her refusal to travel was affecting her career.

She was a very easy hypnotic subject and went into a deep state of hypnosis. As always, I sent her to the root cause of the inexplicable reasons for these night attacks. Immediately, she began to report on a life as a woman married to a man whom she recognized as her husband in her present life.

They were very much in love and lived in a small log house. This house was located in the present historic Frank Slide area, in the town of Frank, Alberta, Canada which was partially buried by a devastating avalanche which occurred in the early morning hours at 4:10 AM on April 29, 1903.[1] Her name was Julia and her husband's name was John.

That very night, her husband, who was a miner in the coal mine in Turtle Mountain, and because of his friend's request to change shifts with him, as the due date for his friends wife's delivery of a new baby was the next day, stayed home with Julia.

It was at about 3:15 AM when Julia was woken up by the violent shaking of their log home and then also when she heard a loud roar of sound from Turtle Mountain. She grabbed her husband, woke him up suddenly, and dragged him into the farthest corner of their small home. He wanted to leave the house but she convinced him that it would be safer to stay inside. They both thought that it was an earthquake. She was

1 https://en.wikipedia.org/wiki/Frank_Slide

standing in front of her husband, pushing him into the corner. They cowered there for over 45 minutes.

Then suddenly the whole cabin shook and massive boulders started to fall onto them. The two walls were crushed into him and she was catapulted forward and the logs ended up on angle where there was a space big enough to protect her and she somehow survived.

Her husband John was killed. She felt so guilty that she couldn't save him. She lived to age 48 and never remarried. I feel that she died of a broken heart.

Failing to save him in that lifetime caught her in a vicious cycle in which was doomed to repeat the experience in her present lifetime. Her psyche was also protecting her from pregnancy in the unconscious fear that a child would be left fatherless. After the session was over, and I sat with Gloria talking about it, she was in awe about uncovering the real reasons for her night terrors, which helped her feel at ease and released. I then took her hands for a moment, and looked down at her palms. I told her I saw not one child, but two different children, one a boy and a girl. Six weeks later her mother announced to me that Gloria was pregnant.

Within four months I got a distress phone call from her mother again, as the doctors found some type of recessive gene on her husbands side — a history of birth defects on his mothers side, and suggested that they could do an invasive surgical procedure to confirm their preliminary diagnosis. However, the probability of a miscarriage if this was done was close to 80%.

So, Gloria, sadly, was left with two choices: either go ahead with the surgery and take a real risk of losing the baby, or accepting the situation and pray that everything would turn out fine.

She came to see me, and I placed my hands around her tummy and mentally connected to the fetus. I could not detect any abnormalities or defects in the baby boy, of which was known by then.

I told Gloria not to worry, because she was going to have a healthy, beautiful baby boy.

When the announcement of the birth came, I wasn't surprised that they had a healthy and strong 9 pound baby boy. Neither was I surprised that two years later Gloria gave birth to their second child, a little girl, which I had also predicted.

*The people have always some champion whom they set over them and nurse into greatness...This and no other is the root from which a tyrant springs; when he first appears he is a protector.*

— Plato, *The Republic* —

## CHAPTER TWENTY-ONE: 9/11

Even now when I'm writing this chapter I can still feel the indescribable dread and grief that I felt on that memorable weekend prior to the 9/11 disaster.

And one of the most powerful group premonitions that I've ever had.

It started out for me on the Friday evening, September 7, 2001 that instead of doing what I normally do with my sister, Lidia, whom I was living with at the time, that is to watch a few movies and have a couple of glasses of wine together, and just enjoy the conversation, I went to bed at an early hour without explanation to Lidia. For a night owl like me this was perhaps only the second time in my life that I've done that.

Saturday morning when I awoke the dark cloud that was around me became even darker and tighter. And it only continued to grow more intense as the weekend progressed.

I should mention here that I had purchased an airline ticket for my flight to the States the upcoming week to visit a friend.

I somehow felt and knew that this trip would be canceled. I couldn't put a finger on the reason why I felt this way.

I went downstairs for breakfast, now crying, with my heart heavier than a bucket of lead.

When my sister asked me what was going on, I said, "I don't know. I don't understand. But I feel like I'm grieving for everybody at once."

The first thing that we thought was that something had happened to our loved ones or our parents back in Poland.

Though having a conversation with my sister in the past would always make us both feel better, this particular morning that wasn't happening. I didn't touch my breakfast as I had no appetite. I told my sister that I wouldn't be going to the States and she replied:

"Why, are you planning on canceling?"

"No, but I just know I'm not going and I don't know why!"

I retreated back to my bedroom. I continued my incessant crying and cried throughout the entire day with only a few short breaks. By evening both my eyes were red and swollen.

I hardly slept that night, It was like some kind of nightmare. I wanted to sleep but the heaviness I felt in my chest prevented that. It became even more oppressive as the night wore on. I would lie there staring at the shadows on the walls and at the dark ceiling.

By morning I woke up even more tired and depressed than before. My sister suggested that I do meditation or prayer but I simply couldn't do it. This had never happened to me before.

I had a few bites to eat but had to force myself, I went outside to clean my van as a distraction, but wept the whole time.

My sister really started to worry about me and gave me a hug.

"I don't understand what's happening. I feel like I'm grieving for the whole world!" I lamented.

She didn't respond, after all what could she say?

I wasn't working on the Monday and was on my third day of tears and angst. There seemed no hope and no purpose to life to anything. Only the darkest, heaviest pain, sorrow and despair. And the helplessness.

The period between Monday night and Tuesday morning was as restless and sleepless as the two previous ones. Even worse.

On Tuesday morning at around seven I was driving my van to work and a voice inside my head told me to turn on the radio, which I have to mention I *never* do.

What I heard on the station chilled me to the bone. I heard the broadcaster screaming:

"Oh, my God, the second tower has been hit!"

My first thought was that this must be a live radio theater program that I often listened to back in Europe. All of a sudden I just knew that something terrible was happening though I had no idea what. I pulled the van over to the curb and sat there crying for over half an hour. My hands were shaking. I was finally able to collect myself enough to drive. When I reached my work, my boss who was a Syrian Catholic, a very nice and graceful man, greeted me at the door and explained what had happened.

He said: "They will blame all of us for what has happened here!"

We watched the whole attack on the small TV he had during which they were reporting how many people had likely died. Now I understood the feelings of loss and grieving that had tormented me that weekend.

Late that day, the airline called me saying that all flights had been grounded because of the directive and would I like a refund. I obtained a full refund on my ticket.

As everyone now knows, by 2003 the Americans made the decision to go to war against Iraq in retaliation and under the pretext of Iraq developing and having Weapons of Mass Destruction (WMD).

The World seemed to be convinced that this was true, even my husband, with whom I had a very heated argument on the subject. I said to him, "Michael, there are no Weapons of Mass Destruction. These people want food and to live. This war will cause many people to suffer and die for nothing. You will see."

In hindsight everyone knows the real truth of what happened over there.

*If you want a vision of the future, imagine a boot stamping on a human face — forever.*

— George Orwell —

# CHAPTER TWENTY-TWO: CLIENT WHO WENT INTO THE FUTURE

Rene came to me mainly to understand some anomalies and compulsions with others and in particular with German Shepherd Dogs. And her deep disdain for the German people and the German language. Since the woman didn't drive, my husband offered to pick her up and bring her to the session in our home.

As always I had a short interview before we started about her expectations for the hypnosis and explained the nature of the process to her. As she went under very quickly, I asked her to go to the root cause of her dislike for the German people and their language. And for her obsessive love for the German Shepherd Breed. She wanted to know if she should get one, if the right reasons could be found.

She went to the existence of a Jewish man, Ishmay, in a small town in Poland, my old country in the year 1942. He was one of the Jews hiding in the building once owned by a prominent Jewish Industrialist who owned a manufacturing plant that produced yarns.

The owner was long dead. It had a hidden access and held over 30 Jews including women and children.

Unbeknownst to all of them the Germans found out about their hiding place. They came with a big army truck and the Gestapo captured them, loaded them on the truck and took them to the forest. There were over 400 Jews gathered there by the Nazis. They were ordered to dig a deep mass grave for themselves.

They shot the children first so their parents were forced to watch their children die.

The women were next, falling into the pit as they were murdered.

Then the men. The Jewish man was in the first row. He was shot in the abdomen, having several machine gun bullets rip into his flesh. He fell on top of the bodies some of which were in the final throes of death's grip.

He fell further towards the back wall of the pit. Many other bodies fell on top of him. More agonizing than the searing pain of his own wounds were the screams and wrenching groans and moaning of the nearly dead.

Rene was showing visible signs of great physical and emotional pain and distress.

We were both in tears. When the execution was over the Germans brought their German Shepherd Dogs on long leashes to walk over the stacked corpses to detect if anyone was still alive. The dogs would bark if they found a person still breathing. A stream of bullets would then make sure that they were very dead. He could hear the sharp orders and shouts from the German officers as the people were slaughtered.

He was covered by other bodies except for the head and neck. One particular dog stood and looked straight into his eyes knowing that he was still alive. The German Shepherd licked his face and in total silence quickly jumped out of the dugout.

After night fell, he managed to slither out of the mass grave and make his way to the forest where he was found by Polish Partisans.

The man died of complications from his wounds in 1952, she told me.

We took a break for 10 minutes to recover from this taxing exercise.

When we resumed, Rene had asked me previously that she was worried about her 17 year son, whom she was having some difficulty with and asked me to help.

I decided, under hypnosis, to send her into the future.

She went at first seven years or so into the future. I asked her to look at a newspaper, the Calgary Herald in a newsstand and find the date of the issue she was looking at. She told me September 19, 2009.

She was in some type of auditorium where her son was receiving some sort of diploma in Engineering. She was very proud of him and her comment was:

"I'm so proud of him. I don't have to worry about him. He'll get there on his own."

I then left her to choose where she wanted to go next. I asked her, "What is the date?"

I was absolutely floored to hear the date she responded with, "2309."

I asked her to tell me what the world around her was like. She said, "I'm inside somewhere, a big box. There are big screens all over. I think they are windows, but they are projection screens.

I think its a view of an ocean with a beach, but its only a screen. Everything is white. The furnishings are simplistic and square. All white.

Everything that I want responds to voice commands. I couldn't see doors or handles; no appliances are in the kitchen. Everything is austere and clinical. Food is dispensed from the wall in the form of pills. My clothes are straight and white. A tunic. I have no shoes, my feet are bare. The floors look like a white solid tile. They have no grooves, and are cold and slippery. I talk with someone and their face appears on a screen. Their voice comes from all around me.

No one smiles. I am feeling in total isolation and loneliness. Women get pregnant in some artificial way with robotic equipment. She is unconscious when the baby is born and never sees it again. I don't want to be here.

I hope mankind never gets here!"

At the end of this session, before she left she told me she was going to go to an Animal Shelter and adopt a German Shepherd dog.

*Feel the fear and do it anyway.*

— Susan Jeffers, *Feel the Fear and Do It Anyway*, 1988 —

## CHAPTER TWENTY-THREE: EDYTA

Edyta, who was my best friend's daughter, struggled for awhile with depression which deepened after her natural fathers' sudden death. She also suffered with an irrational and obsessively morbid fear of snakes.

She went very quickly and very deep. The first thing that she reported was a picture in her mind that was split: one side was very light and the other was very dark. And immediately she sensed the presence of her father, who was pulling her from the dark side.

I asked her if there was anything she wanted to say to her father. I could see him there.

Part of him was in the light and the rest in darkness... I could sense that the full awareness of him being dead was not real to him, as he had had a massive heart attack and died suddenly in Europe after only being there for a few weeks. People who die in this manner often are not aware that they are dead, in my experience. I asked Edyta to say to her father the things she wanted to but never had a chance to tell him.

She responded, breaking into tears and said: "I'm so sorry that I never got to Poland in time to see you! You know I love you and your dying doesn't change that."

I interjected here to ask Edyta to set her father free and ask him to go to the light.

"Are you ready to let him go?"

She nodded anxiously. I prompted her further, "You need to say it out loud."

She said, "Dad, I want you to go. There is nothing more for you here. I'm sad and I don't want to be sad anymore."

I asked her to let me know when her father had disappeared to the bright light that I made them both aware of.

As always I let her breathe and relax before we delved further into the session.

Shortly after I asked to search for the reasons and causes for her morbid fear of snakes.

"I am here," she said after a few minutes.

"Who are you?"

"I'm a woman, my name is Elizabeth."

"What are you wearing? Can you describe yourself to me?"

"I have a big, white bonnet, a long skirt, white blouse and I have a little boy with me. He's my son."

"Where are you at the moment as you see yourself?"

"I'm in the farmer's market. I'm buying fruit." The date, she told me, was in the early eighteen hundreds.

"What language are you speaking?"

"English."

"Where are you?"

"I think I'm in the southwest area of the United States."

"Who is the boy's father?

"My husband." She sounded disappointed.

"Tell me about your husband."

"He's twice my age, and now I know he married me for my father's money. He's not a good man. I'm afraid of him."

"Take me to the next serious event in your life as Elizabeth. How old are you?"

She says, "I'm twenty eight. We are just coming home from the market."

"Where are you now?"

"I'm standing in front of our home, but I'm afraid to go in. I think something bad is inside."

"Go into the house," I told her.

She walks into the first room and sees her husband standing there, holding a small trunk.

"Glad that you are home," he says while approaching her.

"He's looking at me strangely. He's got something evil in his eyes, I know he wants to hurt me!"

"What happens next?" I prompted her. All of a sudden her husband opens the trunk and throws its contents straight at her face. It's full of snakes.

"Oh my God, he's going to kill my son!", she exclaims. The snakes bite her on her face, neck and hands. To ease her fear I ask her to move out of her body and watch the scene from above.

She says, "It's too late, I'm dead."

"What else do you see? Where is your son?"

"Oh my God! He's on the floor. He's dead too! Why did he kill his own son?"

"Looking back at your life, what have you learned?"

"I've learned that people lie. They lie all the time to get what they want. He wanted this house and now he can have it!"

"Do you see your husband? Where is he and what does he do?"

"He killed the snakes and now he is standing above my body and he is laughing like the devil!"

"Breathe deeply and as I count back from 5 to 1. I want you to find another lifetime connecting you to your fear of snakes."

"OK, I'm here. Everything is gilded in gold. I'm in a big chamber."

"Who are you? What are you wearing?"

"I'm a man, a High Priest. I'm wearing a headdress on my head. I have gold bracelets on my wrists and a heavy skirt. I'm wearing sandals…my skin is dark. My head is shaved."

"What is your status?"

"I'm very important. They fear me." There was pride in her voice as she said this.

"What is the reason people fear you so much?"

"When they break my rules, I punish them."

"What do you do to punish them?"

"I throw them into the snake pits."

"What happens next to you?"

"I've been poisoned."

"Once you are out of your body as this high priest look back and tell me what you've learned."

"I learned that no bad deeds go unpunished and there is a time to pay for all the wrongs we've done."

The session was going on 2 hours and we were both spent and tired. I brought Edyta out of her trance. Her awful fear of snakes was finally conquered after so many years of being in paralyzing fear of the creatures.

*Most people get a fair amount of fun out of their lives, but on balance life is suffering, and only the very young or the very foolish imagine otherwise.*

— George Orwell —

## CHAPTER TWENTY-FOUR: FAILURE OR FATE?

I keep reminding myself that there are those who are meant to mend their broken lives and those who are condemned to accept their fate blindly and without resistance. Sometimes as an acceptance of karmic debt, and sometimes as a surrender to evil.

These cases always left me feeling a failure.

One of these cases will be thenceforth known as:

### Bonaventure Drive Massacre

I left out this case as long as I could because I consider it the hardest case I have ever dealt with and the one with most tragic ending. Also for many years I blamed myself for not being able to help my client and that at one point of time seriously considered abandoning spiritual counseling for good.

Lynn was referred to me by one of my clients whom I had done some extensive healing work dealing with her childhood sexual abuse. She fully recovered and began rebuilding her life, even though at the time she was almost 50, she felt that she had so much more to do and so much more to accomplish. Her tremendous improvement was just short of miraculous and everyone in her circle couldn't help but be astonished and impressed.

That is why Lynn, who was my client's best friend for many years asked for my telephone number to set up an appointment to see me. Lynn had struggled with bouts of depression on and off most of her life and for years attended psychological counseling with zero improvement. Desperate for help, she called me and waited impatiently for my next trip down to Calgary. Due to my other arrangements and responsibilities I was unable to give her a firm time commitment as to when my visit could take place. She called me almost weekly to make sure that I wouldn't forget about her.

It was around late March of 1997 when we were finally able to set up our first appointment. She was very excited about it and I sensed that she was also pretty desperate at the same time.

During our telephone conversation I had a strange and unsettling feeling in the pit of my stomach that someone else was on the phone with us.

It was the first time during this telephone conversation that, by mistake, I referred to her as 'Linda' several times, for which I apologized profusely. She only could smile, saying that it was OK.

She gave me her address and we set 10 AM Tuesday morning as the time for our appointment. After we hung up I sat there for a moment looking at the phone receiver.

I had just placed it in it's cradle, when a feeling of inexplicable and unreasonable dread washed through me like a gust of cold, north wind sweeping through the Alberta plains in the winter months. It was a very strange feeling that took me awhile to shake myself out of. It was Saturday, and I needed to pack for my trip to Calgary.

I used to stay with one of my good friends and she would afford me the peace and quiet of her nicely furnished condo. Having lived for many years in Calgary I was quite familiar with the city's layout and two of the four quarters of the city were better known to me, the southwest and the southeast. I was pretty sure I knew where the address was, or at least how to get to the street where she lived. The particular address I would find by just slowing down as I drove to find her house number.

It was a cool but very beautiful and sunny day. I enjoyed the drive from northwest Calgary where I was staying to the southeast where my client lived. As I reached the street Lynn lived on, I slowed down and started to read the house numbers which in Calgary are organized in very simple order. Once you know in which direction the numbers go, smaller or bigger, it is very easy to find the address you are looking for. What happened to me that day was beyond weird. I passed by her house three times and failed to see her house number which was quite large and very visible. It was almost as if some force was hard at work to send me away without finding my client's address…

To this day I wonder if this was the work of an angel or a devil trying to prevent me from seeing my client. Nevertheless, due to my stubborn character I found a place to park and decided to walk to try to find her house. I finally found it and it struck me as strange how I could miss this place three times in the row.

The number was not only on the house itself but also on the cement block right by the sidewalk. As I rung the doorbell, I heard someone rushing to the door. Lynn opened it for me and with her was a large beautiful dog, covered in cognac brown short hair, its ears hanging down on both sides of his intelligent looking face with its velvety brown eyes. His short tail shook excitedly as he tried to lick my hand. I gathered from Lynn's face that her dogs behavior was pretty unusual.

"I can't believe that, he's never before allowed anybody close to this house without going crazy, barking and growling. He didn't make a noise or bark once when you approached. He was actually sitting in the hallway as if he was waiting for you!"

The first time this happened to me was when a friend of mine was forced to move out of her house after separating with her partner and had to rent a place for herself, and faced the dilemma of what to do with her beautiful Border Collie/ Australian Shepherd dog that she had had from the time he was a tiny pup.

The new landlord would not allow any pets into her place and she was facing either giving the dog away or putting it down. I knew she loved this dog too much so putting this 5 year old vibrant and lively dog to sleep was out of the question. She decided to try to find someone that would take him from her. The first person she thought of was of course, me. It was a huge surprise to me, since I had never owned a dog and had never even thought of getting one due to my busy schedule.

"Please consider it?" she pleaded with me. "Bear will love you, he is such a beautiful, smart and good dog..." She was presenting her case to me.

"Look, I have never had a dog in my life I wouldn't even know or understand when he would need to go pee or what he eats…" I tried to get myself out of this situation. "Maybe he wouldn't even like me?"

"Bear will love you and he knows how to talk. You would have no problem understanding what he wants," she insisted. "You live in the country, so he will have more freedom and it will be healthier for him to be there than here in the city."

"Ok," I finally agreed "I'll come tomorrow to your place to meet your dog, but if he won't like me and tries to bite my head off, then that will seal his fate. I won't take him then. Is that OK?"

"Absolutely," she said finally. "If he doesn't like you then that is OK, but he might bark a little…" she said with hesitation. "You know dogs do that, hopefully it won't scare you." She was hoping.

"Tomorrow…" I said I would be there, and hung up the phone.

The next day around 3 PM I knocked on Emily's door. It was very quiet around her place, and for a moment I thought she was not at home. I assumed the dog would raise a hell of a racket if she was, so for a brief moment I felt relief that maybe I would be off the hook. But then the door opened and Emily asked me in.

"Where is your dog?" I asked not seeing or hearing the very reason I showed up there.

"He's right here…" she pointed to the right. "He has been sitting here for the past two hours." I craned my neck and saw what she was talking about.

There was this beautiful black dog with a white spot on his forehead sitting like an Egyptian Sphinx, staring right at me. I could hear in my mind what these eyes were saying to me. "*I was worried you wouldn't come for me!*" It was a strange thought but it dawned on me that maybe I could communicate with a four-legged creature as easily as I could with people.

"I can't believe it!..." Emily said, her eyes opening wide, "Bear never lets *anybody* close to the building, even less to my door. Not even my boyfriend who he knew all his life."

I sat on the sofa as we had coffee. The dog moved away from the door and sat right by my feet. He never moved once, only stared me down.

"He is already your dog...he knows his life is in your hands." she said, tongue in cheek. "There is no denying it, he has already dumped me."

"Oh, don't exaggerate! ." He wouldn't know any of it." As the words came out of my mouth a voice in my head said, 'You know she is right, this dog knows you are the one that can save his life.'

"All right." I finally agreed, "I can't take him tonight, but I will be here tomorrow around nine before heading back North."

"Thank you so much...you will enjoy having Bear, he will be your best friend and protector."

As I walked towards the door to put my shoes on, Bear followed me, ready to go when Emily grabbed his collar to hold him in place. There was this whimpering sound that he had finally made. It was his entreaty, 'Don't leave me, please!' At that moment I knew I could hear his thoughts!

"Bear." I padded the dog's head, "I will be back for you tomorrow. I promise!"

He sat on his hind legs and even though his eyes were still pleading with me, he made no other attempt to follow me. He trusted I would keep my word and that he was safe. He knew I would come back for him. So I did and he lived for another 11 years to the ripe age of 16, when my ex-husband was forced to put him down.

—

What I was feeling from Lynn's dog was a little different. What he was saying to me was "Help her, I know that you can. Keep her safe!"

"Please come in." Lynn was of medium height, a rather slim woman in her early forties. She had shoulder length, blond straw-like hair and blue, tired eyes. Her complexion was showing signs of prolonged use of drugs that she was taking for her depression.

She had a nice face and I could sense that she was a kind and gentle woman who had the bad luck to have been born into the wrong family. She was dressed in tight fitting jeans and a dark blue sweatshirt with a sign on the front that said: 'You think you have problems?' And on the back, 'Look at me!' I couldn't help but feel that this was Lynn's cry for help.

"Let's go downstairs to my meditation room. I have everything prepared."

As she started walking in front of me through the kitchen and then through the living room towards the staircase leading downstairs, a man appeared out of the blue, coming up from the sunken family room where he had been sitting by a large black baby grand piano.

He passed by us in the narrow passage by the wall behind the stairs leading down to the basement. As he was passing us, looking much like a stranger in a crowd, he almost brushed against my shoulder. Suddenly I felt as if a cold breeze had passed right through me and just one look into his dark brown eyes, sent shivers down my spine. Those eyes were the coldest and deadliest eyes I had ever looked into.

"I'll back in two hours," he said this in this low, matter-of-fact voice. "I'm taking the dog." he added, grabbing the collar of the dog that was following Lynn.

"Ok…" Lynn answered with a slight hesitation in her voice. The last thing I noticed was the dog trying to pull away from the man's grasp but was unsuccessful in freeing himself. In retaliation, this man tugged at his collar so forcefully that the dog, in response, made a low squeal, then stopped resisting.

As we walked downstairs I could not shake off this weird, cold feeling which became even stronger after noticing the rough treatment of the dog.

"That was my boyfriend," she felt obliged to explain, "he takes Buddy for walks every day after his music lessons. He teaches music…"she continued talking."He has students come to the house, but today I told him we needed peace and quiet. He moved today's lessons to after three." Lynn felt compelled to clarify this to me, for some reason.

Lynn led me through the wide open space of the main part of the basement, and to the left, where her small meditation room was located.

Following her closely I tried to figure out what was happening in my head.

I had two different voices inside my skull arguing in the weirdest way and I wasn't even a party to this argument.

One of these two voices would say: 'This is the deadest house, everything here is wrong. This house is a trap.' Then the other would argue. 'You must be crazy, there is the door to the garage.' As if in response to the second voice, I looked to the left where indeed there were three pairs of doors. One of them lead to the garage, the other two I learned shortly after were a laundry and a washroom door. The main part of the basement was covered in a rusty quite dingy shaggy-type of wall-to-wall carpet. There was no furniture that I noticed. There were two tiny windows placed so high that a person of average height would have to step on a stool to be able to look out.

What I could see were cement blocks laid by the side of the house leading to the back where the garage was located. There were metal bars in the two windows creating an impression of total entrapment.

As we entered the small, sparsely furnished and windowless room, a shelf filled with books of various sizes, and subjects from psychology to self-help books like 'Hands of Light', 'Spiritual Journey' and similar lined one of the walls. There was a small mattress on the floor and one chair, I assumed, prepared for today's session. As we entered the room one of the voices said: ‘This is the only safe room in this whole house! .’ The other voice would respond, ‘And how would you run from here?’

These unrelated and strange statements made no sense to me at the time. I understood everything all too clearly three months later.

“What do you think about my meditating room?”

“It is nice.” I gave her this laconic answer, afraid that she might probe for details. I couldn’t tell her about the strange conversations that were taking place in my head.

“I see that you are reading lots of book on spiritual healing, psychology and parapsychology?” I said, changing the subject.

“For years I have been trying to find out what is wrong with me. Five years of visits to psychologists have not helped me. When I saw what you did for my friend, I had to see you. I am glad that you could finally make it to Calgary.” She smiled at me. “Thank you for agreeing to see me.”

I wasn’t sure if she wanted to have an hypnosis or a reading, but for some reason deep down in my heart I prayed she would not ask for the reading. As we sat down, she on the mattress and I on the chair, facing each other, the door to the room was on my left. On the same side next to the door stood the tall book shelf filled with the books that I had made a note of right after walking in. At the top of the unit Lynn had some small porcelain figurines, one of them being a small statue of a Smiling Buddha.

“Let’s get started,” I suggested but not quite sure for the first time in my professional history, where to start.

“Tell me…is there anything there that you have to or need to know?”

I realized that as soon as this was said, my heart started to pound inside my chest as if wanting to get out and run. She took a very long time to answer, and stared intently into my eyes, as if trying to penetrate my mind to find out what I was so afraid of.

"No," came her truncated answer that made me sigh with relief. It was inconceivable to me why I was going through these ridiculous motions and why I felt so frightened that she just might request a reading before proceeding on to hypnosis. Never before had I ever felt this way with any of my clients except for one, which was long dead, but never forgotten.

"I will ask you one question after the session if this is OK with you?" she said.

"I suppose so..." Why I was so reticent and couldn't figure this out bothered me immensely. As I was battling my internal hesitancy a sudden loud thump made us both jump out of our skins. With my peripheral vision I caught something large flying from the shelves and landing on the floor with a loud and violent sound.

"Oh, my God what was that?" She looked at me with eyes wide open, then we both looked to the left noticing a large volume of the Webster Encyclopedia originally propped at the very top of the shelving unit, laying up against the wall, on the floor maybe three feet from the shelf unit. What struck me even more was that every small figurine that was placed in *front* of it was still in the very same place as they were when we came into the room. There must have been an incredible force that could lift at least 2 kilograms worth of hard bound book high enough to throw it to the floor that far from the shelf, and at the same time not touch anything that was placed directly in front of it.

It took awhile before we looked at each other and neither one of us was able to speak.

"Linda," I stumbled and blushed "I am sorry, Lynn." I corrected myself, "I don't know why I continue calling you Linda?" She shrugged her shoulders without saying a single word as if to say: "That's OK don't worry about it."

"Have you had any strange occurrences like this in this house before?"

"What do you mean? What strange occurrences?"

"Out of the ordinary, like lights going off and on, or the TV turning on or off by itself and such?"

"No," she said at first then she thought further about it, "Come to think of it, yes"

"We had some electrical problems a few weeks ago. The bulbs would burn out right after they were changed, lights would flicker and things like that. We called in an electrician, he checked the wiring and couldn't find anything wrong with the wiring."

"How long have you been living in this house?"

"About 8 months now."

"Do you own this house?"

"No, my boyfriend does. He said he needs a home for his two girls when they come every other weekend to stay with us."

As I listened to her words, I continued having this internal silly conversation, or rather argument, inside my head. The two voices that I started to hear after arriving at the house were presenting very opposing opinions for every word I heard. One would say 'She has no idea has she?' Then the other one would say, 'It doesn't make any difference who owns the house.'

"Do you need to go to the bathroom before we start?" I shook off this weird internal conversation.

"No, I am OK" she said.

"I think I need to go quickly."

"Go ahead. It is to the left. It's the middle door. The one on the right is the garage door and the one on the left is our laundry room." She explained in great detail where I would find the bathroom. This hit me as a bit strange but everything that day was nothing if not strange.

"I'll be right back," I said opening the door, stepping outside. Little did I know I was to be back faster that I would have imagined.

As soon as I left the room heading towards the middle door as she said, I felt an incredible oppressive heaviness clutching to me like a thick fog. The room seemed so much darker in spite of all the ceiling lights being on and the stream of daylight slipping inside through the small window at the far end of the basement.

I opened the second door as instructed and as I crossed the threshold of the little windowless room that was freezing cold, it felt as if all the air had been forced out of my lungs. It was so difficult to breath there so, even though it was against my better judgment I didn't close the door behind me. As I sat there, . I felt freezing cold hands grab both my both ankles and squeeze them in an iron grip. I had never done that before, but the fear by itself was enough for me to shorten my visit to the ladies room, though I wasn't finished. I literally ran from the bathroom. As I headed back to her meditation room, I felt as if there were a thousand demons following me.

My skin was covered with goose bumps and the hair at the back of my neck stood straight up. All this must have shown clearly on my face, because as soon I got back to the little room where Lynn was waiting for me, and anxiously closed the door behind me, she asked, “What’s wrong?”

“I am sorry but this house just feels so dead…” I blabbed before realizing how inappropriate my answer was.

“What do you mean?”

“I am sorry, I don’t know why I said that. Let’s get started, I have another appointment today on the North side of Calgary and I might hit rush hour traffic if I am too late.”

“Yes, I have a few things to do after as well.”

Lynn laid down on the mattress and covered herself with a warm blanket.

“Now, Lynn, close your eyes and start breathing…” We began the session with my regular routine of relaxing my client and instructing them how to breath properly and deeply to help them let go of the tension and stress. As I knew from our prior conversation what the most urgent issues were that we needed to review, I directed my client to regress to a time when she was a little baby. I asked her to go to exact time and place where the roots of her estranged relationship with her two-year older brother, began.

“Where are you?”

“I’m in my crib, “she said with a tiny voice indicating that she was emotionally in the time of her life she was describing. It was a voice of a very small child.

"Tell me more about what you see around you?"

"I can't see too much, it is dark. The door to the room is closed."

"How old are you?"

"I am eight months old. I'm lying in my crib. I feel wet…my diaper is heavy and it burns my bottom."

"Are you crying to attract attention, so someone can come and change you?"

"No…"

"What is the reason?"

"I am afraid, I don't want anybody to be angry at me…" she whispered and I sensed great anxiety in her tiny voice.

"Take me forward in time and tell me what is happening next."

"I hear the door open and I see light from the other room coming in."

"Who is there, look carefully and tell who you see." I directed her gently.

"It's my brother and my mother. She is holding him by the hand…"

"How old is your brother?"

"He is two years older than me." As my client was saying this I noticed her countenance change as if she was ready to cry.

"Please continue."

"My mother has a pillow under her arm…"

"Why does she carry a pillow?"

"They are coming close to my crib, my mother is handing the pillow to my brother and is lifting him off the floor and putting him in my crib…She has never done that before…"

I see fear twisting my client's features.

"What is happening?"

"My brother puts the pillow over my face…oh my God, I can't breath he is pressing the pillow hard to my face…Lynn begins to thrash around and her breath becomes labored and punctuated as she relives the scene. Her face grows dark red and I can see the physical symptoms of one being suffocated…" Then suddenly she stops thrashing around and takes a few deep breaths like a person who has just emerged to the surface of water after being under way too long.

"Lynn, tell me what is happening now?"

"It stopped. My mother is pulling my brother from the crib and he is still holding the pillow in his hands."

"Tell me what is your mother doing?"

"She is very, very angry…but…" her voice breaks and I see shock mixed with disbelief spreading all over her face.

"Oh, my God, she is not angry at my brother for what he was doing in trying to suffocate me…She is mad because he was so lousy in doing it!" By now I see my client is really crying.

"She hates me so much that she wants me dead! She has hated me from the day I was born. Why…?"

"We will go back further in time to find out… Take a few deep breaths and relax, , , just let go. Breath and go deeper." As my instructions flowed I see Lynn responding and become very still. Her face grows serene and her breath even and deep." As I count from 5-1 you will move back even further in time, even further and search for the lifetime that can show you the reason for your mother's hostility towards you. You are moving towards the time when this volatile relationship between you two began."

"Yes, I found it," she finally tells me.

"Who are you?"

"I am a young Catholic priest."

"What year it is?"

"1859." She gave me a very fast and decisive answer.

"Where are you located?"

"Boston." Another amazing response.

"Where are you right now?"

"I am in Church."

"What are you doing there?"

"I came to take confessions from my parishioners. I am sitting inside the confessional."

"Who is there on the other side to confess?"

"A young woman. She comes very often, more often than needed."

"Are you going to tell her that?"

"Yes I must tell her. She is disturbing me…"

"How can she disturb you?"

"She is a good looking, virile woman. I might be a priest but I am still a man…"

"Then what happens next?"

"I am listening to her confession."

"Tell me what is she confessing?"

"She tells me that she is in love with me and that she can no longer fight her temptations. She disgusts me. Doesn't she know how hard it is to be in presence of the flesh and deny yourself from all that Satan brings to torment me?"

"Are you blaming her for your weakness of the mind and inability to resist?" Isn't that what you are supposed to forgive of those who come to confess?"

"She is trying to clear her conscience at my cost, so she can go home with a light heart and her dark secret off her shoulders, when I have to fight with it with all my might…!"

"What is she saying?"

"She asked me to forgive her the sin of lustful thoughts. She must be punished."

"How are you going to punish her?"

"I am going to mention her name during my Sunday sermon and warn all the unaware men about the devil that lives in their neighborhood."

"What is happening next?"

"I am storming out of this confessional and grab her by the hair. I am pulling her away from the confessional. I push her down to her knees. I am ordering her to repent and pay for her sin of the flesh…"

"She has not done anything, , she just expressed how she felt, did she make any attempt to act on her feelings?"

"No, but it's not good enough."

"What is it that you do next?"

"I tell her how disgusting she is, how worthless. And I tell her God will never forgive her. All she can do is cry and cower like a slime…" An expression of disgust and repugnance pours over my client's face.

"I want you to see now how the negativity and hostility between you and your mother started. Can you see it? You condemned her for being honest and open, for something she barely felt and never acted on. Can you see how the same soul reborn in your mother returned the same hostile and hateful feelings towards you, an innocent, defenseless baby?"

"Yes, yes I see it now. It was all wrong. I started it. I was not a good man and even worse priest. I was to be about love and forgiveness, yet I chose to condemn this woman for my own weakness of the flesh. I am so sorry. I am so sorry."

"It is Ok. That is the reason why we all return to repair the damage we have done to others, sometimes it comes with lessons we need to learn and sometimes we need to feel the pain we have caused. But it is never God that punishes us. It is ourselves. Can you let go of the old and unwieldy feelings? Can you forgive your mother and brother for what they have done to you in your present life as Lynn?"

"Yes, I can." She whispered this and a few tears again found their way to freedom.

It could explain all the dynamics that governed Lynn's life and her pathological relationships. Her close attachment to a father who was so painfully ripped apart from her when her father was stricken with cancer and dead in 8 months. Proper grieving never occurred and this was the very trigger that pushed her into a depression that would plague her for most of her life. Lynn never developed a close attachment to her mother and was always afraid of her older brother, even though the man again and again throughout the course of their adult life tried to get closer to his sister. She would never allow that, as she never, until now, understood the real reason for her fear.

There, was another nagging thought that was on Lynn's mind. It was Lynn's tumultuous

1 1/2 years old relationship with her boyfriend whom I met briefly walking through their house. Eight months of the eighteen that they knew each other was spent in the house. Later on I found out that Lynn had tried to break up the relationship and stopped seeing him for a time. During that period, he would stalk her and frequently be spotted sitting in his car, watching the house she lived in at the time. Somehow he managed to talk her into getting back together with him. And this was the disquieting reason I wanted to know why.

"I want to do one more thing before bringing you back to the present…"I started "If there was a lifetime in which you knew your present boyfriend I want you to go and find it now. I will count…"

"No!" She interrupted me with a firm and stern response to my request. "No, I never knew him!" she added, which was very strange and left me a little unsettled, yet very relieved.

After that I went through the positive programming I always do with every client, then brought her out of the hypnosis. She sat down on her mattress, and a big smile shone across her face.

"I feel so different, light and peaceful." she said, "I don't remember ever feeling so good inside. Thank you, thank you so much."

As I was still sitting on the chair, she leaned forward and took my hand in both of hers.

"You make me feel so light and safe."

"What do you mean — safe?" I couldn't help but ask this question.

"I don't know, this is how I feel." She shrugged her shoulders and got up. "When can I see you again?"

I am going to meet my publisher in Ottawa. I will be gone for 8 days, so do you want to set an appointment in two weeks?"

"Can I see you the next day after your return?" There was a hidden urgency in her request but I decided not to ask the reasons.

"Sure," I agreed and made a note in my calendar.

"You are doing such a fantastic job, the way you work is so different from any psychiatrist or psychologist I have ever seen…and I have seen a few over last five years. I have never felt so good after seeing any of them as I feel today…" Her blue eyes appeared brighter and filled with an incredible peace that radiated from her entire being.

"Maybe when I get better and stronger you could teach me your ways of healing?" she asked shyly.

"Absolutely, they say, 'pass it forward.' If you are willing to learn then I am willing to teach." I answered.

She walked me out to her door and took my hand again when I put on my boots and stood in the open doorway.

She held my hand so tightly that it was almost awkward for me to pull away.

"I can't wait to see you in nine days. I will call you to confirm our appointment. I don't understand why you make me feel so safe!" She said it again and as she let go of my hand, I felt prickly pangs of fear rush from the top of my head to my feet and stayed there until I got to my car. As I drove off I still tried to shake off the strange feeling that lingered for another 15 minutes before it finally released me from its hold.

The eight days I spent in Ottawa, I went to see my publisher whom I had never met from the time we worked on editing my first book. How I got my ticket to be able to do that is another interesting story that proves how the power of mind and guts to ask for what you want can bring about incredible results. The event that made it possible for me to travel to the other side of Canada to meet one of the most incredible and wonderful human beings that I was given the honor and privilege to know, took place in late February 1997, the year my first novel was published by an Ottawa private publishing house. I had a reading set up with a woman who was referred to me by another client who had seen me a few times in the past. She was a nice Polish lady who lived in an upscale part of Calgary with her husband whom I hadn't had the pleasure to meet. I got there around 10 AM on a nice summer day. The reading took longer than an hour, which is not unusual for me. By the time we were done, my client was extremely happy with the outcome of the reading, it was almost 12 PM. She asked me if I had another appointment I needed to get to right away. I told her that my next three appointments were between 5 and 7 PM that day at my home. She asked me if I would like to have lunch with her. I accepted her nice invitation, and as we sat down by the table to eat, she asked me out of the blue, "What was my deepest wish?"

Surprised at her question I said that my deepest wish was to be able to fly to Ottawa to meet my publisher so I can give him the biggest hug and thank him for what he has done for me.

"When are you going?" was her next question.

"Well..., as soon as my finances will allow me to buy a ticket and pay for the hotel."

“So when are you going?” she asked again almost as if she did not hear what I just said.

“Well…” I stumbled over my words “like I said, when I can afford the ticket.”

“You have the ticket…when are you going?”

“What do you mean I have the ticket?”

“I am going to give you the ticket and a 50% discount for your hotel.” It was then that she proceeded to tell me that she owned a travel agency and that she was giving me the ticket to Ottawa. I could not believe my ears.

“You are serious?”

“Absolutely. Give me the date and I will issue your plane ticket and a voucher for the discount for the hotel. We work with a number of hotels across Canada that we have special deals with. I think one of the better ones is Novotel hotel. I’ve stayed there and I would recommend it to anybody.

“It is Novotel then and the time I can be off from my work is the end of March next year.”

“OK, I will get your reservation in place, then we can get together for lunch and you can pick it up.”

This was exactly what had happened and I will never forget the feeling of gratitude that flooded me and did not leave for a very long time. Even today when I think about it I see it as proof of positive thinking and LA (Law of Attraction) dare to dream and you should receive what you desire. I have to make sure that I think about it more often and use it in my life more frequently than I have been.

I had a wonderful trip to Ottawa and met the man who changed my life. At the time I had the privilege to meet Robert he was 87 years old. He was a tall, distinct gentleman with bright, clear blue eyes and a straight posture. The moment he walked into the hotel lobby, even though I had never seen him before, I knew it was him. The only difference between the real man and the picture in my mind, was his weight. I saw Robert with the 90 pounds he lost within the last year due to the stress caused by taking care full time of his wife of 47 years. For the last thirty years of their marriage and shortly after they had their second son she had been diagnosed with Huntington Cholera. She became totally unable to take care of herself and her condition deteriorated steadily until it got to the point that Robert was no longer able to take care of her by himself. She finally was approved to be placed in a facility with 24 hour medical care.

We had the most wonderful 8 days and I will treasure them forever. Robert would pick me up from the hotel and we would go to a nice quiet restaurant or cafe and sit for hours talking. It was during these long conversations that he said things that meant the world to me. The first evening when we were having dinner in a nice, classy but small and private restaurant he said:

"You can't even imagine how nice it is to talk to someone knowing that they not only understand what you are saying, but respond to you. I am not talking about every day conversations like talking much about nothing, but about what sits deeply within a person. We have been here for four hours yet I don't want to stop talking. I am almost afraid that this is the last time it'll be possible. It feels so good just to talk and know you are not talking to yourself.

"You have such a different and wonderful way of expressing…your words can say so much more than any other person I have known. You can reach deep into someone's psyche and even deeper into their soul, yet I have not felt threatened by you walking *into* my soul, when even my wife of many years never could."

"Robert…" I said putting my hand over his, "you will never know how much what you did for me changed my life and how much it means to me. Publishing my book was a dream I have had since I was 9 years old and you made it happen for me…" I felt the tears coming.

"I haven't done anything. It was your talent and your work that did all that, and I was privileged to see that!"

This answer made me swallow my tears, I was too moved to say anything for a while. I could not fathom the depth of this man, his humbleness that neither the 2 World Wars he fought in nor people could manage to change or destroy.

Twenty years have passed since my first novel was published and these words replay in my head, I spent 7 days in the presence of this man and it felt as if we had known each other for hundreds of years. I never met Robert again, but we spoke on the phone ever so often. During one of these telephone conversations he told me that he had read my book six times since it was published and that every time he did, he found something new, something he missed during his previous readings and he said something else that I keep very dear for all the years that have since then passed. He said that my writing would make him cry and laugh every time he re-read my book and that his heart was forever changed. For the first time he saw Native people of North America the way he had never seen them before. He saw them as fellow human beings and felt ashamed for what was done to them by the race we both represented. He said that I showed him in my book all the reasons and true depth of their pain and the extent of the destruction done to their spirits that still echoes today.

I remember the night I knew Robert left this world. That night I had a dream that I was in my house when somebody knocked on my front door. I went to open it and saw Robert standing in front of me. He wore a black formal suit, white shirt and multicolored silk tie. His face was serious and solemn.

"Oh my God, Robert how good to see you. You look good." I smiled at him and gave him a hug, then he moved me away, placed his both hands on my shoulders and looked deep into my eyes.

"I have come to say good-bye and ask you to never stop what you doing, it will only get better." Then he turned and started to walk away from me. He then vanished, leaving me dumbfounded and stunned.

"Robert, Robert don't go!" I shouted after him and with these words I woke up abruptly. I sat on the bed, wide awake and felt my heart grow heavy with sadness. I knew he was gone forever and that had I lost a very special friend, someone who changed my life and the way I felt about myself. I tried to call him many times since then but his phone was no longer in service

## Lynn's Case Continued

I flew back from Ottawa the evening of March 16 and had a message from Lynn left on my answering machine. The message was left on the day of my return. She sounded very tense and anxious to see me, as soon as I would be able to, I called her right away but a male voice answered the call.

"Hi, may I speak with Lynn?" I asked.

"Sorry, she is not at home right now." the man's voice was cold and unfriendly. "May I ask who is calling?"

"Ula." I said without providing any further information. "Could you please ask her to call me when she gets back?"

"I will, bye" The man hung up the phone rather abruptly and rudely." I waited three hours but Lynn didn't call me back, so I decided to call again hoping that this time she would pick up the phone. After the second ring my client answered.

"Hi Lynn… Thank God you are back. An hour later and it would be too late to call you."

"I was home all day, I didn't go anywhere. I didn't hear the phone ringing…" She was noticeably surprised.

"I called three hours ago, I think I spoke with your boyfriend. He was to pass my message to you." As I was saying this, the disquieting impression that there was someone else listening to our conversation washed over me like a cold wave.

"He never told me you called…"Her voice sounded visibly shaken. I detected a slight note of anger in her words.

"Don't worry about it, Linda." I tried to change the subject and again I slipped calling her by the wrong name.

"I am sorry I keep calling you Linda…"

"That's OK," she brushed it aside "I want to see you as soon as I can." She sounded tense and nervous. "I have some questions I have to ask you, I do not want a reading…but"

"No problem, how is your day tomorrow?"

"It is good, what time can we start?"

She was real anxious to set up our appointment.

"How about 10 AM?" I suggested.

"Great, I will see you tomorrow then." There was a slight audible click on the line before she hung up the phone. Something made my skin crawl. I could not shake this weird feeling long after our conversation was over.

"Supper is almost ready." My sister came into the room as I hung up the phone.

"Were you on the other phone?"

"When?"

"Just now."

"No, I was in the kitchen getting our dinner ready," she answered, and then I knew who was listening to our conversation.

I left home by 9 AM knowing that Lynn's place was on the opposite site of the city and I needed a good 40-45 minutes to get there.

What really told me something was amiss was that for the second time I missed her house twice and was forced to turn around. This was more than strange that knowing her address I missed the house both times, as if something was trying to keep me away from getting there.

She was waiting by the door like a little puppy waiting for its master to return home.

"Hi Linda, sorry I'm 15 minutes late but I missed your house again."

I apologized without even noticing that I called her by the wrong name again. This time it appeared that she did not notice my slip up. She looked stressed and pale. There were dark circles underneath her eyes as if she had not been sleeping well.

"I was worried you wouldn't show up."

"Why would you think that?"

I did not see the dog so I assumed my client's boyfriend took it for a walk.

"Let's go downstairs." Lynn led me down to her little meditation room. As we walked downstairs she started to talk.

"You know right after last session I got this terrible headache as soon as you drove off. Right here..." she pointed her finger at the back of her head right behind her ear. It never stopped and I still have it today. All 8 days you were away I hardly slept because of it."

I stopped and looked at her.

"We will find the reason for it and we'll make it go away. I promise."

She didn't say anything, just nodded her head.

I sensed that my client was tense and subdued and that she was very glad I was there.

"Before we start can I ask you one question?" she asked me timidly.

"Go ahead..." I said but deep down I knew what the question was all about. I wasn't sure if I was too anxious to hear her question and quite apprehensive about giving her an honest and straight-forward answer.

"What do you think about my boyfriend?"

I wasn't sure but I had the impression that she wasn't sure if she was ready to hear the answer.

It took me a long moment to answer her question. I stared right into her eyes.

"I know that you know..." I took a deep breath before continuing, "that you are in the wrong relationship. It is up to you how quickly you can get out of it."

"But please whatever you decide to do, just do it and tell no one what you are doing! ! !" I felt that I needed to repeat this message to her as it was the only thing I could tell this woman so she could have enough knowledge and awareness to save herself. This was as much as my internal guidance would allow me to say. Never in my wildest dreams did I realize how much dire warning was locked into my last words. And the reality was that I wanted to be out this house as soon as possible.

"I will..." My client finally blinked, then looked down at the floor. There was an uncomfortable moment of silence lingering in the air.

"Let's start our session." I finally broke the silence trying to lighten the heavy atmosphere hanging in the room,"Let's kick this headache out and get you on the way to feeling better...it's high time." I faked a smile and she bought it.

"Let's", she said lying down and covering herself with a colorful fleece blanket.

As soon as I felt Lynn had gone deep enough, we again began our journey into the past.

"I'll count from 10 down to one and with every number you will begin to move back in time as far as you need to, to find the reason and root cause for this severe headache," I counseled her gently then began to count backwards. I could sense that she was going back. At one point her closed eyes shifted and it was evident to see them darting around.

"Who are you?"

"I am me," she answered.

"Can you give me the date?"

"Sept 14, 1993…" her answer was immediate and very precise. I was surprised that she was taking us back in time barely 7 months prior to the session.

"And where are you?"

"We are in Fish creek Park." This is a Provincial recreation area south of Calgary.

"Who is "We"?"

"Me and my boyfriend. A month ago we moved into this house…"she was giving me more information than I was asking her for.

"What are you doing there?"

"Ian, my boyfriend, asked me to come with him for a walk."

"What time is it?"

"It is about noon. It's a very nice, sunny day. The trees in the park have already changed their colors to yellow and red. It is very pretty here, lots of leaves on the grass and pathways. Oh, it hurts!" Both of her hands flew to the left side of her head. Pressing against her skull right behind her left ear.

"Tell me what were you doing when the pain came?"

"I was standing and staring at the creek."

"Where is your boyfriend? Is he there with you?"

"No, we had an argument so I walked away leaving him behind."

"Where is he now? Turn and see where Ian is," I instructed her.

"Oh, my God!" She gasped," It's him.He threw a large stone and hit me right behind my ear!"

"What is his explanation for doing this?"

"He is laughing!" There was pain and disgust in Lynn's voice as she continued describing this to me. "He is laughing and saying he didn't know that he had such great aim. He is telling me that he really didn't think he could throw a rock that far. He is pleased with himself..."The tone of distress and sorrow deepened in my client's voice. "It's a joke to him, to hurt me like this. It is a joke to him..."

"Lynn, I want you take a deep breath in and calm down. As the air enters your lungs I want you to feel peace and tranquility entering your mind and the pain going away. When you exhale, all the emotions you are feeling right now will leave your body and mind. Everything negative will be extracted from your body. When you take another deep breath there will be a beautiful wave of peace and calmness filling your entire being. You will relax more and go deeper into the center of yourself where you are going to be safe and nothing negative can touch or effect you in any way, shape or form."

The changes on my client's face were tell-tale signs that my suggestions were working. Her body relaxed and her face became serene. Slight indentations showed in the corners of her mouth as a soft gentle smile crossed her face.

"Continue breathing gently and normally." I gave further instructions trying to get her into an even deeper state.

"How are you feeling now?"

"The pain is gone…I feel good now…Thank you."

"Lynn, I would like you to let go of the past so it will no longer have a hold on you. That is necessary for your healing to occur and allow your life to shift in a better direction.It is sometimes karmic connections that we need to release in order to set ourselves free."

I was coaching her in an attempt to embrace the reason for what we were to do next. I knew that there was a Karmic hook between her and Ian and she needed to clear it in order to set herself free from what tangled their lives in the unhealthy, pathological knot that was squeezing the joy, optimism, and happiness out of her body and life.

"If there was another life that connected you and Ian in the past, I want you to go and find it now."

My client became still and her face immediately drawn.

"No!"

Her voice came slow and filled with cool determination that told me right away that she would not want to go anywhere, and even her subconscious was dead set in preventing this regression to her past from happening. I have never had a client do that. I realized that both on a conscious and also subconscious level she was aware that there *was* a past connection but for some reason refused to go and see what it was. I knew then that there was something she was meant to embrace and accept into her life, and that awareness and realization was both new and illuminating.

The rest of the session was spent on positive programming and re-framing. This was all I could do for my client. I couldn't help her to lead her life back in the right direction. When I brought her back from under the hypnosis, she sat on the bed and her face was bright and peaceful. Her headache was gone.

"I feel so good," she commented. She drew closer and took my hand from my lap.

"I don't know how to thank you. You have lifted such a dark cloud from me, that I have felt for so very long."

"I am glad that I could help," I responded, but it was only my voice saying this. My heart felt heavy and sad.

"When are you leaving up North?"

"Tomorrow morning. If you would like to see me again let me know, though I really think we did all we could. You will not need to see me again. Now you'll have to continue your healing by yourself. I think you are good to do that?"

"I think I am." She smiled and squeezed my hand. "You are such a wonderful person. You have an incredible power to bring people to you…could you teach me how to do that? I would like to be able to do what you do."

"If you want to learn I am willing to teach you what can be taught."

"Let me know when will be the next time you're coming down to Calgary. I would like to set a time for our first lesson. I will pay you…I can't expect you doing it without charge. I took many other courses and not one proved able to help anybody. You would not believe how many therapists I have seen over the years, but not even once have I felt like I feel today."

"I am happy that I could do something to elevate the load you've carried for so many years." As we continued our conversation I began to feel somewhat uneasy and restless. I wanted to leave as fast as I could. I just wanted to go.

Lynn walked me to the front door and again the same way as on our first visit she held my hand in hers tighter than she should. I felt a desperate urgency vibrating from her hands and lodging into my consciousness like prickly needles.

"I don't want to let you go. You make me feel so good and safe." As she said this I felt a powerful shiver run through my body like an electric shock.

"Are you cold?" she asked with concern.

"A little bit. I need to grab some lunch, I haven't had anything to eat this morning," I lied.

"I could prepare something for you."

"It's nice of you, but I have another appointment in an hour so I need to get going. I will grab something on the way." Another convenient lie, because I couldn't imagine staying in that house for another minute. I just wanted to get in my car and get away from there as far as I could.

"That's too bad, I would love to talk to you for a bit longer, but maybe on your next visit when I take my first lesson we will have plenty of time for that," she smiled, finally releasing my hand.

"For sure." It was all I said and I started walking away towards my car. Half way there I stopped and turned around.

"Lynn… remember to do what you need to do and do not talk about what you are going to do to *anybody*… just do it."

She looked at me surprised but didn't respond. All she said was, "Have a safe trip back home." After she closed the door, I sat in my car and tried to rationalize my rather rude and strange behavior. Even being out of the house and in the sanctuary of the car didn't wash off the funny and creepy feeling I had both times when I was inside this unassuming suburban home.

I didn't have any other appointments that day, so on my way home to my friend's house where I was staying the night, I stopped to grab a quick lunch. I sat for a while in a little coffee place. After I finished eating I replayed in my mind everything that had happened that day. I felt somewhat sad and depressed. It felt to me as if I was grieving over something but couldn't figure out what it was. I couldn't think of any reason in my own life which would make me feel this way. I should mention, incidentally, that the place I was staying another night, was home of my client whom I had known for a few years and who had referred Lynn to me. She was Lynn's best friend, Brenda.

Brenda was a hairdresser who converted one of the rooms in her house to be her hair salon. That day she was finished with all her appointments, so when I came in she was glad to see me.

"How did it go?" she asked, taking my coat to hang in the closet.

"It went well…" I said but there was no conviction in my voice to support my answer.

"Something wrong?"

"Have you met Lynn's boyfriend Ian?" I asked, instead of answering her question.

"Yes, but I really don't like him. There is something about this guy that's creepy, even Doug (Doug was Brenda's live-in boyfriend ) can't stand him. Have you met him?"

"I only passed him in the house for maybe 5 seconds when we had her first session and he gave me the biggest goosebumps

I've ever experienced. This man has the deadest and coldest eyes, when he looked at me it was as if he was not even inside…"

"Join the club. I told Lynn that she should break up with this guy and be done. He managed to drag her back into the relationship she terminated after a month of barely knowing him. But he kept stalking her and begging for her to come back. I couldn't believe that she gave into him like that. She doesn't even love the guy. She likes his daughters, you know about that, don't you? They stay with them every second weekend. Nice girls, 9 and 13. They both come here for their haircuts."

"Where is their mother?"

"She lives not too far from the school they go to. I never met their mother but I heard from Lynn that she is a nurse and appears to be quite a nice lady."

"I have to ask you about something funny,"

"Sure, go ahead," she encouraged me.

"From day one I continue calling her Linda. It was embarrassing but I couldn't control this strange urge to continue using the name Linda." As I was finishing this sentence I noticed a broad expression of amusement spreading over Brenda's face.

"Isn't this strange?" I assumed that she found this as peculiar and almost comical as I did, but as I would find out in a moment the whole story was even funnier.

"You are kidding me." She started,"You must have known on some level that Lynn"s real name was actually and correctly Linda. Five years ago she legally changed her name to Lynn. Since she was a child she hated her name, so she decided to change it…I guess you can never change your name?" She raised her brows at me.

"Not energetically." I explained. "I guess I was tapping into her energy fields, knowing that her name was really Linda." I myself was quite amazed with the way this proved to me once more that I must always trust my internal guidance. Once before I had a very similar situation back in the St. Paul area where I used to live for a few years. I had a client from Bonnyville come to see me. Right from the start I knew she was married and to boot she was happily married, yet through the entire reading I kept seeing the initial D of the first name of the man that I knew she was supposed to be with. I told her that the man she is supposed to be with has the initial D in his first name. She was surprised and a bit disturbed by my statement.

"My husband's name is Larry and we are happy…"

"I know that and I don't see you ever divorcing or having another partner yet I keep seeing it as clear as the hand in front of my face. That the initial of the man you are to be with is D like Douglas."

She looked at me without responding to what I said, visibly disturbed.

"I am sorry, I don't understand why this just sticks in my mind. I keep seeing the ID in front of me that has a name starting with letter D. I am pretty sure it says Douglas.

But please don't let it bother you, sometimes I might be receiving somebody else's information. Or I may be wrong…" I dropped the subject and made a real hard attempt not to bring it up again to the end of the reading.

Two days later I received a phone call from my client and right from her tone I sensed that she was excited.

"Hi Glenda, what is happening?"

"I can't believe what just happened today..." Her voice was shaking, her voice giddy.

"Do you remember during our reading when you kept repeating that I should be with a man who has the initial D in his first name, not L like my husband?"

"Sure, I remember. I felt like a moron repeating the same statement over and over again like a broken record."

"My God, you were right!" After she said this, there was a prolonged moment of silence on the phone. I held my breath because I was surprised and didn't know what to say.

"This morning my husband asked me to go to Staples to fax his driving license that he needed to provide to his new employer. He was hired by an oil company to work on an oil field close to Rainbow Lake in Northern Alberta. He was busy getting things wrapped up in his present job and couldn't do it himself. I took his driving license and was standing in line waiting for the next clerk to help me fax it. To kill some time I started to read his DL and what I saw just blew me away. The man to whom I have been married to for almost 21 years and have always known him as Larry, well his real name is Douglas L."

"I asked my husband after I returned home, why he is using the name Larry rather than his real name Douglas?"

"He said that he never liked the name Douglas and all his life preferred using his middle name which he got from his favorite uncle Larry. You were right when you said that I was supposed to be married to a man with initial D not L. How did you know that?"

"I told you I kept seeing the ID with name Douglas on it." We had a good laugh after that.

"I knew you weren't going to get divorced and that you were in the right relationship, that's why I was so puzzled with what I saw!"

"I have lived with my husband for such a long time and never knew his real name was Douglas. I can only say that you are really good at what you do."

"Thanks Glenda. That is a great compliment."

It was about 11 AM on a beautiful Monday morning in May 1997, two months after I concluded the second and the final session with Lynn. During the two months she called me once and said that she had stopped seeing her psychologist and she felt better than ever in her entire life. She thanked me for helping her and said that after the summer she would like to take a course with me to have herself trained in the field of hypnotherapy. She was quite anxious to learn as much as she could about the subject and become able to help people the way I did. I told her to call me whenever she was ready and then I would let her know when was my next visit to Calgary was going to take place. Then we could schedule our first lesson during that time. She even offered that I could stay in her home when in Calgary. Without understanding why, I felt a cold shiver running though my body(again) when she presented her offer. I could not picture myself ever going to her house again. My plan was to have her come to my friends house in Calgary where I usually stayed during my visits to the city.

I thanked her for the offer and we hung up the phone. This was the last time I spoke with her until the fateful day when my client Brenda rang my home in May, a beautiful sunny day which in the blink of an eye became the darkest day in my entire career.

"Ula..." Brenda's voice was low and careful, and she sounded very distressed. "Have you seen the news?"

"No, what news?" I answered, a little surprised at her question. I thought she knew that I never watch the news. I found out a long time ago that there was never good news so I decided to make my own news rather than watch the depressing and often disheartening news that the media wallows in. There was never anything good happening: price hikes, armed conflicts, somebody bludgeoned to death, earthquakes in one city, floods or drought in another, political turmoil, murders and more. No, it was definitely not what I wanted to hear as a regular diet.

"Oh my God, then you did not hear..."

"Heard what?" I began to feel agitated and my hands started to shake a little.

"That Lynn is dead..." her voice died and all I could hear was her sobbing.

"What are you talking about?" My mind had totally rejected the words that I had just heard.

"How could she be dead? I saw her two months ago and she just called me two weeks ago. She was feeling great and was very happy."

"Ula...he killed her! He murdered her and murdered his two girls too."

"What are you talking about?" I stammered again. I felt that all the air was knocked out of my lungs and I found breathing almost impossible. I pulled up a chair and sat down. I felt dizzy and nauseous.

"Ula are you OK? I'm sorry, I thought you'd heard?"

"When did this happen?" I could hardly speak.

"Friday… around 1 PM." That is what they said on the news. He killed her then went to school and took the girls even though it was not their weekend to stay in his house. The girls fought and did not want to go with him, but he shoved them into his car. He grabbed them at 3:15 PM after school was finished. Other students saw the girls crying when he was pushing them into the car.

"Lynn left a message on my answering machine at 2 PM. She said that she was leaving him and she was going to stay with me for a few weeks until she could find an apartment. At the end of the message she said that if she wasn't at my place by 4 PM he would have done something to her." It was hard for my client to talk but it was even harder for me to hear this terrible news. I developed a sharp pain behind my left ear. It felt like a long nail was stuck in my skull, crushing my brain. I tried to calm my shallow breathing and gather my scattered thoughts. As she talked to me, vivid and chaotic pictures were flashing in my head. They would manifest, zoom in and then suddenly zoom out, vanish, only to be replaced with other even more sickening images. I knew before Brenda told me how she had died. I knew her head was damaged and I finally understood the headache she felt for the 8 days after I conducted that first session with her. She had foreseen her own death and that was the reason she refused to retrieve a past that connected her to this man she barely had known a year in this life.

One flashback that still haunts me is an image of Ian[1] standing in a cashiers line in a well known department store in Southwest Calgary. I could hear his thoughts and feel his burning hatred and the anger he was filled with. Here is what he was thinking: "They will never know I bought it here and for what reason. Many people buy tools at Canadian Tire every day. I am just one of them!"

"Ula, are you coming to Calgary soon?" my clients voice brought me back to the phone call.

"I was planning to go in the middle of May." I took a deep breath.

"Could you stay with me this time?" she asked. "I need to talk about this. I can't sleep since I heard about this."

"Of course, I can stay with you."

"Please take it easy, there was nothing more you could do to help her…"

"Maybe you are wrong." I felt terrible.

"Last Thursday she came for her color and we talked about the sessions. She was really happy. I have not seen her in such a good spirits as long as I have known her. She called her psychologist that she's seen for the past five years and canceled her appointment. She told him that he should contact you and start using your methods rather than what he was doing, since they were much more effective and helpful."

"She said she was going to study with you and learn hypnosis and your ways of healing…"

"I know, she told me that too."

1 **Calgary Herald Archives.** February, 1998. Math tutor Ian Gordon used an axe to murder his daughters, ages 14 and nine, and his girlfriend Lin Kreis inside a Calgary home on Bonaventure Drive S.E.

"She asked me if I knew what you meant by saying that she should do things she needed to do and not talk to anyone about what she was planning to do."

"She did not listen did she?" I said this with more rancor than I wanted.

"She said she was going to tell him that weekend that they were finished and that she was moving out."

"This is exactly what I told her not to do!" my voiced trailed off. I wiped my wet cheeks with the back of my hand.

"Police found her in the laundry room in the basement, the back of the left side of her skull was cracked with an axe..." Every word felt like a blow to my head. She had her bag with personal things next to her body. She was on her way to the garage to get her car when he attacked her.

"How do you know all these details?" I asked, surprised at how much she knew.

"I was interviewed by the detectives when they came to collect the tape from my answering machine. They knew we had been friends for years, and they found my info on her phone and private notes."

"Who called the Police?"

"He did. After he killed his two daughters he cut himself and said that they were attacked in their home and the two men who did this fled leaving him to die. When the Police inspected his wounds they knew he was lying. All his cuts were superficial and hardly nicked his skin. The detective told me that the crime scene was so gruesome that police were throwing up and they had to call a special unit in from Edmonton to process the house. He told me that the blood was everywhere. Lynn's skull was split behind her left ear, but he had swung the axe many more times after she was dead. His younger daughter, the 9 year old, had her head taken from her shoulders from behind. She didn't know what had happened, but his 13 year old fought for her life terribly. She ran upstairs and he killed her in the bedroom upstairs. The autopsy found sky high adrenaline levels in this poor girl."

"He was arrested and will remain in jail without bail until his trial. I will have to be a witness and I am so scared... I need your help to prepare me for the time I will have to face this monster..."

"I will help you to be ready, I promise."

"Thank you." She said."Let me know when you are going to come to Calgary. Take care...don't blame yourself." She hung up the phone.

I sat motionless by the kitchen table and didn't move for three hours. I felt so cold inside and so empty. If I ever had an idea what the word 'failure' "meant it was that day. I cried until my daughter came from school. When she asked me Mummy what's wrong I could not answer." I just hugged her and kept her in my arms for a long while. She was my life raft and holding her made me feel safe.

I must say that it was my ex husband who helped me through this crisis. He said this to me many times until I finally understood.

"If God meant for you to save her, then he would have helped you to do that. Some people have their destiny and karma to repay and there is nothing that anybody can do to change that. You have saved many people from accidents and illnesses and such. You were not to save Lynn's life and on a subconscious level she knew that and accepted her payment. As unfair as that sounds."

These words really helped me to stop blaming myself for what had happened and feeling like a failure.

Now listen to this: The final event that set me free from the burden of guilt was Lynn herself. Two weeks after her death her spirit showed itself to me during my stay with Linda. I was sitting alone one day in her backyard basking in the nice warm early Spring sunshine while Linda was working in her home based salon.

I sensed her before I could see her, as what normally happens to me. She stood perhaps 5 feet away and close to the back patio door.

"I am sorry to disturb you." I became aware of what she was trying to tell me."I came to tell you that I do not blame you for my death. I knew I had to accept what I needed to set straight. All I want to ask you, is what we did together enough to set me free?"

"Yes, Linda it is." I used her real name for very important reason. It was for her to really understand and embrace who she really was and take that with her to the spirit land.

"You are free. Don't look back, just go to the light." I said it out loud knowing that it would be the last time I would ever see her spirit. I knew she was ready to be freed. Yet, I understood that on some level she knew she had to settle her karmic debt in order to clear her past entanglements and set herself free. I wondered if she knew what had happened to her two step daughters. Decided that if she did not then it would be easier for her to leave this plane and not to be pulled back by that sense of guilt. Either way I knew she would meet the girls in a better place.

## Court Case

As I promised Brenda I stayed with her on my next trip to Calgary. She was still very shaken by the loss of her friend and very nervous at the prospect of having to be a witness in a murder trial. She dreaded the day she would have to stand on the witness stand to testify and be forced to face the man who butchered her best friend and his own two daughters

"You do not look too well." I said after she let me inside the house and took one of my travel bags.

"I don't feel too well..."She responded. "I don't sleep well. That is why I need your help."

"I am here, we will try to make you feel better and stronger." She smiled at me and closed the door.

Since it was barely after three PM and Brenda was finished with all her hair appointments, we had enough time for the session, so we started without delay.

From my previous work with Brenda I knew she was a very responsive hypnotic subject, so we spent barely seven minutes in putting her under and the rest of the time we could work on what we needed to help my client overcome her fears.

"Tell me where you are." I began in a familiar soft voice. This helped her clear the pain of her past sexual abuse by her father and the fact that no one including her mother suspected something like this was taking place in her own home. As a parent myself I have always questioned if it was even possible not to know when something so terrible is happening to your child? As a mother who loves her child and is in tune into her child's energy fields…I must say it is not! Unless one is overwhelmed with her own unstable emotions and too self-preoccupied to see anything around herself. It was my client's own father(spirit) who had been dead for over 18 years that told me what he had done to his daughter. It was difficult to go through all the details when one was worse than the next. Even serial killers have a need to get things they have done to their victims off their chests, which is sometimes how they get caught or even admit to crimes they were not even suspected of committing. The same goes for the victim of incest, the villain will try to make sure that the child is left with the terrible burden of believing that it was their fault and that they have caused this to be done to them. My client's healing once we uncovered the abuse and removed it from her subconscious, and brought it into open view to her conscious mind, was amazingly visible to anyone who knew my client. Maybe for as long as live I will keep asking myself if there was something, anything more that I could have said to her to make her more aware of the danger lurking. And if there was, how would I say it without frightening her to death? Is there a way to say to someone that they were to die in the very near future and the way that are going to die will be as terrible and painful as it happened to my client and the two others that she was looking after? Will I ever know the answer to this question? Is there even an answer to this?

Another question that haunts me is the question if the punishment that this man received equal to the crime he committed? Here I must say that he received only 23 years in jail. This sentence was mainly given for the two daughters he murdered since the prosecution couldn't prove that it was a premeditated crime. As for Lynn, the jury was unconvinced that the crime was premeditated. They called it a 'crime of passion' and he was only given 7 years for killing Lynn with an axe, to be served simultaneously with the 23 years he was serving for his two daughters. I must say here that I, and everybody else in the entire country, was totally stunned at the verdict. It was not only insufficient for the severity and cruelty of this crime but totally unfair to the woman who's life was snuffed so callously in her prime. I know that the axe was in the house when I was there for the second session. I felt grateful for the fact that he didn't decide to use it on me, since I triggered his irrational fear that Lynn was going to walk away from his life and that he was going to lose control over her. A man like Ian would never accept that, never!

It took many long years for me to finally let go of this irrational self-blame.

He is slated to be released from prison in 2023.

"Let's find the life when you and Lynn were together and that started your initial connection."

"I see…" My client's voice sounded excited as she said this.

"Who are you?"

"I am a woman…"

"What year is it, can you read me the numbers your mind can see? Please read the first digit left of your mind's eyes.

"27 5 1678" She rattled off the numbers without hesitation."

"Are you saying the 27th of May 1678?" I repeated wanting to make sure that I was getting it right.

"Yes..."

"Could you tell me how is Lynn related to you?

"She is my daughter. She is 16 and so beautiful..." My clients voice was filled with admiration.

"Tell me about yourself," I prompted her. "Are you wealthy or poor?"

"I am poor and just two years a widow. My husband died at the hands of the noble man who owns the land we live on. He took this land from my family by force after we could not pay the terrible taxes he imposed on us. My husband was working so hard to be able to keep our land, but he got sick and passed away. After that we lost the rights to our land that belonged to my family for over 100 years."

"How many children do you have?"

"I have only Cecilia, my two other children died in their early childhood from the fever. I had two boys. I miss them so much...I am so grateful that Cecilia did not die and she reached 16. We both work very hard to pay the dues, but it is harder and harder... I am afraid that Landlord will show up and will throw us both from our home...and..." Her voice trailed off and I felt she was afraid of something.

"What are you afraid of?" I asked her.

"I am afraid that when he comes he will take my daughter away. He is evil. I heard what he has done to other young women in our village."

"Your two sons that died... do you recognize the two souls of your dead sons?"

"Oh, my God! ..." She was clearly shocked."They were Ian's two daughters he murdered..." She lapsed into a long moment of silence. I gave her the time to recover from the news before I continued.

"You knew!?" She said quietly.

"Yes, but I wanted you to see that for yourself." I gave her an honest answer. "I can see many things but it is imperative that you experience it for yourself to be able to let it go."

Back to 1678.

"This landlord is going to take my daughter away from me, and I am unable to prevent that, the same way as I could not help her in this life!"

"I want you to tell me what happened, please do not guess it."

"He came unexpectedly to collect and he saw my daughter. I was unable to make her look like a boy. He thought that I had one more son...Now he knows the truth...Oh, my God." Her voice trailed off and she started to cry. It was this moment for the first time that I realized how much physically my client looks like Lynn. Both had blue eyes, small, triangular faces and a bush of blond wavy hair. It was amazing how souls can find each other and choose bodies that display the similarities of the previous incarnations.

"He forces my daughter to go with him to his castle. I tried to make him stop but he hits me across my head with his fist. I blacked out."

"What happens next?"

"Two nights later my daughter managed to push him from the window of the castle when they struggled and he attempted to rape her. She was beaten and bruised when she stumbled into my home."

She tells me what had happened.

"He died from the fall, broke his neck, but nobody saw how it happened. People hated this man so nobody did anything to find out how he died. I wanted to make sure my daughter was safe, so I sent her away, so nobody would ever find her even if they learned what happened. He was an evil man and he deserved what he got." I agreed with my client, but said nothing. Finally…

"Can you see the way Ian manged to find the three souls that were connected to you and continued his evil reign over them in his present life. He brought them all together again to take their lives. He wanted revenge and he got it. Cecilia was not brought to justice and did not pay for taking a life and see that neither did he in this lifetime. He wanted her and he would not let her get away this time." Brenda laid still and listened carefully to every word I was saying.

"She left you a message but never showed up. She knew she could have been safe with you or maybe she was afraid that he would come after both of you, if you gave her shelter…Maybe Lynn understood that coming to you would put your life in danger, so she chose to do what I told her not to do…"

"I told her to keep her mouth shut and do what she needed to do without telling anybody about what she was about to do… She did not listen, she told him she was leaving and this way cut off her route of escape. Remember what she said in the last message she left on your machine…She said I just told him I was leaving and that if she did not show up by 4 PM, she wanted you to know that he has done something to her…"

"Yes, yes I see that now…Oh my God neither one of us could help her?" she said startled.

"She knew she had to pay her karmic debt…She knew."

"Yes," I confirmed, and that very moment I felt the load that was pressing my chest for such a long time had been released and I could breathe with ease. It is so amazing that by helping Brenda I was at the same time helping myself to understand the inevitability of what had happened and the simple fact that there was nothing I could have done better or differently that would have changed the course of events. I could not interfere with Lynn's karmic path. Her spirit understood that and accepted her fate.

After this I programmed my client with positive thoughts and brought her back. When she sat on the sofa I could see she was visibly relieved.

"Thank you…It was amazing to see how everything was linked together and helped me understand that there are times one cannot prevent what has to take place,"she said quietly. "I feel so peaceful and light."

"I do too." I said,"I was going through the same emotions as you,"

"You know there were times that I was angry at you thinking that you failed to help my friend. I am so sorry that I felt that way."

"Don't be. And please don't apologize."

"How many days are you going to stay?" Brenda changed the subject while getting up from the sofa.

"Until Friday." I answered her.

"I hope you will stay with me?"

"If you don't mind." I accepted her offer.

"We can have a hot tub tonight so you can relax…"

"That would be great." I was looking forward to it.

"When is the trial starting?"

"Next Monday."

"We will have enough time to teach you how to protect yourself from the evilness of the man you will be testifying against. We will build a very powerful shield he will not be able to penetrate and he won't be able to affect you in any way. You will stand strong and focused on the witness stand."

"That sounds good." She smiled.

That evening when we sat in the hot tub at the back yard of my client's house we had an opportunity to enjoy a gorgeous starry sky. We meditated for a few minutes and allowed ourselves to really unwind and just be in the moment.

"What a wonderful night!" I sighed resting my head back on the head rest. The pitch black sky was swept with thousands of beautiful stars.

"I am so glad you are here."

At one point for no reason, and almost simultaneously, we both looked towards the house. In the darkness of the open upper back patio doors we saw two silhouettes. At first they were light and misty but then their shape became more distinct and clear. We both stared at the two girls standing shyly close to the doors.

"Can you see them?" Brenda hushed.

"Yes, I can…" I whispered back looking at the two spirits of the murdered girls. They were holding each others hands.

"Do not stay here, you must go towards the light," I said out loud.

"Go and never look back." I made my voice louder. "You belong to another side of life and you must go!" I ordered firmly,"Don't be afraid any more, he cannot touch you now." As I was saying this the two apparitions began fading away until they were gone.

My client sat silent and shocked before she spoke.

"Did they really come here?"

"You did their hair for awhile. They felt safe here and it was the place they came to hide," I explained.

"I thought I had seen shadows moving around my hair salon, but I dismissed it thinking it was my imagination."

"They will not be back, they went to the spirit place and are free now."

"Thank you for helping them go."

I looked right at Brenda. "I saw Lynn once two months after she died."

"Did you?" Brenda moved closer to me. "Has she gone to the light?"

"Yes, she said to me that she was not there to blame me, she only wanted to know if what we have accomplished together was strong enough to set herself free of the Karmic connection to Ian. I told her that it was. Then she thanked me and was gone."

"I think I have had enough." Brenda stepped out of the hot tub and covered herself with a large white towel. "You can stay longer if you wish, just pull the cover after you are done."

"Absolutely. I'll enjoy this another few minutes then get out too."

"Your bedroom upstairs is ready," she said then handed me a glass of cold water before heading to the house.

It was perhaps five minutes later when I started to feel dizzy and my heart started to beat more rapidly. Without delay I stepped out of the tub and dried myself with a towel before pulling the cover over the tub as I was asked to do.

The last thing I remember was stepping through the patio door leading to the kitchen of the house. I remember thinking that I felt so weak that I couldn't possibly make it up the stairs to my bedroom. I felt so weak and dizzy. My entire body was shaking so badly that I couldn't take another step toward the staircase leading upstairs. I thought about calling for Linda but couldn't speak. The last thought that flashed through my consciousness was the feeling of the wooden banister in my left hand. It didn't hurt when I collapsed at the base of the stairs without making a sound.

The next thing I remember was being in my bed and someone sitting on the edge of it and touching my forehead gently. It was the large cool hand of a tall male. All I could see was a dark outline that loomed darker against the darkness of the room.

"You are Ok now. Go to sleep. Everything is going to be OK." The voice I heard was soft, deep and masculine. I have never heard that voice before or since.

"Who are you?" I thought. "How did I get to my bed?"

"Shhh…" was all I heard… "shhh… sleep now. I will stay here with you."

"Who are you? Who are you?" I repeated.

"You know who I am. I have been with you for a long, long time… Shhh sleep." These were the last words I heard before falling into a deep slumber.

I slept so deeply that I never moved until the morning light started to seep through a small opening of the drapes. As I opened my eyes I realized that I was naked and my terry robe was neatly hanging in the closet. I had no recollection of how I got to the bedroom, how I managed to hang my robe. I could vividly remember the presence in my room. Trying to shake off the cobwebs of sleep I started to speculate what could have happened, and even allowed the thought that it must have been Linda's boyfriend who had brought me upstairs and touched my forehead. It must have been him. I clung to the thought that it must have been Brenda's boyfriend. I had a shower, dressed and came downstairs to the kitchen. Brenda was having her morning coffee. She was in a good mood and smiled at me.

"I slept so well!" she said to me

"I stayed in the hot tub way too long." I said, "I passed out at the base of the stairs, did you hear me fall?"

"No!" Her face drew serious and upset. "What happened?"

"Thank God Glen carried me upstairs and put me to bed." I said.

"What are you talking about?" Her eyes widened. "That is not possible. Glen will be away for another three days…" A long silence filled the air. I was too shocked to speak.

"I remember someone carrying me upstairs…" I breathed, remembering so vividly being carried upstairs in a smooth gentle way as if there were no stairs to overcome.

"It wasn't Glen and it certainly wasn't me." Brenda's face looked as stunned as mine.

"I don't know… the person who carried me upstairs hung my bathrobe in the closet. I never do that. I always put it at the foot bed for easy reach. I never hang it in the closet. Then he sat next to me on the edge of my bed, touched my forehead and told me to go to sleep and that he was going to stay with me until I fell asleep."

"Oh my God I have no idea who that was or even if it was a person. This staircase is so steep it would be a challenge to carry even a small child upstairs without hanging on, for your life, to the railing."

We dropped the subject right there since the more we talked about it the more mystifying it was for both of us.

What echoed in my mind was the thought that I felt so safe knowing that there was a source as powerful and loving that could carry me to my bed and watch over me when I slept.

All I knew was that whoever or whatever it was, left me with a profound feeling of being loved, cherished and protected and that was good enough for me at this moment.

I helped prepare Brenda to testify as a witness for the prosecution. I taught her how to put a shield of protection around herself so powerful that no hatred was powerful enough to break or penetrate it. Later on, she told me that during her testimony she remained focused and calm and she said in her head she could hear the sound as a bumble bee would when splashing against the windshield of a fast moving car, all the black arrows of hatred that he was trying to send her way to discourage her from telling the truth about him. These she sent right back to him. She stood strong and was able to look straight into the eyes of evil and feel no fear.

Since Lynn's case was the most powerful case I ever worked with, that left the deepest marks on my psyche, it would be also the last one I would describe in my book. I pray that as long as I live and do spiritual work with people I would never have to deal with any similar case that would be so hard to break and embrace. What I know for sure, of the cases that shook my life, Lynn's case and the demonic possession would be the ones that taught me the most about myself and about the unseen side of life. It had taught me to have a healthy respect for what cannot be defined and explained by scientific methods or ways. Something that can strike anyone at any time and any place, and might not have an antidote or solution, something that can leave doctors, scientists, engineers, lawyers, law enforcement officers powerless and unable to do anything to save one affected and in peril. The biggest lesson I have learned from my extensive work with people is that no one is immune from the unseen, no one is safe and no one is untouchable from evil. There is no gun that can kill the devil, no medicine that can cure us when we are afflicted with the germs of spiritual disease. But there are still many things we can do to protect ourselves from the unknown and evil.

First and most important is to be aware that there is another dark side to life and just by accepting it is to make sure we have shields around us at all times, that we have someone else who understands this, that has our back when we are sick, weak or even sleeping who makes sure our shields are up and strong enough to keep us safe and protected. No one is immune to evil, except the devil himself.

What I also learned is that we are naturally beings of light and that love, tolerance and kindness are our best protective shields.

## PROLOGUE:

What I understand is that much of the time if we do not look for trouble and if are lucky enough stay out of it, sometimes that might not be so. We come into this earthly existence with our destiny designed by our karmic past. One would have to ask here, are we coming again to pay for our past deeds if they were unkindly and hurt others? The answer would be yes and no. *Yes…* because we do need to even out our wrongs or be rewarded for our good, but not the way most of us think. We are not punished or rewarded by God or the Divine. We are balancing our Life Bank deed account so everything is accounted for. A similar metaphor as balancing our real bank accounts, the Spiritual Bank account is there solely for our own use. We are the ones that deposit value or lack of it and at the end of each lifetime we need to reconcile everything to know if we are in a surplus or in a deficit position. Further to that we have to make decisions of what is next.How are we repaying our debts and what we are going to do with our surplus? If the balance sheet at end of each life shows a little bit of surplus we are doing well and our spiritual wealth is building which translates into good, happy lives that carry little or no regret and much joy and pride that we did well. Is God anywhere to be found in this Bank of Life? Yes, yet unlike real financial institutions He will never force us to close our accounts even if the deficit we have accumulated is huge. In his eyes it's always repayable…

We are not judged by anyone or anything but ourselves. We are our best friends or worse enemies, it is only a choice that separates us from right or wrong. That choice is always ours and no one else can be held accountable for anything we did right or wrong. To imagine how it feels, put yourself on a road that has no posted speed limit. How we drive on this road is entirely up to us. Not many people drive like maniacs on such roads when only the driver -himself/herself -can be held responsible for accidents and harm done to ourselves or to others. Human nature will always direct us towards self preservation and once we understand that, our lives and what we do with them are our full and entire responsibility. We tend to make better decisions and stay on the right side of the universal law that governs the entire Universe.

It has been a long time since my journey as a spiritual being began and everyday I remind myself that there is so much more for me to learn and embrace. So many more times humbleness will have to take place to show me how I fit into all this that surrounds us and fills us. Just the simple realization that my learning will not end until I reach my last day on Earth in this physical format is both daunting and exciting at the same time. Our growth continues beyond the here and now. We are taking on as many lessons in the spiritual realm as we take here on Earth. Even more so for groups of souls called Sages — the ones that teach in both realities, Physical and Spiritual.

I feel very humble and grateful for being one of those chosen to teach and lead. This honorable choice often comes with pain and defeat, therefore souls chosen as Sages go through a higher number of existences where we have to die for what we believe and stand for. Looking at many of my past lives (139 I'm aware of) I can see why so many times I have been prosecuted and killed for what I embraced as my life path. Healers, seekers, visionaries, artists, scientists, and spiritual leaders possessed wisdom and knowledge in times when the rest of the world was mired in darkness with beliefs so limited and skewed that made them see the world as flat and the solar system and sun revolving around the earth. I know that all these insiders were different from the rest of the population in one respect. The fact that they have receivers and antennas more in tune with the Universal Pool of Knowledge (reference the work of Carl Jung), from all their inventions, visions, prophecies and healing knowledge. They were not different in other aspects of being a human being. They did not create, they re-created, they did not invent they re-invented since every single wisdom, thought, invention, which could appear in someone's mind was already there. Everything in the Universe is energy, our bodies, plants, animals, earth, stars, planets, water, air and our thoughts are pure energy. Mainstream cutting edge science today is, layer by layer, peeling back the onion skin of truth and knowledge about the reality of nature and existence. We mold this energy with our minds and create our reality. It is that process that makes us different from each other, or determines how different our lives and our achievements can become. "We are what we think we are. We are as successful as we think we are. We are as rich as we think we are."

This concept, though so simple, was the most onerous for me to embrace, yet one for which I have repeated proof. I can think of a few life events I went through and how the power of my mind and beliefs really helped me to mold the outcome I wanted. To mention just one of many.

Since I was perhaps 6-7 years old I always saw myself living on the North American continent. I envisioned images of the landscape, people who for thousands of years inhabited these lands from Alaska to the tip of South America. I saw in my dreams at night and often in my daydreams an awesome level of detail pertaining to their clothing, weapons, spiritual ceremonies, and ways of life. I lived in the country of my birth as if waiting for something to happen that would transport me into a different reality, a different place, into a different life. As I grew older these feelings were becoming stronger and preoccupying me more. The most vivid dreams started to appear between the 12-14 years of my life. I had panoramic full color recollections of other lives I lived as a native. This was the real purpose I started to write my first books. Their subject: North American Indians! It became my obsession, all my drawings and paintings were of the same subject. This strange obsession was driving my father half mad and his stock comment would become, "I should give you two revolvers and send you to the Wild West!" My favorite answer was, "I will be there one day!" I can't remember how many hundreds of times I would say this, never realizing that just by repeating it with this strong conviction and the feelings that stood behind it, I was creating my future. In 1986 all this became my true reality. The day I arrived in Calgary, Alberta I felt like I had finally returned home. Everything felt right, the space, the sky, the sun, the mountains…It became even more potent when I had for the first time participated in a sacred ceremony called "Sweat Lodge."

As soon as the opening of the sweat lodge went down, I felt tears streaming down my face and an overwhelming feeling of peace washed over me like tidal wave. I knew just what to do, how to behave. I chanted songs with the medicine man who was leading the sweat ceremony, songs that were so well known to me, yet I had never heard them before. The powerful visions that I experienced during that first sweat lodge shook the foundations of everything I have ever known about the spiritual realm. Later on, the way I was received by every elder, was even more shocking. They accepted me into their circle in spite of being a white woman, as if I have always belonged there, as if I have, always, been one of them. My learning process started in 1987 in the Sweat Lodge in Claresholm in Southern Alberta and it continues to the present day. My hunger for the wisdom of healing will never cease until the day it will be my time to cross over yet again.

What I have learned on my journey into Native spirituality is that it felt most comfortable and natural but also that it allowed my heart to open to all other religions or beliefs that exist in this world, and accept them with respect and humbleness. After all, if one takes a really close look at the ground principals of each religion, it will soon be evident that they are similar if not identical. All pointing at the same aspects of our co-existence. Honesty, tolerance, love, and respect for another human being or for that matter to any other creature that was put on this planet to live! There is no better or worse religion, there is no right or wrong… We all have the same right to be, the same right to be well, to be happy and wealthy to live in dignity and harmony with the rest of the Universe. What makes me sad is the fact that some of us claim the right to be above this Universal Law and are consciously destroying this fragile natural balance and harmony, going to any extent to totally destroy it. Even sadder to me is the fact that there comes a time when we all will have to re-balance our Life Bank deed accounts and the debts will have to be paid equally and by every single soul on this planet. The Universal Law applies to each and every one of us without exception and exclusion, regardless on how much we had or did not have, how much we owned (or we thought we owned) or did not own; what will be due will have to be paid.

If there would be one thing I would like to say to everybody who reads this book it's this: Make the changes when you can and when you still have time to undo what was done wrong so that on the last day on this planet your Life Bank deed account will have a surplus of kindness, love, tolerance and fairness, your ticket to karmic freedom and a free slate to be ready for another happier, healthier and fuller life.

If you would like to contact the author with your comments or questions, please send an email to:

ms954@hotmail.com

Subject: *Attention to Urszula Teresa Kur*

Manufactured by Amazon.ca
Bolton, ON

24921995R00245